NATIVE NORTH AMERICAN RELIGIOUS TRADITIONS

Dancing for Life

Jordan Paper

PRAEGER

Westport, Connecticut
London

Library of Congress Cataloging-in-Publication Data

Paper, Jordan D.
  Native North American religious traditions : dancing for life / Jordan Paper.
    p. cm.
  Includes bibliographical references and index.
  ISBN 0-275-99097-4 (alk. paper)
  1. Indians of North America—Religion.   2. Indian cosmology—North America.   3. Indians
of North America—Rites and ceremonies.   I. Title.
  E98.R3P227 2007
  299.7—dc22

British Library Cataloguing in Publication Data is available.

Library of Congress Catalog Card Number:
ISBN: 0-275-99097-4

First published in 2007

Praeger Publishers, 88 Post Road West, Westport, CT 06881
An imprint of Greenwood Publishing Group, Inc.
www.praeger.com

Printed in the United States of America

The paper used in this book complies with the
Permanent Paper Standard issued by the National
Information Standards Organization (Z39.48-1984).

10 9 8 7 6 5 4 3 2 1

Why we dance:

To dance is to pray,

to pray is to heal,

to heal is to give,

to give is to live,

to live is to dance.

(by flyingheart 2, 2004)
(see Chap. 8, note 9)

To my Native friends – Marilyn Johnson, Kenn Pitawanakwat, Vern Harper, Pauline Shirt, Jim Dumont, Edna Manitowabi, Joe Couture, and Jay Vest – who over the decades and in various ways shared their understanding and lives with me, and to the many other elders of a variety of Native traditions who shared their knowledge and wisdom with me, with the hope that, in some small way, this book recompenses their gifts.

CONTENTS

ILLUSTRATIONS

PROLOGUE

A quarter century ago, I completed a four-day fast, the last of a series I had undergone at an Anishnabe community in northern Ontario returning to traditional spirituality. At the coming-out feast, the elder of the community who had guided me through the ritual directed me to take the understandings I had gained to my people. At first, the directive left me dumbfounded. Who were my people? As a non-Native in a community forced to leave their own reserve because the Christian missionary who then controlled it would not allow the practice of Native religion, I was not really welcome. On the other hand, this mode of spirituality would hardly be meaningful to the Orthodox Judaism in which I had been raised. I eventually realized that my people must be the academic community, of which, as a university professor, I am a part.

As a comparative religionist trained in Chinese language and culture, I consequently also began to teach and write on the subject of Native American religions, along with my studies of Chinese religion and comparative religion methodologies. Shortly thereafter, at the request of Art Solomon, an elder attempting to spiritually assist Native prisoners who were usually prevented by the prison authorities from practicing their religion, I began the research for a book on the history and religious nature of the primary Pan-Indian ritual. That book, *Offering Smoke: The Sacred Pipe and Native American Religion*, has remained in print for twenty years. Subsequently, I wrote some articles, a couple with an Anishnabe friend, Kenn Pitawanakwat, on aspects of Native American religion. But it is the opportunity to write this book, a comprehensive introduction to Native North American religions, that allows me to come to terms with that directive given so long ago and to partially repay the debt I owe to Native peoples for the privilege of participating in their rituals, which has made my life so meaningful.

I have been fortunate over the years to take part in Anishnabe rituals of many types as well as Cree, Pikuni, and Tlingit ceremonies. I have met elders from a number of traditions in Canada, the United States, and Mexico. I have traveled to sacred sites in North America from Alaska to Yucatan, from the Carolinas to California, and I have sought to aid the passing on of these traditions by assisting in Native-way schools and organizing elder's conferences. But it must be understood that this book is being written from a comparative perspective, which means from an external standpoint. It is an introduction to the hermeneutics and history of those indigenous modes of spirituality that continue to be alive in North America. It is not a how-to book on the practice of Native spiritual traditions.

In introducing Native North American religions, I strive to honor traditional sensibilities concerning Native traditions. When I took part in Native ceremonies, I never brought a camera, a tape recorder, or even a notebook with me. These are oral traditions, and what is recorded is a matter of memory. Native traditions have a strong esoteric undercurrent, which is part of its spiritual strength, and much that takes place or is learned is intended only for those present. Hence, what is described in this book will often be general; unessential details will be left unspoken.

The focus of the descriptions will be the ceremonies, for behavior is observable, and rituals tend to remain essentially unchanged, sometimes over many centuries, even millennia. Ideology in these traditions, on the other hand, tends to be individualistic. In all of the traditions to be discussed, it is expected that people will have their own ecstatic experiences of the numinous. Thus, within the range of cultural possibilities, there can be as many interpretations as there are individuals. Symbolism can vary from culture to culture. For example, all of the traditions have an understanding of the "Four Directions," but the colors and other symbolic associations with these directions can vary considerably.

Moreover, no myths per se will be presented. In most presentations of Native religions, the focus tends to be on myths. But none of these myths are ever presented as told. First, of course, they must be translated, and the act of translation necessarily brings in major changes, as translation is not just from one language to another, but from one conceptual system to another. Second, myths in print are necessarily truncated. The actual telling of a myth can take a long time. Myth telling has many functions including education and entertainment. In order that myths be remembered, there is considerable repetition. But this repetition also exists for emphasis. And there is the storyteller's mode of expression, which lovingly crafts words. Hence, a truncated myth is no myth at all. Many myths when written down are expurgated. The love of children for scatological humor and of teenagers for salacious humor is utilized as pedagogical devices in the myth telling. Finally, myths are stories of the sacred and sacred in and of themselves. Thus, the telling of myths, different from legends and other tales, is a ritual act. They are told only at certain times of the year and in a proper setting. In the tradition I am familiar with, myths can only be told from the first snow to the first thunderstorm. While I have told myths to young children in Native-way schools, it was always in the proper season and in the proper setting, after ritual purification. Putting a myth as a myth into print would violate these religious imperatives.

There are so many Native traditions in North America that they cannot all be possibly covered in a work of a single volume. Rather, there will be a sampling of traditions chosen for regional balance and variety. There are new multivolume encyclopedias on Native religion that will provide those interested with more detailed coverage, although even these are necessarily limited in their coverage. No scholar can possibly be familiar with more than a few of these many religious traditions.

In closing, I would but add that I feel privileged to have the opportunity to introduce these beautiful spiritual traditions. I only hope that this work meets with the approval of those elders who have guided me in my journey toward understanding.

PART 1
GENERAL CONSIDERATIONS

· 1 ·

Introduction

PRELUDE

Dancing for Life

Dancing, along with the use of drums and shakers (rattles) and usually accompanied by singing, is ubiquitous at major Native ceremonials. At Native religious rituals throughout North America, it is common to hear the same explanation for dancing: dancing is how "Indians" pray. Native people do not just pray with their voices, but with their bodies as well. In Native oratory, I often have heard "dance" used as a metaphor for life itself.

In 1890, several hundred Lakota were massacred by the U.S. Army because the soldiers incorrectly assumed that they had danced the Ghost Dance. In 1922, forty-five Kwakwaka'wakw (Kwakiutl) were arrested for violating Canadian law by taking part in a Native religious ceremony. The criminal charges were for dancing, giving speeches, and distributing gifts, all illegal for Native people. In their defense, the Kwakwaka'wakw insisted that in their religion "[a] strict law bids us dance," but to no avail. Their ritual paraphernalia was confiscated and sold to American collectors or given to Canadian museums, and twenty-two were imprisoned for dancing. At the same time, in the United States, Native people could be imprisoned for participating in the Thirst Dance (Sun Dance). Both governments well understood that dancing was the means by which Native people expressed their spirituality in religious ceremonies; to exterminate Native religion, it was necessary to prohibit dancing.

Dancing was also a means to surreptitiously maintain Native religion during the many decades of severe repression. The powwow appeared to the dominant culture as a benign form of secular dancing, but for many of the dancers this was their only means of expressing their traditional spirituality. As another example, during these times in Dené communities throughout the Northwest Territories, Tea Dances were held in the parish halls of the Anglican mission churches. To the missionaries, the Dené were carrying out a British tradition of afternoon social dances, but I have been told that the Dené were in fact dancing their spirits, which was their traditional way of reinforcing their relationship with personal guardian spirits.

Native ceremonies, as in any religion, have many functions. They create and enhance a sense of community, not just with their fellow humans but with the spirit realm. The continuity and intensity of a typical four-day ritual leaves one utterly elated; they are profoundly moving. These ceremonies are also the means by which traditions are imparted. They are learning experiences not only for the young—learning by doing—but because when these ceremonies bring forth ecstasy, even the most experienced elders can receive teachings from the spirits, not only from their own special relationships, but also from those dreams shared by others. Most important, they engender life; they make it possible for us to live despite all the travails of this world.

Decades ago, when I first began participating in Anishnabe Midewiwin rituals (to be found in the northern Great Lakes area—Chapter 4), I had an epiphany concerning the meaning of the ceremonies. At one point during the winter ceremonial, the Little Boy (the sacred water drum) went around the circle of the many people in the lodge. As it came to each person and they held it, they spoke whatever was in their hearts. Some said but a few words; some went on and on giving their life stories. It was a long wait until it would come around to me, and being new to these practices and unsure of myself, I thought and thought about what I would say. But when it was my turn to embrace the Little Boy, everything I had planned to say was wiped away, and I too found myself speaking from my heart, thanking the spirits and all those participating for the gift of life itself.

Thus, "dancing for life" can be understood to sum up Native spirituality. These religions are not ones of passivity, of sitting quietly singing prearranged hymns or listening to a religious professional sermonize or pray for one. Rather these are traditions of dynamic religious lives, where one actively involves all of oneself, including the body. These are religions of doing, of spontaneity, of taking active responsibility for one's spiritual life, and of encountering the spirits with one's entire being. And these are also traditions that are inherently this-worldly. The spiritual quest is not for another or next life; it is for this very life, not just for oneself, but life for all one's relations: family, clan, people, and even the spirits themselves.

Native North American Religious Traditions

In the United States, the common term for the indigenous peoples is "American Indian"; in Canada it is "Native American" or "Native Canadian," although, for political reasons, it is being replaced by "First Nations." As I prefer not to perpetuate Christopher Columbus's major blunder, in distinction to geographers of his time, in insisting that our planet is half its size, and thus the land he reached is India, and as "First Nations" is a term specific to the postcolonial period, I will use the term "Native American." Here, "American" does not refer to the United States, but to all of the American continents, North and South. The border between the United States and Canada, and between the United States and Mexico, is either arbitrary or a product of war between Euro-Americans. It has no meaning for Native traditions, and both borders cut across many traditional indigenous cultures; indeed, the U.S.–Canadian border cuts across several large reservations.

This book focuses on those indigenous traditions that belong exclusively to the American continents. For this reason, Inuit (Eskimo) religion will not be discussed. The Inuit, by language and culture, have a consistent tradition that stretches from Siberia, across Alaska and northern Canada, to Greenland, and involves cultures under the control of the Russian, American, Canadian, and Danish governments. Hence, it is a topic best dealt with separately.

There are more indigenous languages and traditions to be found in the Americas than in the rest of the world combined. Although there is continuity of religious traditions to be found in North and South America, it is necessary to limit the coverage; hence, this book is only concerned with North America or Turtle Island, as it is known in many Native traditions. Moreover, as this book is written for an English-reading public, the focus is on those traditions found in Canada and the United States, with but occasional reference to those traditions found in Mexico and further south.

Native American traditionalists today tend to use the word "spirituality" in place of religion. To them the word "religion" evokes the Christian churches, who, until recently, sought to destroy Native traditions and force Native Americans to become Christians. Christian missionaries were accorded control over reservations ("reserves," in Canada) for routing out all aspects of Native culture. Children were torn from their parents and forced into Christian-controlled boarding schools, where those who did not die of disease were brutally beaten for speaking their language and many were sexually assaulted. Christian missionaries had the governments pass laws prohibiting the practice of Native religions on pain of incarceration. Moreover, Christian missionaries told Native people that their religion was not a religion, that they had no religion at all. Hence, it is no wonder that

Native traditionalists today do not wish to apply "religion," a negative term for them, to their traditions. Thus, it has often been replaced with the word "spirituality."

Since this book is being written from the standpoint of comparative religion, however, the word "religion" will be used. In a sense, to not use the word implies that the missionaries were correct, that Native Americans have no religion. More important, to understand Native religious traditions comparatively, it is necessary to use like terms and analytical approaches cross-culturally.

The word "traditions" in the title is also important, for it deliberately limits the scope of the book in order to have a manageable topic. Given the half millennium of domination by European Christian powers, there have been many religious developments within indigenous cultures. In Spanish-controlled Mexico, being the time of the Inquisition, it was simply convert or die. In the French- and English-controlled area, conversion was on a voluntary basis until control was gained over the continent, and Native peoples were then forced onto reservations by the national police in Canada and the military in the United States. At that point, it was assumed that all Native people must live a Christian life, whether converted or not, and the traditional religions were made illegal. During these times, Natives were not passive. There were Native prophets who preached an indigenous Christianity, and various syntheses took place between Christianity and Native traditions (a few to be discussed later in the book).

Most Native people today are Christians, but the traditions did not completely die out, and over the last several decades, there has been extensive revitalization. As there are many excellent books on the missionary enterprise as well as on Christianity among Native people, this work concentrates on those Native traditions with no or negligible influence from Christianity, although being in all other respects modern versions of, in most cases, traditions with considerable antiquity. The focus of this book is on living traditions, but in doing so, there will be discussion of the past.

In the early phases of the revitalization, many of the young Native people seeking their traditional spirituality were often in contact with developments taking place in the dominant culture from the late 1960s through the 1970s. This led to a degree of fusion with what became New Age movements and concepts. A number of new ideas became so ubiquitous that they seem to have had a long history, when in actuality, they were often but a few years in age.

In this book, there is no desire to disparage these developments or concepts that are due to fusion with Christianity. Since the focus is the continuation of traditional religions in the contemporary context, they simply will not be mentioned or but referred to in passing as necessary. Hence, this book is a comprehensive introduction to the ongoing traditional religions of the indigenous peoples of North America.

COMMON FEATURES

Although there are numerous indigenous religious traditions in the Americas, all were in varying degrees of contact with others. Different from the interrelated monotheistic traditions (Judaism, Christianity, and Islam), polytheistic traditions, including all Native American religions, do not have a concept of absolute truth. Other traditions, rather than being threatening, were perceived as interesting. Native cultures continually borrowed from each other, and raiding cultures, at times, stole sacred items as war trophies and incorporated them into their own rituals. Thus, although there are differences between the traditions, there are also important commonalities. For this reason, Native traditionalists are often at ease with the rituals of other Native cultures. I have observed visiting Natives from the Andes comfortably and knowledgeably taking part in Native ceremonies in northern Canada. As well, to be discussed in Chapter 8, there are pan-Indian rituals that were designed to be used cross-culturally.

The Number Four

All cultures seem to have a predilection for a particular number. In early Chinese culture, for example, the preference was for the number six, but this later changed to the number five. Chinese culture kept both numerical systems (5/10 and 6/12), so that the traditional mode of year counting was a sixty-year cycle (6×10). Thus, there are the Five Phases (*wuxing*) and the twelve zodiacal symbols that were central to early Chinese ideology. Indo-European–language cultures, ranging from Northern India to North America, focus on the number three, hence the Trinity in Christianity, the triad of Brahma–Vishnu–Shiva in Hinduism, and the Three Jewels (*triratna*)—Buddha, Dharma, and Sangha—in Buddhism. Early Semitic cultures had a preference for the number seven; hence, Western culture, and no other, has a seven-day week, and Catholicism has seven sacraments. For Native American traditions, the predilection is for the number four and its multiples; one of the simplest indicators of a Native American tradition is the predominance of the number four.

Hence, major ceremonies last for four days, preceded by four days of preparation. Repetitions in ritual are fourfold, and most aspects of religion occur in sets of four as well as their multiples of eight, twelve, and sixteen. Thus, symbols, such as sacred colors, occur in sets of four. As Indo-European–language speakers tend to think in sets of three, so Native traditionalists tend to think in fours. Not only is the use of the number four ubiquitous, but where one finds in religious thinking or rituals sets of three or seven, it often, although not necessarily, indicates subtle influences from the dominant culture. This use of the number four, of course, did not influence the development of higher mathematics in complex civilizations as the Maya, which based their numerical system on the number twenty.

Every culture, save those in the polar region, understands the path of the sun to bisect the earth and that the perpendicular to that line creates the four directions. One of the earliest Chinese texts, for example, speaks of the ruling city, the ceremonial center, as the "pivot of the four quarters." Because of the importance of the number four, most Native traditions in North America have taken this notion a step further, deifying these quarters as the Four Directions. When offerings are made, particularly tobacco offerings, they tend to be made to the Four Directions (sometimes Four Winds) as well as to the nadir and the zenith (Earth and Sky). In some Catholic-influenced traditions, a seventh offering, to the center, is made.

Again in virtually every human culture, Earth and Sky are female and male complementary deities, who in their conjoining create all living things. The major exceptions are the monotheistic traditions, who in order to have a single numinous realm have exclusively made the male Sky the deity (Heaven or the one who reigns in Heaven), who is also the Creator, and deemed the female Earth (Hell) to be the locus of evil. Using China again as an example, before the fall of imperial government in 1911, only the emperor and his consort, as the chief priests of China, could sacrifice to Sky and Earth. This sacrifice was so important that it was the mark of imperial prerogative.

Thus, in traditional ceremonies throughout North America, one will find, at a minimum, offerings being made and prayers directed toward Earth, Sky, and the Four Directions. Together, they sum up the numinous realm of the entire cosmos.

But the preeminence of the number four has also led to some peculiar developments. In the 1970s, as young Native people were rediscovering their religious traditions, they latched onto the long-discredited anthropology of race. The nineteenth-century anthropological and biological understanding that there are four races—black, red, white, and yellow—fit the sacred number four. To counter the hurt from forcible Christian conversion, it began to be understood that "[t]he Creator made four races and gave each a religion." Red people should follow their own indigenous religions, all white people should be Christians (and not take part in Native ceremonies), yellow people should be Buddhists, but I never heard what black people should be. On the other hand, I have never met a red human being, save for sunburned people of Celtic background, or a yellow one for that matter, save for someone suffering from a liver disease. One theory as to why Native Americans were perceived as red is that when Native people were first met by northern Europeans in the northeastern part of North America, they were wearing the common face paint of red ochre mixed with bear fat, and the Europeans thought that was the color of their skin. In particular, the Addaboutik (Beothuk in the literature; literally, "The Red People"), who lived in present-day Newfoundland, coated themselves with red ochre during the summer to save themselves from the swarms of mosquitoes.

Reciprocity

Virtually all the religions of the world have an understanding of reciprocity, that we must symbolically pay back for the many gifts we receive from the deities to make manifest our thankfulness. As described in the Bible, Israelite religion focused on sacrificial offerings of meat and grain. For political reasons, these sacrifices which had taken place at many altars were consolidated into a single one at the temple in the capital of Jerusalem. When the second temple was destroyed by the Romans after a failed insurrection, Judaism ended the practice of sacrifice and awaits the coming of the messiah to rebuild the temple to again offer sacrifices. So too Christianity and Islam do not have sacrificial offerings. But in Chinese religion, Hinduism, central African religions, and so on, food is offered to the spirits and deities on a daily basis, and all ceremonies involve sacrificial offerings. Similarly, in Native American traditions, offerings to the spirits are of major importance.

Thus, for example, in Pawnee and Mandan dwellings, there was an altar with a bison skull and an ear of corn. Each day, corn was offered to the skull and dried bison meat was offered to the corn (Chapter 6). Today, traditionalists in many cultures, before eating, will take a morsel from each of the foods of the meal and offer it through the fire, if there is a wood stove, or save it for a later offering, perhaps by burial in the earth. At major Native ceremonies everywhere there will be feasts, and these communal meals are first and foremost offerings of food and water to the spirits. Reciprocity is not just a matter of food; the most important offering is tobacco (see *Tobacco and Other Sacred Herbs*).

But in some Native American traditions, reciprocity is often taken further than elsewhere. For the continuing gift of life from the spirits, some traditions offer the very essence of human life, human blood, to the spirit realm. The Maya ruling couple offered their own blood at major ceremonials—the male through the piercing of his penis and the female through drawing a roughened cord through a hole in her tongue. In many of the Thirst Dance (Sun Dance) ceremonials of the Plains cultures (Chapter 8), participants attach themselves to the sacred center pole with a thong attached to the skin of their chest or to bison skulls attached to the skin of their backs. On the fourth day, having danced since the first without food or water, they dance until the thongs tear from their bodies. Thus, they offer their blood, pieces of their flesh, their exhaustion, and their dehydration and hunger to the spirits. As the Maya rulers, they then collapse and await visions. But it is not only the thirst dancers who offer their flesh and blood. In the Lakota tradition, sisters and wives of those taking part or fasting may cut small pieces of flesh from their arms as an offering in support of their brothers or spouses.

Whenever a spirit—animal, plant, stone, or water—is needed, especially for sacred tasks, it is asked to offer itself. One speaks to it and offers a token gift, usually tobacco. One asks that it give itself for one to use in seeking life for one's family and community. When I fast according to the traditional way, I have been taught that every item needed is to be treated in this way. Each of the willow branches needed for the framework of the fasting lodge (a miniature wigwam), the basswood roots needed to tie the framework together, the maple stick needed to create holes in which to insert the poles of the framework, the cedar boughs on which to sit and from which to pick leaflets to create a protecting circle around the fast area; the earth on which the lodge is constructed; the four traditional foods and the water which is placed outside the fasting area to placate unwanted spirits; all are spoken to, asked to offer themselves to be used and to bring their energies to assist in my fast, and are offered tobacco in recompense for their sacrifice.

In gathering–hunting traditions, every animal hunted, every plant used for food, shelter, healing, or ceremonial use is spoken to and offered tobacco. In horticulture–hunting and agricultural situations, it is the Mother of the gardened plants that is asked for its assistance and offered a gift, such as the Corn Mother. In Native American traditions, as in most traditions worldwide, it is recognized that humans are dependent on the spirit realm for every aspect of life and that gratitude is shown through symbolic gifts in turn.

Tobacco and Other Sacred Herbs

While many cultures have sacred substances, such as herbs and incense, only in the Americas is tobacco the premier sacred substance for offerings to the spirits. The ritual use of tobacco smoke (a variety of tobacco is chewed but not smoked by Native Australians) is unique to American Indian religions. Tobacco is the primary sacred plant throughout the Americas, save for the Arctic and the southern tip of South America.

Tobacco is a mild psychoactive substance and used in healing practices among Native peoples in Central and South America in ways similar to their use of more powerful entheogenic plants. Nicotine, the active substance in tobacco, liberates the neurohumor norepinephrine, chemically related to mescaline found in peyote [discussed under *Native American Church (Peyote Religion)* in Chapter 8], and releases the hormones epinephrine, dopamine, and serotonin. However, the tobacco used throughout much of indigenous North America is milder than the forms grown further south, and during rituals when the Sacred Pipe circulates around the circle, participants generally take but four puffs each. Thus, in most North American ritual usage, the importance of tobacco is in its role as a symbol of the sacred rather than as a psychoactive substance.

While Euro-American domestic tobacco is derived from *Nicotiana tabacum* L. from the Caribbean, in eastern and central North America the native tobacco is *Nicotiana rustica* L. Three other varieties were grown in the Plains, and several other varieties were cultivated on the West Coast.

Nicotiana rustica L. is an attractive plant that varies in height from two to four feet, depending on climate and soil, having medium-sized leaves and small, yellow blossoms. In shade, the leaves dry green, this preferred color being the symbol of healing, and the blossoms are also smoked. The self-seeding seeds are quite tiny, similar to mustard seeds in size.

When tobacco itself was not available or in short supply, other substances were either mixed with tobacco or smoked in its place. Alternatives include the inner bark of certain trees of the genus *Cornus*, such as red osier, the leaves of one of the sumacs (*Rhus glabra*) when they have turned red in the autumn, and the leaves of bearberry (*Arctostaphylos uva-ursi*). All these plants have an association with red, symbolizing blood, the essence of life. Bearberry has red berries, and the dried leaves are similar to the green of shade-dried tobacco leaves. The Algonquian-language word "kinnikinnick" is applied to smoking mixtures as well as individual substances.

Tobacco is the oldest domesticate in the Americas, dating to over eight thousand years ago in central South America, and reached the middle of North America some four thousand years ago. The cultivation of tobacco is generally distinct from the growing of plant foods. In some Plains cultures, only tobacco is grown. Tobacco horticulture invariably requires special rituals and is an especially sacred act; those who grow it often belong to special ritual societies.

The primary purpose of offering tobacco, either directly or as smoke, is for communicating with the spirits. When herbs, trees, animals, or stones are taken for use, especially sacred use, tobacco is directly placed by the requested substance as it is asked to offer itself for human needs; this is the simplest mode of using tobacco. The common means of offering tobacco smoke to spirits is the most direct: throwing the leaves on fire or placing them on coals. Next in complexity is the bringing of tobacco smoke into oneself and then blowing it toward the spiritual recipient. The sharing of the smoke between the one making the offering and the spirit receiving it creates communion between the two.

Not only is tobacco offered via fire, but so are the sacred fumigants: cedar leaves in the east, sweetgrass in the central region, sage in the Plains, and juniper and sweet pine needles in the southwest. Nowadays, the use of these substances is not limited to specific geographic areas. The smoke of these sacred fumigants is used to purify the place, participants, paraphernalia, and offerings used in ceremonies.

There are several methods of smoking, often indicating regional preferences. The simplest is to place one's head over burning leaves and inhaling. Next in order of complexity is the cigar, a roll of leaves ignited at one end, with the smoke drawn into the mouth through the other. This was the most common method of smoking in the Caribbean and southern North America, and cigars are still ritually used by the highland Maya. Next in complexity is the placing of shredded tobacco in a tubular, combustible container as a reed or rolled cornhusk. This method of ritually smoking tobacco is found from the American southwest through much of South America. Finally, there are manufactured smoking devices, that is, pipes, which is the most common method of containing tobacco for smoking throughout North America. (The Sacred Pipe is discussed in Chapter 8.)

Experiential Religion

Most religions involve varying degrees of experiencing the sacred. The notable exceptions are the mainstream Protestant churches and Roman Catholicism, which focus on belief in theological dictums rather than knowing the divine through direct experience. In contradistinction, the fastest-growing Christian movement worldwide is the Pentecostal Church, which emphasizes experiencing the Holy Spirit. Virtually all of the Native American traditions stress the necessity of personally experiencing the sacred and do so perhaps more than others elsewhere.

From the southern part of North America through South America, entheogenic substances are the primary means of eliciting ecstatic religious experiences. Native American traditions utilize a far greater variety of these substances than traditions elsewhere. Often these substances are taken in a communal ritual setting, which enhances the possibility of communal trance. For example, the Huichol in northwestern Mexico use peyote in all of their ceremonies. The Papago in the southwest United States, when the sahuaro cactus fruits ripen, ferment the fruit and become ritually inebriated once a year.

But throughout the central and northern parts of North America, the traditions use other means than psychoactive substances, save for the Native American Church (Chapter 8), which ingests peyote. In the southwest United States, traditions such as the Hopi and Papago utilize running long distances as the means of engendering trance and visions. Hopi males run on a pilgrimage to the Grand Canyon, and Papago males run on a salt-gathering pilgrimage to the head of the Gulf of California. Apache and Navajo young women, at the time of menarche, run daily during the menarche ritual, which is their major cultural ceremony (Chapter 5).

For most of the North American Native traditions, the ubiquitous mode of seeking visions is through fasting. A common misunderstanding prevalent in most of the literature is that only males vision-quest. This is due to the understanding of late-nineteenth-century anthropology, based on Christian attitudes of the time, that religion is purely a male activity and that anything women do, by definition, could have nothing to do with religion. Thus, they ignored the obvious fact that traditionally women sequestered themselves during the time of their menses, usually for four days, in a structure identical to those used by men for fasting, and that time was one for seeking visions. Thus, women vision-quested on a monthly basis, far more frequently than did males. And women's visions were essential to many facets of the traditional religions. Before menarche, girls fasted as frequently as did boys and in the same way.

In gathering–hunting traditions, children were often sent into the woods to fast through the day while their father and older brothers were hunting. This was to impress upon the spirits through their hunger the need of the people for food, but it also prepared the children for the longer fasts they would undertake when older. When the children reached their teens, they would begin fasting for the usual four full days or longer.

For the full fast, one builds a small shelter or, as in some Plains traditions, digs a fasting pit. Those with or seeking relationships with avian spirits often build a nest in a tree; those with terrestrial spirits build lodges on the ground. There one stays in complete isolation without food or water and without sleeping, awaiting a spirit to take pity on one and initiate a special relationship. Even if one has a vision early in the fast, one completes the length of the fast that one has vowed. This relationship, so long as it is maintained as taught by the spirit, will continue for many years, sometimes for life. Such relationships are understood to be essential for life. Humans are weak and need the power of spirits to survive. The specialty of the spirit becomes a power for the individual, and it is common to have relationships with two or more spirits. Such relationship is understood to be so essential to life that when children are born, an elder who is understood to have powerful spirit relationships is asked to dream a name for the child. This name will transfer to the child sufficient spiritual power to live until the child is old enough to fast and develop relationships with spirits on its own. Fasting continues throughout life, especially when one needs to reenergize one's relationships or is to begin an arduous task, such as healing or leading a raid, that requires the assistance of spirits.

Other means of vision seeking include the Thirst Dance of the Plains and the Salish Spirit Dance. On the Northwest Coast, near drowning in the cold ocean or prolonged periods of isolation are other means of eliciting visions. The most common means of eliciting communal visions throughout North America is the Spirit Lodge, called by the demeaning term "sweat lodge" in the literature (Chapter 8).

It is in these regards that there has been a major misunderstanding in the popular literature and in Hollywood movies concerning those who have visions. European culture and subsequently American culture have become fixated on a Tungus (northeastern Siberian culture) word for a religious specialist: *saman* or shaman. From the Saami in northern Scandinavia to the Altaic language cultures of western Siberia, and stretching across the northern fringes of the Americas among the Inuit, ritual specialists, male and female, while in a trance of varying depths, with the assistance of helping spirits, work in various ways for the good of their community and families. Shamans are social functionaries who may or may not have special status in their communities. This concept has been applied to Native American traditions, usually portraying a single person in a community with religious power over his community, for the shaman is invariably depicted as a male, with a role similar to that of a Catholic priest in a reservation.

In the 1930s, the anthropologist Robert Lowie pointed out that this depiction is far from the actuality of Native North American traditions, that in these traditions we have "democratized shamanism." By this, Lowie meant that every member of the community to varying degrees works with helping spirits in a state of trance to assist their communities, for every member of these traditions fasted for visions, and these visions were always for the community. To so act for oneself was considered the epitome of evil, and such action could lead to the death of oneself or of members of one's family. What one often found is that various individuals would have particular specialties. So for the healing of broken bones, one might go to one individual, but for the healing of a skin disorder to another, for healing one's horse, to a third person, and for leading a raid, yet another. As well, some people were more prone to having powerful relations with spirits, often several, than others. Just as all healthy people can run, some can run faster than others. So some were more effective at assisting others through functioning in trance. Those traditions that do not focus on individual trance experiences for all have elaborate ceremonials in which costumed and masked dancers embody the deities and make them manifest to the community, blessing the participants in the ceremony and being blessed in turn (Chapters 6 and 7).

Thus, throughout the Native traditions of the Americas, there were many means to engender trance and subsequent visions or dreams—trance and dreaming were often denoted by the same word, for it is understood that no one can live without a particular relationship with spirits and such relationships come from trance experiences. Native religious traditions are completely experiential. There is no need for faith—belief in the truth of what one has not experienced—in the existence of spirits when one directly encounters the spirit realm and sees and talks with the spirits.

WESTERN PERCEPTIONS

Western perceptions of Native religion run the gamut from nonrecognition to romanticized approval, but few perceptions are based on an accurate understanding. Part of the reason is that there is little information available on Native religious traditions that is reliable. Many of the classic works in ethnology were written by scholars who spent a few weeks over one or two summers in the vicinity of Native cultures, often living in the closest hotels which may have been a considerable distance from reservations. Usually, these early missionaries and later anthropologists did not speak the language and relied on translators who were almost invariably Christian converts and presented the information based on what they thought the anthropologist wanted to hear or should hear. Second, given an understanding that women had nothing to do with religion and that deities were necessarily male, most studies studiously ignored half of the spirit realm, half of the rituals, and half of the religious participants. Overall, most studies were highly skewed. Fortunately, there are a few reliable studies. Especially important are those imparted by Native participants or non-Natives who became participants and were asked to present what they learned to the non-Native population (see, for example, McClintock 1910).

No Religion: The Heathen Savage

To his death, Columbus believed that he had reached China, which he called the "Indies." Thus, on first contact he was disposed to assume that the indigenous people had religion, and he recorded some passing observations in these regards. But subsequent Italian mariners understood that they were not in Asia and consequently that the indigenous peoples might not even be human. These mariners were not disposed to observe religion, and some were quite adamant that the Native people had no religion. Giovanni da Verrazzano, in attempting to find a westward route to China, in 1524 reached the coast of the Carolinas, which he understood to be a new land and not China, and sailed north as far as Labrador. Although he infrequently went ashore and had little contact with the Native peoples, he concluded:

> We think they have neither religion nor laws, that they do not know of a first Cause or Author, that they do not worship the sky, the stars, the sun, the moon, or other planets, nor do they even practice any kind of idolatry. . . . We consider that they have no religion and that they live in absolute freedom, and that everything they do proceeds from ignorance . . . [1]

The Spanish came to fully understand that they were conquering empires in the southern part of North America and in the Andes, with cities grander than their own. When the Spanish decided that the indigenous people had souls, they were accepted as human beings, but being consequently subject to the Inquisition, it was convert or die. The Spanish intermarried with the Native peoples, creating populations in Latin America that are in large part mestizo (mixed heritage). The French were primarily interested in trade, rather than colonization, and saw the indigenous people as partners not only for trade but for marriage. The latter eventually led to a new culture of its own, the Metis in the middle of Canada. The English, and particularly the Puritans, saw themselves building a New Jerusalem in a wilderness. Accordingly, North America was not being conquered, but unused wasteland was being turned into a garden by the civilizing British influence. The indigenous people were a hindrance no different from wild beasts, and the children from sexual relations between humans and savages were anathema.

The latter attitude became part of the foundational mythos of the United States. I was taught in the schools in the 1940s and 1950s that Daniel Boone discovered a route to the Midwest, a vast wilderness inhabited by wild animals and wilder humans, both best exterminated. What was not taught was that Boone followed a route well used by Native peoples to a land of villages and farms. The Euro-Americans did not clear the land; they stole it. But it was much later in my life that I discovered what has been long suppressed in public education, that in the midst of North America there had been a city, as large as if not larger than any in Europe at the time (twelfth to fourteenth centuries). The remains, with huge temple mounds, similar to those at Teotihuacán near Mexico City, are just outside East Saint Louis, at the confluence of the Mississippi and Missouri Rivers. There is only one reason for a city to be there: trade. Clearly, at the site called Cahokia was a mercantile city. It seems to have ended with the Little Ice Age of the fourteenth century. The direct trading network extended from the Gulf of Mexico to the north shores of the Great Lakes and from the Appalachians to the Rocky mountains; indirect trade went as far as the Pacific and Atlantic Oceans and Central America. This means that the people colonized and displaced by the British and Americans were far from being savages; they were aware of cities, extended trading networks, and political hegemonies. And they had special religious rituals to enhance long-distance trade (Chapter 8).

With Native cultures deliberately misunderstood to be utterly primitive, missionaries could comfortably say that they had no religion or that in place of religion they had the ignorant work of the devil. Such an attitude justified making Native ceremonies illegal—their being by definition not true religions—and forcing Native people under missionary control to become civilized, meaning to Christianize them. Children were forcibly placed in missionary-controlled boarding schools to be trained to become Christian servants of the dominant culture. This understanding of Native peoples as primitive continues to inform the Western understanding of Native religions. Even today, the Canadian census, which does ask about religion, has no option for choosing any of the Native religious traditions.

Animism, Totemism, and Other Nineteenth-Century Fallacies

The discovery of the Americas and of assumed "primitive" humans by the British and the French led to a reexamination of history and of religion. Many theories developed, particularly since Darwin, of evolutionary concepts in the development of religion. Some have remained in the world of scholarship to this day.

One of these terms is "animism," frequently used to designate a pre-stage to real religion. Primitive humans are often termed "animists." *Concise Oxford English Dictionary* defines "animism" as (1) "the attribution of a living soul to plants, inanimate objects, and natural phenomena" and (2) "the belief in a supernatural power that organizes and animates the material universe." The second definition assumes that monotheism is the only possible theological understanding and thus denies the reality of polytheistic religions, which means denying the reality of all Native American traditions, which are poly-theistic. But the first definition in effect assumes that animists have no discriminatory powers and accord equal sacredness to everything, and that certainly is not the case for Native traditions. For example, many cultures would understand certain rocks and stones to have spiritual power, but not all rocks and stones.

Since the Jesuit missionaries began the study of non-Western religions in the sixteenth century, religion has been understood in an evolutionary sense. This historical understanding of evolution long predates Darwin. It was assumed that cultures move from polytheism to monotheism to Christianity. This notion, however, implied a developmental truth at odds with the Christian understanding of Truth as absolute, even across time. Accordingly, there arose an early concept of ur-monotheism, to be more fully developed in the late nineteenth and early twentieth centuries. The earliest cultures were understood to have been monotheistic but lost the Truth, until it was rediscovered by the Israelites and fulfilled by Christ. It was a revision of the "Adam and Eve and the Fall" story, of "Paradise Lost." With regard to the understanding of Native traditions, those who looked approvingly on Native cultures assumed that there must be an underlying monotheism; else Native people would be detestable savages. We will return to this theme in Chapter 3 on theology.

A term that developed in early anthropology and became a mainstay of Freudian theory is "totemism." Without going into the meaning and impli-cations of the term in psychoanalytic theory, it can be pointed out that this term and its understanding is based on a mistaken understanding of the rel-evant Native language.

The word "totem" is a variant on the Anishnabe word "dodem." It is first found in a work written in 1791 by John Long, an English trader traveling north of the Great Lakes: *Voyages and Travels of an Indian Interpreter and Trader.* In his slim book, Long somewhat accurately describes a personal dodem as a "favorite spirit . . . they never kill, hunt or eat the animal whose form they think this totam bears." Long also coined the word "totemism." John Ferguson McLennan, in an article on law in the eighth edition (1857) of the *Encyclopædia Britannica*, used the term in its second Anishnabe meaning of a clan symbol, with no specific ritual aspects. Hence, he dis-cussed in this usage, quite properly, "endogamy" and "exogamy." Following the application of the then recent theories of Darwin to culture, he also wrote of a "totem" stage of human evolution.

In the late nineteenth century, the term began to be used in discussing cultures other than Native American ones. Robertson Smith, in his *Lectures on the Religion of the Semites* (1889), discussed "totemism" in terms of Biblical sacrifice. In his major compendium of religious phenomena, James Frazer, in *The Golden Bough* (1890), linked "totem" with the Polynesian term "tabu." This linkage was picked up by Sigmund Freud. In *Totem and Tabu* (1915), Freud used these two terms to refer to a primitive stage of the human mind in its evolution to its high point: early 20th century, Viennese, upper middle class, Caucasian males. Finally, one of the major founders of sociology and the sociology of religion in the West, Émile Durkheim, in his *Les Forms élémentary de la vie réligieuse* (1912), used "totemism" as the label for an elementary social institution, focusing on Australian Aboriginal culture for his example. As has been demonstrated by more recent scholarship, this particular aspect of his theory was highly flawed, because his understanding of Australian Aboriginal religion and society was skewed by Eurocentrism and androcentrism.

In Anishnabe culture, where the term was originally found, there are two meanings for "dodem." First, it refers to the clan symbol. It does have religious connotations, but these are linked to specific clan origin myths and rituals. Clans do practice exogamy, but in this meaning of dodem there are no dietary restrictions. For example, members of the Deer clan do eat deer; it was originally the major source of meat. Clan members would have eventually starved if the primary source of meat in the diet were forbidden to them. On the other hand, many clan symbols are not eaten by anyone from any clan, as it is not considered edible, for example, the Loon clan.

The second meaning of "dodem" is a personal *manido* (manitou: spiritual being). Each Anishnabe, following the cultural and religious traditions, through rituals designed to elicit contacts with the spirits, develops a personal relationship with one or more manido, which is also understood as a dodem, but a personal not a clan one. Each person will have specific ritual behaviors associated with that relationship, taught to the individual by the particular manido. This might, but not necessarily, include dietary restrictions, such as not eating a particular part of the manido, if it is one of those manido with an animal or vegetable aspect.

In neither case does the term "dodem" refer to a mode of religion. Moreover, it certainly does not refer to a stage of human evolution. I know several Anishnabeg with M.A.s and Ph.D.s who function as traditional healers and ritual leaders and a larger number with a university education who practice the traditional religion and, hence, use dodem in both senses. Would we consider these people, some university professors, at an elementary stage of culture?

This brings us to the problem with the term "totem" and others words of similar ilk, and why it is no longer considered viable in the world of modern scholarship. First, the term becomes irrelevant with the dropping over a half century ago of the notion of the evolution of society (with Western Europe as the highest type of culture) or religion (with Western European Christianity as the highest religion). Second, the Anishnabe term "dodem" when combined with a Polynesian term "tabu" becomes a fictitious cultural mishmash which reflects no cultural reality. Finally, the term does not at all reflect an understanding of the culture from which it derives, given that Western scholars confused the two meanings of dodem.

The Noble Savage

While many Europeans understood the newly found Native Americans to exemplify a brutal primitive human culture, others saw a pristine primitivism with humans in a state of purity before civilization led to their fall from a state of natural grace. Native cultures were romanticized, especially after it was assumed that they had been obliterated, into a vision of innocence and undiluted virtue.

Since the early twentieth century, the Boy Scouts of America has had an honor society called the "Order of the Arrow." The initiation consists of a number of supposed Native spiritual practices, rituals, and dances, all quite powerful to impressionable eleven to thirteen year olds, as I was in the early 1950s. A non-Native pretender to being Native, Grey Owl had considerable influence on the Boy Scout movement.

In Germany and the former Czechoslovakia, some people take their summer vacations imitating the assumed Native life on the Plains before the imposition of reservations. They wear archetypal Native dress, live in tipis, and hire Natives from North America to lead them in religious rituals, such as the sweat lodge. They are seeking not only physical recreation but spiritual renewal.

But all of these perspectives, whether of the Noble Savage or the Heathen Savage, are based on imaginings with no reference to actuality. And they have led to interpretations of Native religious traditions that are pure fantasy, epitomized in recent bizarre B-grade Hollywood films. There seems to be no realization of how demeaning this is to real Native traditionalists who seemingly are not consulted about their own culture and religion.

New Age Hucksters

The romanticizing of Native religious traditions as pure religion unpolluted by the often depressing history and the continuing institutional focus of the mainstream Western religions reached its height with the growing New Age Movement in the second half of the twentieth century. The paperback publication in 1972 of Mircea Eliade's *Shamanism: Archaic Techniques of Ecstasy*, the English translation of *Le Chamanisme et les techniques archaiques de l'extase*, with its romantic presentation of shamanism as ur-religion, stimulated those seeking religious meaning outside Western religions toward the assumed shamanistic religions of Native Americans. At the same time, Carlos Castaneda's fictional depictions of Yaqui religion of northern Mexico became well known to a large segment of North American readers, the earliest of his many volumes being best sellers. In 1980, Michael Harner, who had carried out excellent ethnology, with a focus on religion, on the Amazonian Jivaro, published a how-to manual on becoming a shaman (*The Way of the Shaman: A Guide to Power and Healing*). In the mid-1980s, Harner began the Foundation for Shamanic Studies, which for a substantial fee offers weekend workshops all over the world for becoming a shaman. By that time, Lynn Andrews, a self-styled "medicine woman" trained in secret by otherwise unknown Native women, began writing highly popular books, especially among women, and offering workshops on aspects of Native American religion, some now available online.

Many Native persons, the most notorious to Native traditionalists perhaps being an Ojibwe who called himself Sun Bear, began to offer weekend sessions, which for a price promised an "Indian name" and vision-questing fasts. Sun Bear, with non-Natives, founded the Bear Tribe Medicine Society. One of my students showed me an advertisement of theirs in the New Age journal *Shaman's Drum*, which boasted of the quality of the food provided while fasting! Sun Bear (who died in 1992) began Medicine Wheel ceremonies held all over North America and Europe. In 2005, a typical simple weekend workshop, promising "Sweat Lodge, drumming, dancing, singing, talking circles," costed $200. Another woman who claims to be a Cherokee "princess" (a culture that had no royalty) through a relative, and distantly taught by holy people in Tibet (the basis of Theosophy), founded the White Buffalo Society. Composed of non-Native people, the society puts on "Sun Dances" and other Native rituals, charging many hundreds of dollars for participating.

The wording of the above may bother some readers, but it must be understood that these people have raised the considerable ire of traditionalist Native elders. Their concern is that non-Native people, often going by seeming Native names they have given themselves, are not only putting on what is claimed to be Native religious ceremonies, without the ritual right to do so, but are literally selling Native religion and charging participants substantial fees. Although gifts are often given at real Native ceremonies and voluntary donations for support anonymously collected, fees are never charged by these elders. Offerings are made from the heart, not as payment for the services received. Elders have publicly condemned in the strongest possible language those carrying out these practices, naming such persons as the "late king of the plastic medicine man," Sun Bear, and his non-Native wife, now "Chief" of the Bear Tribe; Lynn Andrews, the "Beverly Hills shaman"; and Wallace "Black Elk," "who scandalously exploits the Black

Elk name for profit (his real name is not 'Black Elk' and he is not related to Nicholas Black Elk of Black Elk Speaks fame) . . . "[2]

Many years ago, at the request of an elder to check it out, I took part in a New Age sweat lodge as a guest. The non-Native ritual leaders knew the Lakota version of the ritual in every detail. But it was carried out in a mechanical way, without the spontaneity and occasional humor one would expect. The ceremony was a mixed sex one entirely in the nude. Although nudity does not personally bother me, mixed sex "sweats" are simply not done in Native traditions, save for family "sweats," and certainly not today in the nude. During the ceremony, the ritual leaders summoned the spirits of Atlantis and Mu as well as alien spirits from far-off planets. The participants were severely chided for not having "faith," thus preventing their appearance. But the ritual leaders were oblivious to the actual presence of traditional Native spirits who did come; they were unaware of the Earth Mother on whom they sat and of the Grandfathers residing in the red-hot rocks. What personally bothered and saddened me was that not only this ceremony was a gross parody of what it was supposed to be, but the participants were denied the real experience they could have had if the concentration had not, from the Native perspective, been on ersatz spirits.

These New Age appropriations of Native religion are typical of the Western responses to Native American religion. Assuming one can take Native rituals and claim them, as Native rituals, for one's own, with no regard for the entire religious context, is taking the position that Native religions in and of themselves have neither meaning nor value and that Native people have no rights to their own traditions.

On the other hand, some Native youths have taken the extreme opposite position that non-Natives cannot have rituals that may be similar to but are not claimed to be Native rituals. For example, heat rituals, as discussed in Chapter 8, have a circumpolar distribution. To state that non-Natives have no right to carry on such rituals as non-Native rituals, in effect, is saying that Finns cannot have their sauna or Turks their hamman.

FURTHER CONSIDERATIONS

A few final considerations will introduce the complications involved in the study of Native American religious traditions. These complications when combined make the study different from the study of virtually all other religions.

Esotericism

Traditions that have ecstatic religious experiences as a major aspect tend to be esoteric. This is the case for the institutional Daoism of Chinese religion, for the Sufi tradition in Islam, for the Kabbalah in Judaism (not the

New Age version), and for the Tantric aspects of Buddhism and Hinduism. In all of these traditions, the written texts do not reveal the entirety of religious understanding. They must be used with a master who knows the oral teachings of which the written aspects are but an outline, often meant to be deliberately misleading to the uninitiated. The oral tradition is only available to initiates.

This is also the case for many aspects of Native American religious traditions. For example, in all the traditions with which I am familiar, one does not reveal the contents of visions, except to an elder guiding one, unless the vision is for a community or someone else. One does not directly reveal through speech the spirits to whom one has a relationship, but this will be known to one's community through symbols one might wear, through the apparatus one might use in healing, through the songs one has been given, or through the activities one might lead. It is understood that to directly reveal these relationships is to violate them, leading to one losing the relationship and the resulting powers. The solitary exception is becoming old. Hopefully, with age comes wisdom and the knowledge of when it is permissible to reveal esoteric understandings. Thus, elders might reveal far more than a younger person, but it will be done subtly.

Sometimes knowledge is but symbolically esoteric. For example, in the Midewiwin (Chapter 4), the ceremonial lodge is a completely covered large oblong structure. The teaching-initiation lodge, however, has the same framework, but only the lower part is covered, and that but loosely with boughs. Those who are not being initiated may sit outside the structure and listen to the teachings being imparted. And although only those initiated or being initiated will be within the lodge during initiations, far more will be sitting outside observing the initiation ritual. But I know of no noninitiate present at these ceremonies who has revealed the teachings or the details of the initiation rituals, even though these are readily available in a late-nineteenth-century publication.

Accordingly, it is rare to find details of visions or of rituals by participants. The exceptions are so notable that I will list a few important ones, as they are a precious resource for understanding Native religion and they are readily available, some still in print and others in libraries (see *Further Reading* for bibliographic data).

Bull Lodge was a noted warrior and holy person of the A'aninin (White Clay People of Montana). Most of his life was spent before the domination of the Plains in the late nineteenth century by Euro-Americans. Toward the end of his life, he told his daughter, Garter Snake, the visions that informed and determined his life. Toward the end of her life, Garter Snake related this material to Fred Gone, another member of her community, who wrote it down. She did this so that the knowledge would not be lost as her culture was rapidly losing its traditions. This material was much later edited and published by George Horse Capture for the same purpose (*The Seven Visions of Bull Lodge*).

In the early twentieth century, a Winnebago, Crashing Thunder, converted to the most Christian of the Peyote religions [see *Native American Church (Peyote Religion)* in Chapter 8] sweeping the reservations. In doing so, he felt it necessary to "give away" his traditional religion. It happened that a young ethnographer, Paul Radin, was in the vicinity, and Crashing Thunder dictated a number of the traditional rituals to Radin as his means of getting rid of it. This eventually led to two books, the verbatim dictated rituals (*The Road of Life and Death*) and an autobiography (*The Autobiography of a Winnebago Indian*).

In the mid-twentieth century when Mountain Wolf Woman, his sister, had reached old age, she told the story of her life, including her visions, to the anthropologist Nancy Lurie (*Mountain Wolf Woman*). Similarly, a Papago woman, María Chona, told her life story, including the religious aspects, to Ruth Underhill, in the early part of the twentieth century (*Papago Woman*). Slightly later, the Hopi Don Talayesva told a rich and full story of his life to Leo Simmons (*Sun Chief*).

These biographies and related material provide insights not otherwise available. These are the understandings of Native ritual leaders and holy people gained from visions, pilgrimages, initiations, and participation in rituals that provide more about Native American religions than any other resource. In particular, they provide an understanding of that which is usually left unspoken but is at the heart of Native spirituality.

Suppression and Secrecy

Although Native religions were made illegal in Canada and the United States from the late nineteenth to the middle of the twentieth century, and were ruthlessly suppressed by the Inquisition in Mexico earlier, in much of North America they continued to be practiced in secret. I recall a story of an anthropologist in the 1920s riding on a buckboard on the Plains with the local Indian agent and clearly hearing drums far off in the nearby hills. On asking the agent about the drums and its implication, the sympathetic agent stated that he could hear no drums. Had he admitted to hearing the drums, he would have had to have stopped the ceremony. But by pretending not to hear, he could allow the ceremony to go on in peace. Needless to add, he was not about to take the anthropologist to the secret ceremonial grounds.

Some Native people were prepared from childhood to maintain the religious traditions despite their illegality. The Lakota Leonard Crow Dog (to be discussed in Chapter 2 with regard to the American Indian Movement) was prepared from childhood to gain spiritual powers to be a ritual leader and healer. In his later life, he functions as a leader in guiding vision-quests, in the Thirst Dance, in the Ghost Dance, and in the rituals of the Native American Church.

But the need for secrecy led to an accentuation of esotericism. A religious life of continual secrecy made it difficult to bring the rituals to the light among the people even after it was possible in the latter part of the twentieth century. An elder heavily involved in the revitalization told me of going to northwestern Ontario reserves to facilitate the revival of the traditions. But being an outsider to the community led to the community keeping it secret even from him.

This attitude, gained from nearly a century of suppression, had led, in many areas, to considering everything regarding Native religious traditions to be secret. And this, of course, handicaps the introduction of Native religious traditions to the general public.

"Stealing Religion"

When I first began participating in Native ceremonies, it was at the very beginning of the revitalization (Chapter 2). The rituals were led by elders who had long hid their awareness of the traditions or by younger people who were being trained by them. There were always a few non-Native participants in those ceremonies where participation was not based on specific clan affiliations, as sincere interest was the criterion for inclusion. But as more and more young Native people, especially those who had been abused because of racism and were trying to recover from the resultant alcoholism and other ills, took part, they brought with them the racism with which they had been imbued by continually suffering from it. As this racism correlated with the new teaching of four races matched with four religions previously discussed, there was increasing resentment against the presence of non-Natives at ceremonies.

There was also bitterness toward the then anthropological practice of observing Native ceremonies without participating and then writing them up in detail without the permission of the elders or community. This is a practice now understood in the social sciences to be unethical. It was felt that the anthropologists were unfairly making their living off of Native culture. On the other hand, some of this material has served to preserve important aspects of the traditions. For example, Frances Densmore's early-twentieth-century wax-cylinder recordings of Midewiwin songs (housed in the Library of Congress) served as a source for young ritual leaders in the 1970s to learn many of the songs that had been lost.

The identification of Native American religion with race was also finding its way into the scholarly world. In the early 1990s, I was chairing a panel on Native religious traditions at the annual meeting of the American Academy of Religion, when a young scholar who had just delivered a paper on the problem of preserving the sacred site of the community with which he was involved was lambasted by a well-known academic in the audience for having the temerity to speak about Native religion. The person excoriating the young scholar was only part Native, had not been brought up in a Native tradition, and did not take part in Native religion, but she had dark skin. The young scholar was blond with fair skin, but both his parents were Native, and he had been brought up in an eastern Native tradition, been adopted by one of the most respected elders and ritual leaders of a Plains tradition, and sundanced several times. Yet none of the scholars in the audience seemed to think anything was wrong with a criticism regarding speaking about Native religion based solely on skin color or spoke in the young scholar's defense. Subsequently, some similar panels were limited to those who claimed to be racially, but not necessarily ethnically, Native.

It was at this time that Native authors began to complain that novels and short stories about Native cultures written by non-Natives were being readily published, whereas Native authors writing on the same topics found it difficult if not impossible to find a publisher. Specifically named in these denunciations were authors such as Ann Cameron, for books of claimed Native myths that Natives of the relevant culture understood were made up by her, and W.P. Kinsella, who published some collections of short stories about reservation life, stories both true to their subject and hilarious, perfectly capturing the spirit of Native humor. Both types of writing were deemed to be "stealing" from Native authors.

This term was picked up by young Natives opposed to non-Native involvement in Native religions. It was said that these participants were "stealing their religion." Attitudes began to develop that only Native people should study or write about Native culture and religion. Of course, if only those of a religion could research and write about it, this would mean the end of religious studies, which is inherently comparative rather than confessional.

My book on the Sacred Pipe was so considered by a few critics, even though it was written at the request of Native elders, it was vetted by Native scholars, it was praised by Native traditionalists, and all royalties went directly to a Native-way school. Similarly, this book will undoubtedly be deemed by some to be "stealing religion." Because of these attitudes, several comparative religionists who had written excellent studies of Native religions in cooperation with Native elders have shifted their research to other cultures. Fewer and fewer good scholarly studies of Native religious traditions are being published. Thus, readers interested in the topic are left with often outdated and misleading studies or studies written by scholars based on these books who have no direct experience with Native religious traditions or elders.

Avoidance of Photographs and Recordings

I hold to the viewpoint that one cannot fully participate in ceremonies and remain even partially an observer. Traditionalists consider photographing or recording Native ceremonies to be sacrilegious, with some notable exceptions. Sometimes if a researcher sponsors certain types of ceremonies, filming or recording might be allowed under tightly controlled stipulations as to who can view the film. Some elders are less concerned if a documentary were to show glimpses of but not the full ritual. Personally, I have refrained from even bringing cameras and recording devices with me, so as not to inhibit my learning in a traditional way. For this reason, the few photographs to be found in this book are of objects that are not involved or are no longer involved in rituals or of the exteriors of structures used for ceremonial purposes.

· 2 ·

From Past To Present

It is common in studies concerned with the past of Native American traditions to begin with the peopling of the Americas. Upon reflection, this is a strange custom. I do not recall a history of religion in Britain beginning with the peopling of the British Isles. In any case, it cannot be done, because we do not know who first peopled those islands and when. And the same is true for the Americas. *Homo sapiens* have been here as long as they have in northern Europe. While it is obvious from the genetic standpoint that many of the Native peoples, who came in waves to the Americas, are from northeastern Asia, humans have also been capable of coming to the Americas by sea from both the west and the east. There have been numerous arguments that Native American traditions are imports ranging from China to Egypt, but all of these studies, usually based on highly selected art decor, ignore chronology. The assumed influences, usually a matter of a stylistic element or a guess at the meaning of a symbol, are often off by a thousand years or more. There has been no compelling argument that Native American religions are essentially anything but Native American.

All traditions everywhere share commonalities based on religio-ecological factors, that is, there are commonalities worldwide among gathering–hunting, horticulture–hunting, agricultural traditions, mercantile traditions, and so on. How much of these commonalities are due to diffusion and how much due to the religio-ecological situation, in large part, is unanswerable. Certainly, when people began to arrive in the Americas perhaps some thirty thousand years ago, they had culture and religion. But whether this or later diffusion explains the few, specific circumpolar rituals to be found in the Americas cannot be determined, and there is little point in attempting to do so. This preliminary discussion is to simply counter the arguments that, in effect, Native American peoples had no religion because it came from elsewhere, whereas in British Isles, for example, we know that what survived did come from elsewhere.

NATIVE TRADITIONS BEFORE CONTACT

The east coast was the first part of North America to be colonized by Europeans. The earliest to arrive, about a thousand years ago, were the Norse, whose encounter with Natives, who were probably Dorset (pre-Inuit) but may have been Beothuk, led to skirmishes, and the Norse evacuated their small colony in northern Newfoundland.

Later, Basques fished off the coast of Newfoundland and interacted with the Native people there probably before Columbus reached the Caribbean. After Columbus reached what he understood to his dying day to be China, which he called the Indies, the Spanish rapidly colonized the Caribbean islands and the southern part of North America, building settlements as far north as present-day California and Florida. They were followed along the east coast by the French, English, and, for a short time, the Dutch.

The English settlers were little interested in Native religion, considering the Native people heathen savages, and many considered them simply vermin to be exterminated. For example, in Newfoundland, as the English did in Tasmania with the indigenous people there, a bounty was placed on the Beothuk who inhabited the island. The last Beothuk died in 1829. (Later, Micmac from the mainland settled in Newfoundland.) Earlier, the Puritans massacred the Pequot who lived near them—and who kept the Puritans alive through their first winter—in 1637, killing hundreds of women and children, most of the men being away. With these attitudes, early recording of Native peoples' religions by the English is not to be expected.

On the other hand, the Spanish friars were fascinated by the Devil and his religion as they understood Maya and other cultures and wrote books on the subject from their own perspective. A very small number of the Maya books escaped the massive book burnings by the Spanish priests, and more written material has been discovered through archeology. With the very recent decipherment of the written language and expanded archeology, the understanding of Maya religion has been considerably revised from what is to be found in most of the literature.

Similarly, the French Jesuit missionaries wrote meticulous descriptions of Wyandot (Huron) religion from their missionary post on the south shore of Georgian Bay (northern Ontario) which now fill many volumes. Typical of the representatives of a misogynist male monastic order, their descriptions are highly skewed, particularly in their ignoring the female aspects of a matrifocal tradition.

In summary, what we can learn from European sources on the nature of Native religious traditions around the time of contact is partial at best. Yet most studies of Native religious traditions have relied entirely on European and Euro-American sources. We can learn much more from the Native peoples themselves who have extensive oral traditions about their past. We must also recognize that we are dealing with a past that is now a half millennium in age since contact with Europeans, if the Norse are excluded.

In the following brief depictions of Native religious traditions on the eve of contact with Europeans, representative cultures will be mentioned for each of the geographic regions. A complete list is not feasible as it would fill this book and preclude discussing religion itself. Readers will find complete lists on maps in the reference works discussed in *Further Reading*. No disrespect is meant with regard to those traditions not individually mentioned.

North and Northeast

Those who lived in the eastern part of the boreal forest, south of the Inuit, were the ancestors of the Naskapi and Montagnais north of the St. Lawrence River and of the Abnaki, Malecite, Micmac, Passamaquoddy, and Penobscot between the St. Lawrence and the Atlantic Ocean (present-day Labrador, Québec, the Atlantic Provinces, Maine, New Hampshire, and Vermont). Further to the west were those who became the Cree, who in various subcultures, depending on the terrain, inhabited the region to the mountains (Québec, Ontario, Manitoba, Saskatchewan, and Alberta). All of these people speak Algonquian languages. On the west side, between the Pacific Ocean and the Cree, are the Athapaskan-speaking Dené (British Columbia, Yukon, and the Northwest Territories).

For all of these peoples, the lifestyle was a gathering–hunting one, following a seminomadic round over a set territory according to the availability of food resources depending on the season. Transportation was by canoe in the summer and snowshoe during the winter. Religion focused on relationships with those spirits on whom their lives depended (moose, caribou, deer, and elk), spirits who were models for hunting (wolves and eagles), and spirits who were both a food resource and powerful spirits of life itself (bear). These relationships were based on vision-questing, usually by fasting, and use of the Spirit Lodge ("sweat lodge"; Chapter 8). Rituals toward those animal, bird, fish, and plant spirits who gave their lives so the people might live were extremely important and frequent. For every animal received through hunting, there were rituals upon their death and upon feasting on them, especially the larger mammals. Communication from the spirits was primarily by use of the drum and, in the eastern part, pyroscapulamancy (divination by reading the cracks that appear on shoulder blades of certain animals after heat is applied). Also there were binding rituals (Chapter 8). All of these modes are most ancient, as they are circumpolar rituals. For example, before the Saami ("Lapps"—far northern Scandinavia) shifted from hunting reindeer to herding them, they used the drum for finding the animal herds as do the Montagnais, and the Chinese 3500 years ago were basing government decisions on pyroscapulamancy, which was also utilized by the Naskapi.

South of the boreal forest in the Northeast (Massachusetts, Connecticut, Rhode Island, New York, and Pennsylvania), one finds the ancestors of such peoples as the Massachuset, Wampanoag, Narragansett, and Pequot, and further south, the Lenape ("Delaware," named after Lord Delaware). They lived the horticulture–hunting lifestyle typical of the temperate zone throughout much of North America. Their residences were large matrilineal–matrilocal clan houses in walled towns, surrounded by extensive gardens, growing a variety of corn, various squashes including pumpkins, and a variety of beans. The women gardened the fields that belonged to the clans, while the males hunted, traded, and raided, all activities which took them away from the villages. Save for the Lenape, whose traditions partially continued in Oklahoma, details on their religious lives are sparse, but it would have been similar in outline to those of the Iroquoian-speaking peoples to their west.

Great Lakes and Midwest

The peoples who inhabited the eastern and central parts of the Great Lakes area (Ontario, Québec, New York, Michigan, and Wisconsin) were the ancestors of the Algonquian-speaking Anishnabeg (Ojibwe, Odawa, Potawatomi, Algonquin, and Menominee), aside from the Iroquoian-speaking peoples. In the western part were Siouan-speaking peoples (Minnesota); some of the Winnebago at their eastern extent are still in Wisconsin. South of the Great Lakes area were Algonquian-speaking peoples as the Miami and Illini (Ohio, Indiana, Kentucky, and Illinois).

The lifestyle north and east of the Great Lakes was a seminomadic one, as described above, with a similar religious life. In the western part among the Siouan speakers, there was a focus on sacred bundles. Before the adaptation to the horse, these were small skin-wrapped packets of sacred items. There were clan bundles specific to clan spirits and to spirits related to individuals and bundles particular to spirits such as Thunder. These bundles were opened ritually under specific circumstances; attached to the items in the bundle would be songs, dances, and origin myths of the bundle or items in the bundle.

South of the Great Lakes the lifestyle was one of horticulture–hunting. Their religious life would have been similar, although not identical, to that of the Iroquoian-speaking peoples, with elements related to the religious life of the people who lived in the Mississippi and Ohio River valleys, for we find both burial and "effigy" mounds as far north as the north shore of Lake Ontario, in Wisconsin and in the Iowa River drainage area. Also, these peoples were part of the Hopewell Interaction Sphere, that is, shared rituals, including the use of a similar pipe shape, over an extensive area from south of the Ohio River to the Great Lakes area and as far west as the Mississippi valley from 2200 to 1500 years ago.

The Iroquoian-speaking peoples resided from Georgian Bay off of Lake Huron (Wyandot) through what is now southern Ontario and over all of upstate New York (Haudenausaunee: Five Nations—later Six, when the Cayuga, Oneida, Onondaga, Mohawk, and Seneca were joined by the Tuscarora from the Southeast). These people lived in walled villages of matrilineal–matrilocal clan houses, some as large as a modern football field, surrounded by extensive gardens, as did horticulture–hunting cultures on the east coast. Every sixteen years or so, the villages moved when the gardens lost their fertility, perhaps to be returned to again after a generation had passed. Semipermanent dwellings meant that ritual paraphernalia could be elaborate and that formal ceremonies could be staged throughout the year.

The society was egalitarian, with the clans headed by "clan mothers" who chose someone to speak for them from among the male warriors. The clan mothers in council appointed male chiefs who in their own council, especially among the Five Nations, made plans for war and relations with other peoples. If the chiefs did not act in accordance with the wishes of the clan mothers, they could be replaced.

In this tradition, there are four major seasonal rituals, based not on a calendar, but on the coming forth of marker foods. The spring festival took place when the wild strawberries ripened; the midsummer festival or green corn ceremony celebrated the early harvest, while the fall festival celebrated the ripening of mature corn, pumpkins, and beans. The most elaborate festival was that of midwinter. As in most human cultures in temperate climate zones, the dark winter days, when the fields are resting under a blanket of snow, is a time for extended celebrations, including feasting, dramatic performances, storytelling, and ritual dancing.

A second difference from gathering–hunting traditions is a greater concern for the dead and ancestral spirits. Seminomadic traditions tend to avoid the resting place of the dead, but for those in villages the dead remain in close proximity to the living, and the clan comes to be perceived as including both the living and the dead in a relationship of mutual support. It was understood that the dead were present at the ritual feasts. Every eight or twelve years, there was a major feast for those who had died in that period. Their bones were removed from the cemetery and reburied in an ossuary, a large common grave. Many people attended as this was the major renewal ceremony of the entire community.

Southeast and Mississippi and Ohio River Basins

Charles Hudson, in his definitive *The Southeastern Indians*, writes, "All people have blind spots in their memory of the past, but the Southeastern

Indians are the victims of a virtual amnesia in our historical consciousness."[1]
There are a number of reasons for our lack of awareness. The indigenous
peoples of the southeast were the first to be colonized by Europeans, beginning with the Spanish and then the English, and thus were the first to mas-
sively suffer from the introduced Eurasian diseases. When de Soto reached
the Carolinas in 1540, he found empty towns that had been completely wiped
out by disease two years earlier. Euro-Americans who traveled through these
Native lands were poorly prepared to accurately and comprehensively record
their observations. Later Euro-Americans farmed the rich area through a
plantation system, preferring to eradicate the resisting indigenous inhabitants
and replace them with slaves from Africa. In the early nineteenth century,
those who remained were driven *en masse* from their homelands west of the
Mississippi to Oklahoma. The few who escaped these removals fled to the
mountains, where they learned to hide their Native identity, particularly in
Virginia, so they would not then automatically be enslaved, or to the Florida
swamps (the Seminole).

Major groups include the Cherokee of the highlands of present-day
Tennessee, North Carolina, and South Carolina, with the Catawba along
the coast of the Carolinas and Georgia, the Muskogee (Creek) of Alabama,
the Chickasaw, Choctaw, and Natchez of Mississippi, and the Caddo of
Louisiana. But there were many other traditions whose list would fill an
entire page—this was a richly settled area with a relatively dense population
prior to contact. The area was linguistically quite diverse, but the major language family was the Muskhogean. All of the abovementioned groups spoke
Muskhogean languages, except the Caddo, who spoke a Caddoan language,
and the Cherokee, who spoke an Iroquoian language.

In general, the peoples of the Southeast cultures, different from those
cultures to their north but similar to those in the Southwest, lived in permanent towns, often palisaded, surrounded by their farms. As with all settled traditions in North America, social groupings within the towns were
matrilineal–matrilocal clans. With regard to religion, they belonged to what
is called in the literature, the Southeast Ceremonial Complex. The
Complex also included those cultures along the Mississippi.

Ceremonies included a Spring Festival, at the first new moon of the solar
year, which was a year-renewal ceremony, including such typical traditions
found worldwide as renewing the fires. (The ceremony seems to have been
similar to the Chinese Spring Festival, called the Lunar New Year in the
West.) This was followed by the Green Corn Ceremony around June, the
Ripe Corn Festival in August, and the Great New Moon Festival of autumn.
There were other major festivals as well. These festivals included stomp
dances and other practices still continued in the Green Corn Ceremony carried out today by the Muskogee and others who were removed to Oklahoma
(Chapter 5). In these ceremonies, not only was the ubiquitous tobacco uti-
lized, but what has been called the "black drink" as well. The black drink

was made from the roasted leaves and stems of a variety of holly that is very rich in caffeine. In effect, it would be similar to drinking many cups of very strong coffee.

Mississippi and Ohio River Basins

The Mississippian cultures include the lower Mississippi River Basin cultures and extended up the Mississippi with cultures whose relationship to post-contact cultures is uncertain (Missouri, Illinois, and Iowa), and along the Ohio River Basin with a macro culture that archeologists label as Hopewell. The latter's influence extended as far as the Great Lakes and the upper Mississippi and as far north as present-day Minnesota, Wisconsin, and Ontario.

Here were not just palisaded towns but small cities with satellite towns that must have had a state government over a large area. The leaders seem to have been chosen from the matrilineal Sun clan, which was at the apex of the sociopolitical hierarchy (as in Japan). Large artificial mounds are a distinctive feature of these cultures.

Mounds, particularly burial mounds, are found all over eastern and central North America. But in the area under discussions, there were two distinctive types of mounds: large mounds or mound complexes and what have been called effigy mounds, mounds in the shape of sacred animals. All of these mounds would have been part of the religion of the relevant cultures, although their religious role is far from understood in many cases.

The earliest large mound known is dated to over five thousand years ago; it consists of eleven mounds, one over seven meters in height, connected by ridges to form an oval structure one hundred meters in length. This complex is near Monroe, Louisiana, at a site called Watkins Break. It has raised many questions, in part, because it precedes horticulture by over a thousand years. Archeology, as at the Koster site in Illinois, has demonstrated that the Mississippi Valley area was sufficiently rich in wild seeds as well as marine life to support permanent settlements long before domesticated plants diffused northwards from Mexico. A second major early mound complex is at Poverty Point, Louisiana, which dates to over three thousand years ago. It consists of concentric half circles, the outermost one a quarter kilometer in diameter. In the middle is a mound forty meters high and covering two hundred square meters.

Dating to over 1700 years ago, in the heart of what will become the Hopewell culture area, at Newark, Ohio, is the Great Circle Earthworks. This structure, ten meters high and four hundred meters in diameter, seems to be connected to other great earthworks, some over two kilometers distant, into a complex megastructure covering a huge area. Later mounds were constructed from the Ohio River north throughout Ohio, Illinois, Wisconsin, eastern Iowa, and southern Minnesota in the shape of animals and birds, including the most sacred, as Bear and Eagle. These mounds tend to be from one to two meters in height, and sometimes a large number will be found in a compact area. The largest of these is known as the Great Serpent Mound in Adams County, Ohio. It undulates over four hundred meters, is a meter and a half in height, and is from seven to eight meters in width. Recent archeological research suggests that it was constructed about a thousand years ago. Almost all of these are near bodies of water—streams, rivers, or lakes.

Rather than a single culture, the associated cultures are understood as an intercultural action sphere. In other words, different cultures, perhaps of different language families, shared many cultural features, along with extensive trade. These features included aspects of religion. This is apparent not only in the making of effigy mounds, but in the use of a common religious ritual apparatus: a pipe of a particular shape, known as the "monitor" pipe, named after the Civil War ironclad ship. The monitor pipe was made of stone with a spool-shaped bowl at its center. It is reasonable to assume that there was a common ritual for using this pipe throughout the large area in which it is found, virtually all of the American Midwest, as there certainly was for a later common pipe shape found over a much larger area (see *The Sacred Pipe: Ritual of Adoption* in Chapter 8). The dates for the monitor pipe—from 2200 to 1500 years ago—coincide with the height of Hopewell culture.

The large trading networks found throughout the heartland of North America, bringing shells and other trade items from the Atlantic and Pacific coasts, feathers from the jungles of Central America, and copper from the small pit mines of the Upper Peninsula of Michigan, led to the formation of a mercantile metropolis at the transportation nucleus of North America, where the Missouri River meets the Mississippi River, not far from where it is joined by the Ohio River. Here, from a thousand to six hundred years ago flourished a city as large as any in Europe at that time, with a population of at least 25,000, plus satellite towns in the surrounding area. Across the Mississippi, from present-day Saint Louis, it was the largest urban and ceremonial center north of Teotihuacan, near present-day Mexico City.

Although nothing of this city known as Cahokia survives save for its many temple platforms, a number of which have already been lost to bulldozers, the largest mound remains a most impressive sight. The mound covers fourteen acres and, rising in four terraces, is thirty-five meters high. The temple which was built on its flat top might have added another fifteen meters in height. It is the largest precontact earthen structure in the Western Hemisphere. This temple platform was at the center of a diamond-shaped city five kilometers east to west and three and a half kilometers north to south, and it is estimated that it was quite densely populated. What led to its demise is uncertain, but it is to be noted that it took place during the Little Ice Age, which also led to the demise of the major towns in the Southwest.

If readers are ever near Saint Louis, they are urged to visit the site. If they do, their understanding of the Native traditions of North America will never be the same. The notion of primitive will be discarded. The Native traditions will be understood to be as civilized as those that came from Europe. All of the Native traditions in the trading web, of which Cahokia was the hub, would have well been aware of urban civilization; the idea of cities was not introduced to North America by Europeans.

Plains and Plateau

For Americans and Europeans, the archetypal Native American is an eagle-feather–bedecked warrior on horseback following the great bison herds across the Plains (Alberta, Saskatchewan, North Dakota, South Dakota, Montana, Wyoming, Nebraska, Kansas, Colorado, Oklahoma, and Texas). Yet these horse-nomad cultures lasted for but a century and a half, from the early eighteenth to the late nineteenth century. Before the adaptation to horses originally brought by the Spanish to the Americas, few Native peoples lived year-round on the Plains. Most either practiced horticulture along the rivers and hunted the bison as they passed by twice each year on their seasonal migrations or lived by the mountains and there hunted deer, mountain goats, and mountain sheep between the bison hunts. The amount of meat that could be carried from the bison hunt was limited by the amount dogs could pull on a travois (a pack attached to two dragging poles tied to the dog's back and later the horse).

The Caddoan-speaking Pawnee, Siouan-speaking Mandan, and related cultures lived in earth-covered log structures on the hills above the Missouri River and its tributaries and farmed the low land by the rivers and streams that were fertilized by the spring floods. Their religious life centered on a complex interrelationship between gardening, especially corn, and hunting, particularly the bison. This is discussed in more detail in Chapter 6. They also had a yearly ritual held inside a large ceremonial earth-log structure that was the progenitor of what has come to be called the Sun Dance, although in the Native traditions a more common term was the Thirst Dance. This was a four-day ritual in which warrior pledgers tied themselves to skewers that pierced their breasts attached to ropes tied to the roof beams (later, the center pole of the Thirst Dance arbors for the postcontact Plains traditions) and danced pulling against or hanging from the ropes until the skewers tore through their breasts. It was a ritual of self-sacrifice for visions of warrior power from the spirit realm (see *From Contact to Reservations* as well as Chapter 8).

The Algonquian-speaking Nitsitapi, who lived on the western edge of the Plains in present-day Alberta and Montana, had rituals that focused on sacred bundles that were relatively small before the adaptation to the horse, but grew in complexity and size afterward. These rituals are more fully discussed in Chapter 6.

The Plateau is the name used to designate the region between the Rocky and Cascade–Coast mountain ranges (British Columbia, Washington,

Oregon, and Idaho). Here people lived off the local animals, similar to the Nitsitapi, but also depended on salmon which traveled up the Columbia and Fraser rivers and its tributaries to spawn. Salish-speaking groups lived in the northern part and Sahaptian-speaking peoples to the south. Until they became more nomadic with the adaptation to the horse, during the winter they lived in earth-covered lodges and temporary shelters during the summer. Their religious practices, aside from the ubiquitous fasting and Spirit Lodge rituals, included a round dance or dancing together in a circle to elicit trance.

Northwest Coast

Between the Cascade and Coast mountain ranges and the Pacific Ocean, and from the westward thrust of Alaska (north of Juneau) to the arid coast of central California lies one of the richest areas in indigenous food resources in North America. This area encompasses the panhandle of Alaska and the coasts of British Columbia, Washington, Oregon, and northern California. Being a northern temperate rain forest, the area is also rich in large, fast-growing straight trees, especially cedar, perfect for the plank houses and large, seagoing dugout canoes of the Northwest Coast cultures. Cedar is light in weight yet strong and flexible, resistant to insects and rot from water, easy to carve, and long lasting. Not only did cedar furnish lumber, but the bark was woven into cloth for clothing and mats, and wooden splints were used for baskets.

In this area, as in the Southeast and Southwest, were permanent settlements. Different from the latter two areas, these settlements were not based on agriculture, but on maritime resources. Some of these cultures, such as the Makah on the northwest tip of the Olympic Peninsula and the Nuu'chah'nulth (Nootka) on the west coast of Vancouver Island, based their economy on whaling; most others were based on salmon, halibut, seals, and sea lions. The area is also rich in berries, oil-rich small fish as well as deer and mountain sheep.

These cultures evidence the longest continuous settled habitation north of Mexico, over seven thousand years, and probably longer, except that the oldest village sites are now under the sea. Being on major ocean currents means that Japanese shipwrecks occasionally reached the shores. One can also reasonably assume that the Polynesians did not find a stop-sign in Hawaii and that some of their exploratory vessels also reached the Northwest Coast. Given that the coast was already inhabited, the influence from these explorers would have been limited, and there is no oral tradition of return trips. Trade items from northwest Asia probably also made their way down the coast from the Aleut, who lived between the Northwest Coast traditions and Siberia. Tlingit armor, for example, was similar to Aleut armor, which was identical in construction to traditional Japanese armor.

Although there was continual interaction along the coast by seagoing canoes for trading and raiding, the largest diversity of languages is in this area. On the other hand, there is considerable similarity of culture, being based on clan longhouses on the edge of the rain forest, where canoes can be pulled up on shore. Inheritance was bilateral and complex. All prerogatives, including such aspects as rights to salmon fishing and clamming areas, were based on inherited rights within a complex hierarchical social system, with slaves, who were captured warriors, at the bottom. These traditions extensively used wood carving to express the clan relationships and affiliations with the spirit realm, some being the famous "totem poles."

The religion had many of the ubiquitous features of Native North American religions elsewhere, such as heat rituals, often in separate wooden structures, and vision-questing in isolation. Their winter ceremonies were more complex than found elsewhere, save for in the Pueblo traditions, using complex dance dramas, with masks and costumes. Called the "potlatch" in the literature, these ceremonials, which maintained the sociopolitical structure, economic rights, oral history, and communal spirituality, are discussed separately in Chapter 7.

Another typical ceremony, with an affinity to the spring festival at the appearance of wild strawberries for the Haudenausaunee and the Green Corn Ceremony for the Southeast traditions, was at the appearance of the first salmon in the spring. For example, the Kwakwaka'wakw (Kwakiutl) had a First Salmon Ceremony when the first salmon of the spring entered the rivers to spawn. As with other Native North American traditions, the Salmon People were relatives of humans who offered their lives so the human people might live. In human form under the water in the winter, in the spring they don salmon masks and scale capes and present themselves for humans to eat. Humans in turn honor the Salmon People with an elaborate ceremonial ending in a feast. The bones are carefully set aside and returned to the sea so that the Salmon People might live again.

The region is different religiously from the other traditions so far discussed in having an affinity with the Aleut and Inuit traditions further north. Not only do they share the ceremonial use of masks and puppetry (also found in the Pueblo traditions), but there were individuals specifically trained as ecstatic religious functionaries, that is, shamans, using elaborate costumes, as is the case for Siberian cultures.

Southwest, Great Basin, and Southern California

It is in the Southwest (New Mexico, Arizona, and southern Colorado and Utah) that we find the third of the precontact North American great cultures, which save for the absence of writing are civilizations. There were several areas of agricultural villages in the Southwest, but the most important, from the standpoint of religion, was the one that surrounded, over a vast distance, the ceremonial center at Chaco Canyon (northwestern New Mexico). Roads were built, some over a hundred kilometers in length, from the various villages to the center, and their outlines can still be seen from the air. The multistoried apartment buildings each consisted of hundreds of rooms facing a kiva (ceremonial pit structures), some so huge they would have held hundreds of congregants. The buildings were aligned according to solar and lunar events, such as the summer and winter solstices. Because there is little evidence of agriculture in the immediate vicinity, it is now assumed that the entire complex existed solely for ceremonial purposes and was only inhabited, except perhaps for priests, during the religious festivals. As with Cahokia, readers are encouraged, if ever in the area, to visit the site (at least two days is needed, as the site is only served by dirt roads). Virtually everyone who has been there has been profoundly moved by the visit.

This culture, called in the literature "Anasazi" (a Navajo term meaning "Old Enemies"), would necessarily have had a large population to support the huge ceremonial complex, as large as the Vatican. As with Cahokia, and around the same time (thirteenth to fourteenth century), climate change—here, prolonged drought—led to its abandonment. The people moved to river valleys that more readily supported irrigation, particularly along the Rio Grande, where most villages, called by the Spanish term "Pueblos," are to be found today. Two large outlying groups, still inhabiting mesa tops, are the Hopi and the Zuni. These two, along with Taos Pueblo in the Rio Grand valley, still have the traditional multistory structures; a single one can comprise an entire village. Here, we also find agriculture, in which males farm, replacing horticulture, in which females garden and males hunt. Major crops included corn and cotton, and subsidiary crops included a variety of hot peppers and tomatoes.

Particularly the Hopi and the Zuni, whose languages are part of the Uto-Aztecan family, have maintained much of their traditional religion to today. Because they have the most complex Native ceremonial traditions now found in North America, more has been written on these traditions than any other. Indeed, I once calculated that more than a page has been published on Hopi religion for every living Hopi. The most popular works, such as Frank Waters', *The Book of the Hopi* (1963), written to parallel the Bible, are rejected as largely ersatz by Hopi traditionalists. These works have become a mainstay of New Age religion, which often posits the Hopi as the most sacred people in the Americas. In the 1970s, Hopi villages were inundated by Euro-American youth and Hollywood movie stars seeking to fulfill their spiritual hunger, leading Hopi elders to become concerned about maintaining the probity of their traditional way of life.

Hopi religion centers on the matrilineal clans and clan-linked ritual societies into which individuals are initiated. Life-cycle rituals begin with birth and continue with initiations into the societies. One of the most unusual features is the linkage of marriage and death rituals. This complex ritual illustrates the complementarity of the sexes and reciprocity typical of all precontact Native rituals.

The major ritual in most Hopi women's lives is the wedding ritual, which enables her to fully realize her personal power and social roles within the matrilineal and matrilocal cultural context. The woman initiates the ritual by proposing marriage. Acceptance of the proposal by the man leads to the first stage of the elaborate marriage ritual.

The bride temporarily moves into the groom's home, where, for the first four days, she is secluded and fasts in the Hopi fashion (abstaining from meat and salt and limiting the intake of liquids). On the last day of the fast, bride and groom are bathed by the females of their respective families, and the groom's mother washes the couple's hair and twists their hair tightly together into a single knot. The bride is then taken out of the house by the groom's mother and exhibited to the rising sun (as is the infant after the naming ceremony). The bride then continues to reside in the groom's home until the groom's family (the males do the weaving in Hopi culture) completes the manufacture of the bride's wedding garments. During this time, the bride cooks for her in-laws.

When the bride's garments are finished, a feast is held. On the following day, the couple move to the bride's family home. After children are born and the marriage is stable, the husband builds a house (or additional rooms) for his wife by her family home, a house which she will own and, should there be marital strife, from which she can exclude her husband. The husband now farms the fields assigned to him by his wife's clan and assists his father-in-law in providing for the family. The wedding is not complete until the bride's family accumulates the payment for the wedding garments and delivers it to the groom's family. The payment includes the making by the bride of a special wicker plaque for the groom.

These wedding garments are very significant in the death rituals, for the wedding-garment bundle is essential for females on their afterlife journey. Without it, they will be forced to grind corn halfway to the Underworld; with it, they will swiftly reach the Grand Canyon, where is located Sipaapuni, the place of emergence and the entrance to the realm of the dead. In turn, the *hahawpi* ("instrument for descending"), the wicker plaque woven by the bride for her husband, is essential for his smooth journey to Sipaapuni.

Not only do the women's wedding garments and the *hahawpi* directly affect the afterlife of both women and men, but the wedding is further connected with death, in that marriage continues in the Underworld. A first husband and first wife remain so forever. Should a person marry again, that marriage is temporary, lasting only until the death of one of the partners, who will again be with the first spouse.

The Hopi ceremonial year is elaborate, one of the most complex to be found among human cultures; most of the ceremonies are centered on the fertility of the fields, the need for rain in the semiarid region, and the harvest. Traditionally, all the Hopi, female and male, were initiated into at least one ritual society and usually several. Most of these societies have their own kivas, the underground ceremonial chambers that are the only non-family, nondwelling buildings in the traditional Pueblo villages. The kiva has a long history, being found in, and central to, the oldest archeologically known towns in the Southwest. Every aspect of the kiva is of symbolic significance; overall, its import derives from the basic myths of emergence as well as birth. The earliest structures in the Southwest were pit dwellings; undoubtedly, the kiva reflects the long habitation of the area by horticulturists. Near the center of the kiva is the Sipaapuni, which represents the *sipapu*, the entrance to the Underworld, the realm of the dead, and the symbolic entrance from the realm below to the present, Fourth, realm into which the Hopi emerged. Offerings are placed in the Sipaapuni for the spirits of the Underworld. The kiva itself functions as a womb in which new or transformed life—initiates, Katsinas (Kachinas), and sacred objects—is created. The narrow exit through which one climbs up a ladder to reach the outside serves as the vagina, from which life emerges. (The kiva also functions, when not in use for ceremonies, as a men's clubhouse—a space for the men, given that the residence is the women's domain.)[2]

From the beginning of snow in November well into the spring, there is, with short breaks, a continual round of ceremonies among all the Pueblo traditions. Most of the activities of these ceremonies, which often last sixteen days, take place in the underground kivas, and the public aspects, which involve but one or a few days, take place in the town square. A major feature of the winter ceremonies is the emergence of the Katsinas; ancestors become spiritual powers who are embodied within male masked, costumed dancers after many days of intense spiritual preparation. A second feature of these ceremonies is the sacred clowns who, during the ceremonies, mock those who have created disorder within the community to bring them back into social and cultural harmony. These ceremonies are rich in symbolism, dance drama, complex kiva altar arrays, and an elaborate theology and cannot be readily summarized. Those interested are directed to *Further Reading* for source material.

A century or so before the arrival of the Spanish, Athapaskan-speaking peoples arrived in the Southwest after migrating from the Northwest: the Diné (Apache and Navajo). Initially, they subsisted in large part by raiding the Pueblos, with some continuing to raid in Mexico until the early part of the twentieth century. Both cultures adopted aspects of Pueblo religion into their own religion brought from the far north based on spiritual power. See Chapter 5 for a description of the Navajo and Apache menarche ritual.

Further west, other offspring of the Anasazi maintained small settlements along the river valleys in an otherwise desert area and adopted their religion to this region. The Papago, also speaking a Uto-Aztecan language, for example, once a year harvest the fruit of the giant sahuaro cactus from which they extract juice and allow it to ferment. They became ritually inebriated on the fermented juice, a ceremony which leads to the coming of the fertilizing rain.

Between the Southwest and the Plateau lies an area called the Great Basin, comprising present-day Nevada and the desert parts of the surrounding states. The peoples there led a marginal, nomadic life, from which later sprang some of the great horse cultures of the Plains (e.g., Ute and Shoshone).

Even further west lived the many peoples of California, speaking a vast array of languages. Those of the northern coast were discussed under the heading *Northwest Coast*. To their south along the coast, many of these cultures used the acorn as their main food source. After leeching out the toxins, they made porridge and bread from it. These peoples early came to be dominated by Spanish missionaries, who forced them to convert, to build the massive mission churches, and to work as serfs on the mission farms. Most died. Those who survived when the area came under the sway of the United States were hunted for sport with dogs. Hence, we have but a very partial understanding of the religious patterns here before contact.

Far South and Caribbean

The Plains, Southwest, and California cultural regions extend into the northern part of present-day Mexico. But it is here that we find one of the characteristics unique in the religions of the world to the Americas: a richness of ritually used psychoactive substances. Best known of the northwestern Mexican traditions are the Huichol, because of both a series of excellent anthropological studies and a very popular series of fictional works pretending to be ethnology. The Huichol have an annual pilgrimage to their homeland (they fled into the highlands to escape Spanish missionaries) to collect the psychoactive cactus peyote, which is ingested by everyone in all of their rituals. The Cora and Tarahumara also use peyote in their ceremonies. North of Mexico, datura is occasionally used in some cultures by those able to handle its potency, and the ritual use of alcohol is found in some of the Southwestern cultures. From the middle of Mexico southwards, further entheogenic substances, some mild such as chocolate, to morning glory seeds and potent tobaccos, are ritually utilized. South of North America, in the Amazonian Basin and in the Andes, other psychoactive plants, some extremely potent, are used in the ceremonies. The use of psychoactive substances allows for all to go into trance simultaneously and for ritual specialists to lead the congregants into shared trances, although, as among the Huichol, in North America the trances are more commonly individualistic. Shared trances encourage social cohesion and enhance group action.

The religions of central and southern Mexico are urban traditions, being, respectively, the Aztec empire and Mayan kingdoms, which were of two aspects: the elaborate state ceremonials and the ordinary rituals of the peasantry. The former, which included human sacrifice and ritual ball games, ended with the arrival of the Spanish, but the latter continue underground within a Catholic Christian facade to today. These traditions are far too complex to treat in a summary fashion, and many books have been written on these topics (see *Further Reading*). Many temple sites and ceremonial cities have been partially reconstructed throughout Mesoamerica and are popular tourist areas.

The Caribbean was inhabited by Caribs in the southern islands and the Taino in the northern ones. The Taino were the first people to meet Columbus. All were thought to have died of disease and brutal enslavement, although recent DNA research suggests that some blended into the introduced African population. The Taino shared religious features with those on the mainland. In Puerto Rico, two ceremonial areas have been partially reconstructed. One is the Tibes Indian Ceremonial Center, just north of Ponces on the south coast. It is a reconstructed village, with ceremonial grounds, on the excavated site of a village. The other, near Utuado in the mountains in the middle of the island, has the most monumental extant Taino ceremonial complex, consisting of large rectangular ball fields flanked by incised stones with many designs. Readers who travel to Puerto Rico are recommended to visit these sites to gain an inkling of precontact life in the Caribbean.

FROM CONTACT TO RESERVATIONS

The immediate consequence of the coming of Europeans to the Americas was massive death from smallpox, measles, influenza, and other epidemic diseases which the indigenous peoples seem never to have experienced, for they had no immunity to even the common cold. Their medical practices, focusing on heat rituals, suggest that they had no experience with respiratory infections. It is commonly thought that of the over 100 million people who lived in the Americas before contact, perhaps 90 percent eventually died of introduced diseases. This is a holocaust unique to the human experience. And this is why such small numbers of Europeans, who carried these diseases yet had built up immunity to them, could conquer on such a vast scale—the armies that could oppose them were dead or dying.

Only those who in modern times have experienced similar holocausts can understand what it would mean to those who survived when most of one's family and community have died. In the Caribbean, where the indigenous peoples first suffered from contact, it seems that those who survived disease only to be enslaved lost the will to live. And it is here that Europeans first replaced the Native peoples with slaves they brought from Africa. The effects on religion would have been equally pronounced.

Among Jews who survived their mid-twentieth–century holocaust, some rejected their traditional religion as ineffectual, while others embraced it even more passionately than before. Similar attitudes seem to have prevailed among Native Americans. In the Spanish-occupied territories, following a debate at the Spanish court on whether the indigenous peoples of the Americas had souls, it was decided that they did and, accordingly, were required to convert to Christianity or be tortured to death. In the northern part of Spanish-controlled North America, in present-day New Mexico, the Pueblos eventually rebelled against Spanish political and religious domination in the late seventeenth century. They were initially successful and drove the Spanish out of their territory, but the Spanish returned a generation later and retook the Pueblos. Learning from their previous failure, the Spanish allowed the Pueblos internal political autonomy and the practice of their religion alongside Catholicism. This maintenance of dual, interrelated religious traditions, Native and Christian, continues to today among the Rio Grande Pueblos, centering around Santa Fe.

In the French-occupied territory, Catholic missionaries sought to convert a people they understood to be without religion to religion, meaning Christianity. At first they were but marginally successful, since the Native people quickly learned that the missionaries brought death by disease. But as the remnant survivors of disease and increasing warfare saw the French succeeding, whereas they were in decline, more and more found the religion of the French to be appealing. Some began to preach to their own people an indigenous understanding of Christianity. After the Puritans and other English killed many of the indigenous inhabitants of their "New World," they began to preach among the few surviving Native peoples, again with slowly increasing success.

On the other hand, Native prophets, to a degree influenced by their awareness of prophets in the Bible, began to preach that the distress of the Native people was due to their adopting the way of the White Man and neglecting their own religion and culture. These prophets sought to get rid of every vestige of European influence and return to a pristine past that probably never existed. The Lenape (Delaware) prophet Neolin preached among his own and other Native peoples in the 1760s. He influenced the Odawa (Ottawa) war-chief Pontiac to unsuccessfully rise against the British in Fort Detroit. Among the best known of these prophets before the reservation period is Tenskwatawa, called the "Shawnee Prophet," whose successful preaching allowed his brother, the military leader Tecumseh, to create a grand alliance of Midwestern tribes to rid themselves of the encroaching Euro-American settlers. This army lost a major battle against the Euro-Americans, the Battle of Tippecanoe, in 1811, and the nativistic religious movement rapidly declined thereafter. The effects of another contemporary major prophet, the Seneca "Handsome Lake," who sought to adopt their religion to the changing circumstances of Euro-American domination, are discussed in more detail in Chapter 4.

The continuing incursion of American settlers into the Midwest greatly affected the quality of Native life, and the use of alcohol spread widely. Like Handsome Lake, the Shawnee Prophet had become an alcoholic and had a series of visions that led to his not only reforming his life, but preaching messages that spread widely throughout the Native peoples of the Midwest. He took the name Tenskwatawa ("Open Door") to symbolize his new role as the prophet of the Great Spirit and preached resurrection, with a Shawnee version of Heaven and Hell. He railed against not only the adoption of Euro-American tools and foods, but also traditional religion, requiring converts to destroy their sacred bundles and to ignore traditional female and male spiritual leaders. He sought to replace it with a highly nativistic version of Christianity. Converts were required to confess their sins and stroke a variation of the rosary. Eventual military failure led to a falling away from Tenskwatawa and his new religion.

A second major effect of contact, after disease, was economic, which affected both society and religion. While the Spanish enslaved the Native people to work in the silver mines or made them serfs on large Spanish-owned estates comprised of former Native farms, the French, followed by the English, were more interested in allying themselves with Native tribes to foster the fur trade. This was not an imposition on Native peoples, as they wholeheartedly entered into the trade, which eventually affected all of the northern half of North America.

In the Northeast and the Great Lakes area, the Five Nations, supported and armed by the English, and the Algonquian-speaking tribes, together with the Wyandot, supported and armed by the French, shifted from traditional raiding for prestige and revenge, to outright warfare to expand their territories to monopolize the fur trade. This seems to be the first full-scale warfare among Native peoples to take place north of Mexico. It led to further loss of life and major movements of peoples who were displaced by these wars. The Five Nations became particularly astute in playing off different European powers against each other to their political and economic advantage.

In the mid-seventeenth century, the Five Nations crushed the Wyandot, who were already decimated by the diseases brought to them by Jesuit missionaries. Many of the remnants of the Wyandot merged with their Anishnabe trading partners, who later were able to push the Five Nations south of the Great Lakes. This merging led to major religious developments among the Anishnabe (Chapter 4). The Anishnabe also pushed westward, forcing Siouan-speaking peoples west of the Great Lakes out into the Prairie, where they adapted to the newly developed horse culture and became the great Lakota nation, which also led to major religious developments.

The fur trade also led to major changes in subsistence patterns, which greatly impinged on traditional gender relationships, particularly among the more northern gathering–hunting traditions. In these cultures, women produced more foods through gathering plants, fishing, and snaring small animals than men did hunting larger herbivores. Women also made blankets, wigwam coverings, cooking vessels, containers, and so on. These were replaced by trade goods: flour, tea, and sugar replaced traditional foods; wool blankets replaced hide blankets; wool serge replaced skin clothing; canvas replaced bark for wigwam covers; and iron and copper pots replaced traditional bark food vessels. Of course, for males, guns replaced bows, and iron axes and knives replaced stone ones. While trapping was added to male hunting activities, women became less important. Gender egalitarianism was replaced by an increasing patrifocal orientation as women were less valued.

A second related factor was one of inheritance. In gathering–hunting situations, there are few possessions and thus there is nothing to inherit. In horticulture–hunting situations, the gardens and longhouses are the property of matrilineal clans. With a trapping culture, families gained rights to large territories for trapping, and being a primarily a male activity, this was passed on patrilineally. Those cultures that remained horticultural also remained matrilineal, even with the increased importance of trapping, but gathering–hunting ones, given the many changes due to trapping, seem to have become patrilineal. This would later be strengthened when the dominant culture demanded that reservation roles be maintained through the male line.

All of this seems to have had an effect on theological understanding; the female aspect of the numinous disappeared and female spirituality declined. This is discussed in the first section of Chapter 3. A further aspect of the effects of trapping on theology was with regard to the relationship with subsistence. The rituals pertinent to hunting remained, with those animals who sacrificed their lives so humans may live still understood to be important spiritual powers. But the attitude toward the desired fur-bearing animals changed. Those animals that were trapped came to be exclusively viewed as a commodity to be traded to Euro-Americans. The precontact trade in furs between Native groups was on a small scale, usually for maize. In precontact times, the animals trapped for their fur were undoubtedly treated with the same respect as those primarily hunted for food. With the fur trade, beavers were killed to the point of extinction in large areas, which suggests that the spiritual relationship between humans and beavers and other animals trapped for trade to Euro-Americans had been broken.

Adaptation to the horse, originally brought to North America by the Spanish, had a major impact not only on lifestyle but on religion. The effects of horse nomadism on the nature and use of sacred bundles as well as the development of sacred societies are discussed in Chapter 6.

The horse allowed for moving permanently onto the Plains, following the migrating bison herds virtually year round. For these peoples, the bison became a major deity, as the bison provided not only rich food but tipi coverings and blankets from their hide, sewing thread from their sinews, and tools from their bones. Thus, for the Lakota, who had previously been a horticulture–hunting culture, White Bison Calf Woman becomes a major deity who gives the Lakota their central rituals. Another major effect on religion was the spread of the Thirst Dance (Sun Dance) as the major ceremonial gathering of entire tribes in late spring when there was sufficient grass for the large herds of horses. This ritual, more than any other, fascinated Euro-Americans, and the Sun Dance came to be seen as the archetypical Native American religious ceremony. It is discussed separately in Chapter 8.

RESERVATIONS AND ENFORCED CHRISTIAN CONVERSION

After establishing the original thirteen colonies, the English, in support of the fur trade, tried to limit the expansion of Euro-American settlements west of the Appalachian Mountains. In the northern part of this area, the Five Nations were able to establish de facto suzerainty, playing the English off against the French, until the French lost to the English. In the southern part, the Cherokee, also Iroquoian speaking, changed their culture to model themselves on Euro-American patterns. They established plantation farming with brick mansions, developed a written language and a printing enterprise, and so on. In all of these Western endeavors, they were quite successful. But after the end of the American Revolution and the Louisiana Purchase, when the infant United States "purchased" from the French a huge Native land that the French never controlled, all changed.

The Americans rushed west of the Appalachian Mountains to take over Native farms and villages. Many of the now Six Nations had sided with the British and fled to Upper Canada (now Ontario). Those who remained precariously held small areas in western New York. The Native peoples of the Midwest, initially successful in some battles, lost war after war. In the early eighteenth century, the U.S. government forced all remaining Natives west of the Mississippi. For the Cherokee, it became known as the "Trail of Tears," as the old, sick, and children died along the route of the forced march. A few Cherokee, and some other peoples, managed to hide in the mountains.

All of these peoples were forced onto what was called Indian Territory, now Oklahoma. Being pushed into areas where other Native peoples already lived created considerable friction. Eventually, even this area was further reduced for Native habitation, leaving small arid areas unwanted by Euro-Americans called "reservations" ("reserves" in Canada). The peoples of the Plains, particularly after the Civil War when the U.S. Army was freed from conquering the Southern states, were reduced by military means, including germ warfare, and forced onto reservations, where promised food often never arrived, leaving people to die of starvation and disease. In

Canada, small reserves were earlier begun by one-sided treaties that left pockets of Native peoples in every province, except British Columbia, where the provincial government refused to make treaties with the Native peoples, considering all of the land the property of the British government. Treaty negotiations there have been ongoing for many decades with no end in sight, as now the Native peoples know better and will not sign a treaty that does not provide local autonomy.

In Canada, the reserves were put under the direct control of the various Christian churches. In the United States, church control was more indirect but still present. In both countries, the police or the army could be called in by missionaries to stop the practice of Native religion. In both countries, laws were passed forbidding Native people, on pain of incarceration, to practice their religion. And missionaries often could control who received food and treaty payments. Obviously, those who did not convert were left to starve. Native children were forcibly removed from their parents and placed in boarding schools under missionary control. There they were only allowed to see their parents once a year at most, their traditional clothes were removed and burned, their hair was cut, and they were beaten for speaking their own language. Many children were also sexually assaulted. And many died of diseases inside the schools, where they were poorly fed.

A modern mode of suppression is to take reservation land, particularly sacred sites, and turn them into public parks. Perhaps the most notorious is the most sacred site of the Lakota and Cheyenne: Bear Mountain in the Black Hills of present-day South Dakota. This was and remains the most important fasting site for several Native traditions. The site has become Bear Butte State Park, where tourists can follow trails to watch Native people vision-questing, the most private of Native spiritual practices! Lip service is given in the park literature to respect the tobacco and cloth offerings, yet their very mention encourages tourists to look for them and take them home as souvenirs. Similarly, the Sun Dance, after it was proscribed by law, was allowed if it was carried out as a tourist attraction. The only encouraged Native dancing was at powwows, which the dominant culture understood to be completely secular, although many Native powwow dancers understood this as a way of expressing their religiosity.

These practices have led to what has been called in the literature "cultural genocide," a follow-up of the earlier physical genocide, and more recently as "religious genocide." The purpose was to destroy Native language, culture, and religion to civilize them, meaning to make the males into laborers for Euro-American farms and ranches and the females into maids to serve Euro-Americans. The actual result for a great many was despair leading to alcoholism, later drug addiction, and suicide. So many teens committed suicide on a number of reservations, even to the present, that some coroners termed it a "suicide epidemic." Particularly after reservations were terminated, Natives found themselves homeless in the cities, where many Native women had no alternative to becoming prostitutes. The image of the "drunken Indian" came to be seen as a Native characteristic rather than the result of deliberate government policies. In all areas with substantial Native populations, far more Native people are jailed than Euro-Americans, often for misdemeanors for which Euro-Americans would not be jailed, and form the majority of the prison populations.

Thus, the first result of the suppression, then prohibition, of Native religion was for it to go underground, where feasible. In permanent villages, it was not possible to hide the ceremonies, and in one notorious case, a missionary, backed up by the U.S. Army, entered Hopi kivas during rituals, confiscated the complex altar arrays, and presented them to the Field Museum in Chicago. The same held for the Northwest Coast potlatch, when Kwakwaka'wakw were arrested by the Canadian national police and jailed for dancing and their religious paraphernalia given away to museums or sold to collectors. Traditionalists of more nomadic traditions could go off deep into the Plains, mountain valleys, or woods to carry on their religion. Some families hide their children to prevent them from being forcibly taken away to the boarding schools, so that they could be raised in a traditional way. One of the most important is Leonard Crow Dog, who is discussed in the subsequent paragraphs.

A second result, found soon after the establishment of the reservations, was the flourishing of new prophets responding to the new crises. Toward the end of the nineteenth century in the western part of North America, new waves of epidemics as well as battles and massacres left many mourning the death of family, relatives, and friends. The traditional way of life had ended as people were forced onto virtual concentration camps, often with little food and shelter, and with every aspect of their life controlled by the military and missionaries. On the Plains, the bison had been deliberately exterminated to erode Native people's subsistence. It is hardly surprising that the new prophets had visions of rituals to bring back the dead and rid the land of Euro-Americans.

In the Plateau region, Smohalla (The Dreamer), whose life spanned the nineteenth century, had visions of death and resurrection. He preached a return to the traditional way of life, of avoiding reservations. For those who followed his vision, with both old and new rituals, life would return to the way it had been, the recent dead would return to life, the Euro-Americans would disappear, and the earth would be renewed. Smohalla was but one of many prophets in this region following contact with Euro-Americans. These movements led to a Native mode of Christianity called the Indian Shaker Religion as well as Spirit Dancing among the Salish that continues to this day.

The best known of these movements is the one termed the "Ghost Dance" that resulted in the infamous massacre at Wounded Knee. During the January 1 eclipse of 1889, a Northern Paiute (Nevada) prophet, Wovoka (Jack Wilson), had a vision in which deities told him that if the people were good, worked together, and performed the dance they taught him, the earth and the Native people would again be in harmony. The dance took place on a cleared circle of land approximately a hundred meters in diameter. The people joined hands and performed a version of the Circle Dance. This dance a generation earlier had been spread by the Northern Paiute prophet Wodziwob and may have been stimulated by the traditional round dance and the Prophet Dance on the Plateau.

Word of the prophecy and dance spread, and a number of Plaines tribes sent delegates to meet Wovoka and assess the movement. Many used the new railroads to speed their way to Nevada. The Ghost Dance found favor and spread rapidly. In the Plains it was understood that the ceremony would rid the earth of Euro-Americans, reunite the living with their recent dead, bring the bison back, and recreate the world as it was before epidemic diseases, massacre by the U.S. Army and militias, and the slaughter of the bison. Among the Plains warriors, it also became understood that the dance, along with a special shirt, would make them invulnerable to Euro-American bullets, and this seems to have "freaked out" the U.S. soldiers, who appeared to have taken the prophecy as seriously as the Native warriors. Thus, when several hundred starving and bedraggled Natives, mainly older people, women, and children, fled the increasing turmoil between the younger warriors and the army in the winter of 1890, they were literally rounded up, encircled by the soldiers at a place called Wounded Knee. Apparently one of the soldiers panicked and fired a shot; immediately the rest let loose with rifles and an early version of the machine gun. The survivors who fled on foot down a gully were chased down by soldiers on horseback and shot. Very few survived.

Although forbidden, the Ghost Dance ceremony survived underground. At the "Second Battle of Wounded Knee," the members of the American Indian Movement (AIM) were taught the Dance by Leonard Crow Dog, and it can be seen on documentaries made during the occupation.

A third result of the reservations and cultural genocide was the creation of new ritual complexes, in effect new pan-Indian (multitribal) religions based not on a single vision but on an understanding of the need for new viable modes of religion to meet the changing circumstances that fit the Euro-American work week and urban and small reservation lifestyles and circumstances. The most successful of these has been the Native American Church (Peyote Religion), which is described separately in Chapter 8.

A fourth result was the merging of Native religious traditions and Christianity. There were two major ways this took place. One was an actual merging of the two disparate religions, either through Native forms of Christianity, such as the Shaker Religion or the more Christian versions of Peyote Religion, or through adding Christian modifications to Native traditions. The second was to practice both Native traditions and Christianity in parallel. An excellent example of the latter can be seen in the life of the

Winnebago, Mountain Wolf Woman, mentioned in Chapter 1. When she died, three separate funerals took place: one Protestant Christian, one a traditional Winnebago ceremony, and one a Medicine Lodge ceremony. (The Winnebago version of the Anishnabe Midewiwin is discussed in Chapter 4.)

The most influential example of the merging of Christian teachings into a Native tradition can be seen in the life and teachings of the Oglala Lakota, Nicholas Black Elk (1863–1950). Brought up in the traditional Lakota religion, he was baptized a Catholic in 1904, apparently not by choice, but he continued the practice of his traditional religion underground and became a ritual leader. Yet he also took Catholicism seriously, and shortly after his baptism he became a catechist (a teacher of Christianity). Nicholas Black Elk and some other Lakota religious leaders came to understand that to save the traditional religion in a time of forced conversion to Christianity the two had to be merged together. Frank Fools Crow, also a Catholic catechist as well as a major traditional ritual leader and healer, spoke of a conversation he had with his uncle:

> Black Elk told me he had decided that the Sioux religious way of life was pretty much the same as that of the Christian churches, and there was no reason to change what the Sioux were doing. We could pick up some of the Christian ways and teachings, and just work them in with our own, so in the end both would be better.[3]

To record the traditions at a time when it was perceived that they might disappear, Nicholas Black Elk dictated material to two Euro-Americans. These led to books that gained considerable popularity. The first, John G. Neihardt's *Black Elk Speaks: Being the Life Story of a Holy Man of the Oglala Sioux* (1932), reprinted many times, had all of Nicholas Black Elk's references to his Christianity expunged. The second, Joseph Epes Brown's *The Sacred Pipe: Black Elk's Account of the Seven Rites of the Oglala Sioux* (1953), also reprinted many times, has functioned as the single true account of Native North American religion in general for many Euro-Americans and as a virtual bible for many Native youths of various traditions seeking their own religious background. Yet in these teachings, White Bison Calf Woman is an equivalent of the Virgin Mary; *wakan-tanka*, a generic term for the numinous, for all that is sacred, is a male, anthropomorphized quasi-monotheistic deity; the seven rites are presented as the equivalent of Catholicism's seven sacraments; and so on.

The above is not meant in the slightest to belittle the sincerity of such great spiritual leaders as Nicholas Black Elk and Frank Fools Crow. But it is meant to indicate that it is incorrect to assume, as is often the case, that Nicholas Black Elk's and similar teachings of others are a pristine version of Native religious traditions uninfluenced by Christianity. Finding Nicholas Black Elk's Christianized version of Native American religion to be theologically similar to Christianity, some teachers of world religions have argued that the Christian truth is a universal one to be found in all religious traditions.

REVITALIZATION OF NATIVE TRADITIONS

The legal prohibition of practicing, even speaking positively of, Native religions was dropped from Canadian law in 1951, although not specifically repealed. But the boarding schools in Canada continued into the 1980s, and in the late 1960s, police still routinely broke up Native ceremonies in the woods when they could be found. Missionaries on Native reserves forbade the practice of Native ceremonies well into the late 1970s and required traditionalist healers to be ostracized by their own community. The Canadian government understood that their Bill of Rights, with regard to religious freedom, did not apply to Native American religions. And provincial lists of hundreds of recognized religions do not include Native American ones. At least until the late 1980s, Native religious leaders could minister to Natives in prisons only with the permission of the local Christian chaplain.

In the United States, the prohibition of Native ceremonies had not been enforced for decades, and in 1978 (amended in 1994) Congress passed the American Indian Religious Freedom Act, which was fine in theory but had no legal teeth. The courts continue to interpret religion on a Christian model, expecting a religion to be institutional and have permanent structures for worship. Thus, there has been little legal protection of Native sacred sites.

In some areas, such as among the Navajo, Apache, Hopi, and Zuni of the Southwest, traditional religion had continued despite legal prohibition. In other areas, they publicly came back as soon as they were legal. For example, the potlatch tradition was again publicly practiced as soon as the legal prohibition was dropped in Canada in 1951. In 1952, the first public potlatch was held in Victoria, British Columbia, hosted by Mungo Martin. By the 1970s, big houses for ceremonies could be found on a number of Northwest Coast reserves. The Kwakwaka'wakw have been able to get back many of the ritual paraphernalia confiscated by the courts from some museums and have placed them in their own museums on two of their reserves. Other Northwest Coast peoples are still trying to obtain from museums ritual items that were stolen by early anthropologists.

By the late 1960s, in much of North America, the practice of Native religions had reached its nadir, and it was assumed by many that they were extinct. When I applied for a research grant in the early 1980s to study the hermeneutics and history of the Sacred Pipe as a pan-Indian religious modality, one of the reviewers, an anthropologist, wrote that the research was pointless as Native religions were "dead," which the reviewer thought was a good thing (nevertheless, I did receive the grant). Just as Native religious traditions had reached its low point, Native youths, the children of those who had become resigned to enforced Christianity, began to seek out traditionalist elders in search of their religious and cultural roots.

At first, the effects of this alignment of youths and elders were primarily political and led to one of the first modern demonstrations against the dominant culture's violation of treaties with Native peoples. In 1969, Mohawk (one of the Six Nations) youth advised and supported by elders of the Longhouse Religion (Chapter 4) blockaded the border crossing between New York and Ontario south of Cornwall. This crossing was on the land of the Akwesasne reserve (which spans New York, Ontario, and Québec), and the Canadian government planned to expand the border crossing by taking Mohawk land without permission. The protest was supported by traditionalists of the Longhouse, such as Ernie Benedict, and was influential in the development of AIM. Thus was born the statement seen on many reservations, "You are on Indian land."

Subsequently, over the violent objections of assimilationists, the traditionalists at Akwesasne created their own school using their own language and a newspaper with a worldwide circulation, and traditional religious practices and sociocultural roles, including the position of clan mother, were revitalized. One of the founders of the school was a clan mother, Ann Jocks, who left the Catholic Church and returned to the traditional religion. Another founder was Tom Porter, who encouraged traditionalists to spread the word of revitalization through public speaking.

A year earlier, in 1968, several Anishnabe, including Eddie Benton, Dennis Banks, and Clyde Bellecourt, founded AIM:

> Although much of its inspiration derived from Indian fishing-rights battles already underway in Washington and Oregon, from Six Nations ("Iroquois") land protests in Ontario and New York, and from the "Red Power" activity that had evolved out of civil-rights activism on the West Coast, AIM came into existence as a direct result of the termination and relocation programs that dumped thousands of bewildered Indians into the cities.[4]

AIM began with social services, legal rights, community protection, and urban education programs in the Minneapolis–Saint Paul area but quickly attracted young Native people from all over North America.

By 1970, AIM also attracted traditionalist religious leaders, including the Lakota, Leonard Crow Dog, who was both a leader in the Native American Church and a leader of the underground traditional ceremonies, including the nonmodified Sun Dance (Chapter 8). Within a few years, older traditionalist elders as John Fire Lame Deer, Frank Fools Crow, Pete Catches, and Wallace Black Elk had become AIM spiritual advisors. Leonard Crow Dog and Wallace Black Elk were at the Second Battle of Wounded Knee throughout most of the confrontation, which was instigated at the request of Frank Fools Crow, as spokesperson for the Oglala traditional chiefs, for AIM's help. The young and the elderly had, in effect, formed a traditionalist-oriented coalition against the assimilationist middle-aged, who were supported by the federal government. In 1973, most of the AIM leaders took part in their first Sun Dance, led by Lame Deer and Leonard Crow Dog. AIM became as much a religious movement as one of sociopolitical reform.

Leonard Crow Dog was particularly influential on the AIM youth. Raised by his family in a traditional way and kept from the schooling of the dominant culture, Leonard Crow Dog, the same age as the AIM leaders, was by the early 1970s a renowned healer and ritual leader. He taught and assisted the AIM members in fasting and sundancing and even reintroduced the Ghost Dance. Documentaries made during the occupation of Wounded Knee show Leonard Crow Dog leading the participants in the circular dance.

Since that time, many young Natives have sought out the elders of their own traditions, and fasting is again becoming the means for youths to come to terms with themselves and all their relations. Elders Conferences became increasingly popular on college campuses with Native students as well as in urban areas with Native populations. Gatherings of youths seeking the tutelage of traditional elders have taken place over much of North America. Many powwows have shifted their focus from dance competitions to a more traditional gathering, including Spirit Lodges.

Some former AIM leaders shifted their energies from political confrontation to education and religious revitalization. For example, Eddie Benton is the spiritual leader of the revival of the Anishnabe Midewiwin tradition (Chapter 4), which has spread from Wisconsin north to Manitoba and east to central Ontario. Eddie Benton is also one of the founders of the Red School House in Saint Paul. One of the major leaders of the Canadian branch of AIM, Vern Harper, together with his former wife, Pauline Shirt, founded the Wandering Spirit Survival School (now the First Nations School) in Toronto, which was the first Native-way school under an urban school board. These schools not only provided an education oriented toward Native culture but added traditional religious practices and teachings to the daily life of the students.

On some reservations, traditional healing practices now take place alongside modern medicine. For example, at the health center on the Wikwemikong Unceded Reserve on Manitoulin Island in Ontario, there is a tipi-shaped wing where traditional healers hold healing ceremonies. In urban areas with large Native populations, Native health centers offer both modern Western medicine and healing circles. In these centers, both modern science and traditional religion support each other.

In areas where the traditions have virtually been lost, as in the eastern New England states and the Atlantic Provinces of Canada, sweat lodges and Sacred Pipe rituals are again being practiced by a growing number of young

Native people. Initially, these were brought to the local youth by traveling members of AIM. While culture-specific traditions such as the Anishnabe Midewiwin or the Northwest Coast potlatch have been strengthened, pan-Indian modalities, for example, the spread of Lakota modes of spirituality, which were important in the development of AIM, also developed. For instance, Raymond Harris, an Arapaho living on the Wind River Reservation in Wyoming and following Lakota spiritual practices, became renowned as a healer in the late 1960s and began to train people from a number of traditions to heal. On his deathbed, he passed on his spiritual authority to his son-in-law, a Plains Cree. He particularly appealed to Plains Cree from Alberta, who had been raised away from their tradition in cities. Joe Couture, a Plains Cree who had been a Catholic monk, and Vern Harper, a Plains Cree who had been raised in Toronto by non-Native foster parents, are among those who Raymond Harris guided through sweats and fasting and have become recognized healers and spiritual advisors.

In some U.S. and Canadian prisons with many Native prisoners, Spirit Lodges and pipe ceremonies are becoming commonplace. But in many prisons, Natives are refused the support of their religion, and Native prisoners have been brutally tortured with confiscated sacred ritual items, such as pipestems. Some of these prisoners were important AIM leaders, who were arrested by the Federal Bureau of Investigation (FBI), convicted through false testimony on trumped-up charges, and given long prison sentences. Although the revitalization has been going on for several decades, there is still considerable resistance by the police and the courts.

Since Vatican II, the Catholic Church has reacted to these developments by attempting to coopt the movement. On some reserves, Churches have been rebuilt along the lines of Native structures and have incorporated Native designs in their decoration, especially on the altars, and the Sacred Pipe has been brought into the Mass. An Anishnabe Jesuit priest also functions as a traditionalist healer. And Catholic priests on reservations routinely fast in a traditional way and take part in Spirit Lodges and other Native rituals. In contrast, some major liberal Protestant denominations have apologized to Native peoples for the way their churches have suppressed Native religion and have supported the revitalization without attempting to make it a part of Christianity.

In summary, despite nearly a half millennium of huge losses due to epidemics, genocide, cultural genocide, and severe prohibition of Native religion by church and state leading to incarceration in the United States and Canada, and burning at the stake in Mexico, Native traditional religions not only have survived underground but are undergoing a renaissance in many areas including Yucatan and Chiapas in Mexico and the Southwest, Plains, Midwest, and Northwest Coast of the United States and Canada. This revitalization has been expanding over the last three decades, but it still involves less than the majority of the Native population in most areas.

The courts have not been kind to Native religion on the whole: many sacred sites remain unprotected and others have been desecrated through development, discrimination is still allowed concerning those practicing Native religion with regard to hiring and firing, Native people are frequently hassled when bringing their sacred items across the border to attend ceremonies, and only in federal prisons are Natives theoretically assured the practice of their religion.

The growth of gambling casinos as the major source of income on many reserves in the United States has also led to friction with traditionalists. After fighting the casino culture with its alleged links to organized crime and associated activities for decades, traditionalists at Akwesasne, under the leadership of Tom Porter, left the reserve in 1993 and founded a new community on ancestral lands in the Mohawk Valley to live according to traditional spirituality. Thus, the fight for religious freedom for Native religious traditions continues on many fronts.

· 3 ·

Theology

Theology means the study or discussion of deities, although English-language dictionaries and common usage would limit the term to the study of the assumed one true God. But the Greeks, and it is a Greek word, used the term and its cognates from their polytheistic perspective (e.g., Hesiod's *Theogony*). Thus, the topic of this chapter is about gods and goddesses, spirits, numinous entities, and, in A. Irving Hallowell's precise use of the term for Anishnabe religion, "other-than-human-beings."[1] Although Hallowell's term is by far the closest to most Native American understandings, deities is simpler and allows for comparison with other religions worldwide and so is utilized in this book.

As discussed in Chapter 1, Native American theologies, especially outside the Maya and Aztec civilizations as well as settled traditions such as the Pueblo cultures, are highly individualized, but all exist within general cultural parameters. And it is these parameters, rather than specific theological understandings, that are here discussed. Thus, the theologies presented under the four categories discussed in this chapter should be understood to apply only generally to Native North American cultures. Specific traditions as well as individuals will have far more nuanced understandings than can be presented in a single chapter.

Much of the following discussion would also be pertinent to many cultures of the world, including the traditional cultures of sub-Saharan Africa, pre-Christian Europe, non-Aryan India, East Asia, and Polynesia. There are two reasons for this pervasive theological similarity. First, given that chimpanzees ritually dance before awe-inspiring phenomena such as lightening and waterfalls, the earliest *Homo sapiens* surely had a religious understanding, and this understanding would have accompanied the spread of humanity around the globe. Second, from the principles of religio-ecology—understanding religion as a response to the gestalt situation of a culture: climate, geography, economy, sociopolitical structure, and so on—cultures at a similar religio-ecological niche—gathering–hunting, horticulture–hunting, agricultural, herding, industrial, postindustrial, and so on—share many religious features.

Native American traditions understand the connection with the spirit realm to be one of reciprocity, discussed in Chapter 1, and relationship. Native deities are neither separate nor distant from humans. Rather they are omnipresent and understood as relations; the connection is familial. Thus, the deities are addressed in family terms: Grandmother, Grandfather, Father, Mother—rarely by name. And the feelings toward the numinous are not only of awe but of love, the same love one has for grandparents. As in many traditional cultures, it is grandparents who raise children, as parents are involved in productive labor. Children in these cultures tend to have both enormous love and respect for their grandparents. The common appellation of the entirety of the spirit realm is "All my relations."

A symbol of great antiquity found over much of North America is that of a cross in a circle. The cross symbolizes the Four Directions, meaning the entirety of this planet, and the circle represents the interconnectedness of all life. The illustration on the cover of this book is a variant of this ubiquitous symbol, being a circle within a circle surrounding the Four Directions and the four semicardinal directions, all together symbolizing that all living beings, including those of the spirit realm, are all related. The image presents in graphic form the statement: "All my relations."

COSMOGONY AND THE INFLUENCE OF CHRISTIANITY

If one went to a typical pipe ceremony east of the Rocky Mountains and excluding the Southwest, after the smudging with purifying smoke, the ritual would begin with inserting the stem of the Sacred Pipe into the bowl, causing the pipe to become spiritually alive. This is understood as conjoining the two elemental complementary energies through inserting the male into the female, the origin of all creative spiritual forces. After the bowl is ritually filled and lit, the puffed smoke and the stem are offered to Sky and Earth and the Four Directions. Some add a seventh offering, either to the center or to all supportive numinous beings, that is, "all one's relations." This contemporary ritual has been noted in the earliest Euro-American writings on Native ritual and undoubtedly goes back many, many centuries. (See Chapter 8 for a fuller discussion of the Sacred Pipe.)

Sky and Earth are, respectively, the male and female cosmic deities, which together are the origin of all that swims in the seas, crawls through the earth, walks on the land, and flies through the sky. The Four Directions or Four Winds represents the surface of the earth or Turtle Island, as North

America is often denominated. Other rituals are directed toward the male Sun, who lights our way and warms us, especially at sunrise; to Moon, who moves the tides and the menstrual flowing of women; to the Morning and Evening Stars, respectively, male and female; and to star constellations, especially the one known in the West as the Pleiades. In some traditions, it is Sun, representative of Sky, and Moon, representative of Earth as an equal cosmic force, that are the dual, complementary, creating cosmic deities.

The Four Winds are also connected to the weather and the seasons. Especially powerful is West Wind, who is connected with Thunder, given that storms tend to come from the west, because of the rotation of the earth. As the Four Directions, they are connected not only with the seasons—East, spring; South, summer; West, autumn; and North, winter—but also with the cycles of life—East, birth and childhood; South, growth and youth; West, maturity and middle age; and North, old age and death. On the other hand, life is also understood to follow the path of Sun, and for many cultures the realm of the dead is in the West (as it is in East Asia and elsewhere). Many cultures have their ceremonial structures open in the east: the direction of the rising sun and of beginnings, while the dead are placed facing the west.

As in virtually all cultures—save for the monotheistic West—Earth tends to be represented by an image of the human female. Most often the image is simply of a vulva, a symbol that is ubiquitous among petroglyphs throughout the world. In some Native languages, the word for Earth and for the human vagina is the same. But in some instances, Earth is represented by a full-figured woman, as the petroglyph in Figure 1. This large image is one of many pecked on a huge horizontal granite rock just north of Lake Ontario on the cultural margin between Algonquian- and Iroquoian-speaking cultures. There are holes and cracks in the rock through which one can hear water flow in the spring. The image in Figure 1 was created around an oblong hole which serves as the vagina. In many North American Native traditions, women when they menstruate sit on the ground in a small shelter, and their blood flows onto the soil, creating an intimate bond between human women and Earth. In some areas, at the time of menarche, the young woman sits in a vagina-shaped cave by a flowing stream and commemorates her coming of age by scratching the vagina symbol on the cave walls.

While Figure 1 represents the image of Earth in the northern part of North America, Figure 2 represents the image of Earth in Maya culture at the southern part of North America. It is unusual to represent the spirit realm in anthropomorphic form in the gathering–hunting and horticulture–hunting traditions of North America, but in the agricultural civilizations all of the deities have been anthropomorphized. Figure 2, painted by a contemporary Maya woman, is of Ixchel, whose is Earth in her mode as the deity of medicine and fertility. Here she is portrayed as an old woman. From the upside-down pot she is holding flows the fertilizing clear, blue water onto growing green vegetation. This water would be from the cool water of the cenotes, the

Figure 1: Earth as human woman. Peterborough Petroglyphs Provincial Park (Ontario). Precontact (undetermined date) Anishnabe. Photograph by the author.

deep underground pools found in the Yucatan Peninsula essential to horticulture in that dry climate. Her headdress is a live snake, the chthonic image of the snake representing the healing arts in many parts of the world. Around her neck and waist and in her ears, she wears large, green turquoise beads indicating her status. The coastal archeological site of Tulum, with its grand temples, was still intact when the Spanish arrived. It was the gateway pilgrimage site to her temple at the south end of Cozumel Island, which is still standing. Pilgrims came to Tulum to take boats to her shrine. At Tulum, one can see where the reef off the coast was dug away leaving a gap that allows boats to go directly from Tulum to her temple.

On the other hand, the primary male cosmic deity tends not to be represented anthropomorphically in nonagricultural settings, although there is a priapic anthropomorphic male figure on the same rock of Figure 1. Instead, one is more likely to find subsidiary elements portrayed, for example, lightening and thunder as zigzag lines or as potent male animals, such as bison bulls. The lack of awareness of the male cosmic symbolism has led some Western feminist theorists to assume that early human cultures were matriarchal and solely worshiped a female monotheistic deity. In fact, no such culture has ever been found.

Figure 2: Ixchel—earth as deity of healing and fertility. Painting on leather by Aurora, a contemporary Maya woman (Yucatan). In care of the author.

In the Americas, time tends to be understood cyclically, following the course of the sun and of the seasons—there is no beginning of time. Sky and Earth are primal; there is no more powerful or earlier deity. Earth and Sky cannot be created; they are the creating forces. Similarly, before the promulgation of Genesis by Christian missionaries, in place of creation myths there were commonly migration myths—how a particular people got to where they are—or emergence myths—how people emerged through several layers of earth to reach the present, usually the Fourth, layer. Creation myths in many traditions are limited to clan origin myths.

For many traditions, in place of creation myths there are re-creation myths, the example in the Bible being the Noah story. In the Anishnabe version, the sacred personage at the center of re-creation is the culture hero/trickster figure (see *Culture Heroes and "Tricksters"*), Nanabozho (Nanabush or any number of dialectical variations). Typical of such mythic personages (e.g., Hercules in Greek myths, Houji or Lord of Millet in Chinese myths), Nanabozho is half human and half divine. The following is a highly truncated generalized account based on elements common to many of the versions of this myth cycle.

Nanabozho's father, the storm deity West Wind, forces himself upon and impregnates Beautiful Woman, who dies at childbirth. The infant is raised by Grandmother, who in some versions is also Moon. He is also a changeling and usually depicted in his most common nonhuman form, a hare. (Some early Jesuit missionaries thought that the Anishnabeg worshiped a giant hare as a monotheistic deity.) Over the years, he brings to Grandmother and her people many important aspects of culture; for example, he steals fire from another type of community and brings it to humans. Typical of such numinous entities in Native American traditions, the primary subject of myths does not figure in rituals and offerings are not made to him.

One winter, Nanabozho's brother, Wolf, although warned not to do so, walks across a frozen Great Lake. The chief of the powerful, dangerous underwater spirits of the Great Lakes—so powerful their name is not spoken even today—causes the ice to crack under Wolf and he drowns. When Nanabozho learns who caused his brother's death, he seeks revenge. He transforms himself into a stump on the shore and, when this underwater spirit comes ashore and sleeps by the stump, kills him. In turn, the rest of the underwater spirits take their revenge by causing the waters to rise. When it becomes apparent that the rising waters will inundate all the land, he places his grandmother and the rest of the village on rafts. Once the waters stop rising, he sends down various animals to seek for mud at the bottom of the waters. The fourth animal, the muskrat, brings up a pawful of mud. Nanabozho causes the mud to expand, re-creating the earth (as the earth on which we stand, but not Earth as an already existing cosmic deity).

There are many versions of the Nanabozho myth cycle, but all have as his most important act Nanabozho's re-creation of the earth after a great flood. In comparative mythology, this is called the "Earth-diver Motif."

Some traditions also have stories concerning the creation of humans. The following is a synopsis of a small part of the Navajo version sung in the Blessingway. The myth is also the ideological foundation of the menarche ritual discussed in Chapter 5.

Talking God and Growling God have turquoise and white shell figurines transformed into the deities Changing Woman and White Shell Woman (who are in many respects a single deity). Impregnated by Sun's rays, they (she) give birth to the twin deities, Born for Water and Monster Slayer. Sun wishes to marry Changing Woman, who makes several stipulations that Sun meets, and she goes off to the home he built for her in the west. White Shell Woman was then lonely. So Talking God, Growling God, Changing Woman, and other Sacred Persons met with White Shell Woman bringing one yellow and one white ear of corn. After a complex ritual, the two ears of corn were placed between two sacred buckskins. Wind enters between the two buckskins and brings the two ears of corn to life, the yellow ear becoming a human woman and the white ear becoming a human man. White Shell Woman takes them to live with her on her home, Earth.

Typical of Native American traditions as well as all other polytheistic traditions worldwide, where there are myths of the creation of humans, they are almost always created by the coupling of a male and a female sacred entities. In the few cases where there is but a single deity involved in the creation, it is invariably a female. In rare cases where a male births, as Zeus does Dionysus, the fetus must be removed from the womb of a female and then placed in a cavity specially formed in the male—in this case, Zeus's thigh. For the human, the understanding, save for the interrelated monotheistic traditions, is that birthing and nurturing (nursing) is exclusively a female act.

The coming of Christianity put enormous pressures on the Native American polytheistic understanding. In the Spanish-controlled areas, a monotheistic overlay was required to continue traditional religious practices. In Canada and the United States, reservations were often put under the actual or de facto control of missionaries, as were the boarding schools. From one to several centuries of constant repetition of a simplistic Christian theology, focusing on the creation accounts in Genesis as well as the values of the dominating culture that include the position that polytheists—Heathens and Pagans—were inferior to Euro-Americans, if not subhuman savages, often influenced the theology of Native Americans.

In response, there developed a notion of a single, male deity who was superior to all the other deities, who were now not considered deities so much as subsidiary spirits, something like angels or saints in Catholicism. This deity was otiose, that is, no rituals, no offerings were directed toward this deity. Nor were there any myths concerning this deity. It was a deity that existed in a few words but no deeds and primarily in words directed toward non-Natives.

The most common English-language term to be heard throughout northern North America is the "Creator." This is a deity that is male, given that the male pronoun until quite recently was invariably used, and is anthropomorphic, at least in terms of human emotions (many Native languages do not necessarily specify gender). The Creator not only creates the earth and humans, but has expectations with regard to human behavior. He directs humans to act according to His will. The term is common among Native youth not brought up in a traditional way, at elder's conferences, and among the generations brought up in Christian missionary–controlled schools. Hence, in the teaching presented in Chapter 1, it is the Creator who creates humans in four colors or races, gives them each a distinct religion, and demands that they follow that religion only. It should be understood that many Native people educated in a Christian context and subject to a monotheistic society sincerely pray to the Creator.

In other cases, a quasi-monotheism is adopted through modifying the language to allow for a high god. This will be illustrated with four examples.

The most common term, the Great Spirit, seems not to have initially been developed by Native people but by Euro-Americans mishearing Native speech. Although the term is not mentioned in seventeenth-century reports, there are confused references to it in eighteenth-century writings, and by the nineteenth century it had become firmly entrenched. In different language-culture areas, the term seems to have arisen somewhat differently.

Among writings on Algonquian-language cultures, a native name for God in the singular is usually provided—Kichi Manitou, meaning "Great Spirit"—and the term was used as a translation for God by Christian missionaries. According to my friend, the Anishnabe (Ojibwa/Odawa) scholar and healer, Kenn Pitawanakwat, the term may have arisen as a confusion over two prefixes: *ke'sha*, meaning "benevolent," and *ki'tchi*, meaning "great," in the sense of "huge" (the pronunciation varying according to dialects). An Anishnabe speaking of the *manido* (Manitou), the deities, as benevolent may have been misheard by a Euro-American listener as referring to the name of an immense deity, which was understood in the sense of "superior" rather than "huge." *Ki'tchimanido* does not mean "Great Spirit," in the sense of the usual translation; rather it means "Gigantic Spirit." The same prefix is used in the Algonquian word for Lake Superior; it means "Huge Lake." On the other hand, the writings of a late-eighteenth-century English trader imply that the term was a French Jesuit invention.

For the linguistically and culturally similar Cree, the term for the deities, *manido*, has come to mean a single, male diety. Owing to major influence from Catholic missionaries, the traditional religion for many has taken on a Catholic theological underpinning. I have been in Cree "sweats" that were identical to the Anishnabe mode, save for the opening facing south rather than east, but were imbued with Catholic theological terminology.

Among Iroquoian-speaking people, the concept seems to have developed with the late-eighteenth-century revision of Six Nations' religion and society by Ganeodiyo, "Handsome Lake," under Quaker tutelage, which led to the Longhouse Religion (Chapter 4). These revisions included a religious focus on a "Great Spirit." One ethnologist, Elizabeth Tooker, has suggested that the latter concept came about through the conversion of Sky into the

Great Spirit or Controller, with the consequent subordination of Earth, and this seems to be the case on listening to the long "thanksgiving" prayer of the Longhouse Religion.

In Chapter 2, the importance of Nicholas Black Elk in fusing Lakota religion with Catholicism is discussed. In the teachings on Lakota religion that Black Elk imparted to Joseph Epes Brown, Wakan Tanka, the "Great Spirit," is a virtual monotheistic, male god. Without its Christian reading, the term originally meant the deities as a collective entity or the totality of spiritual power, of all that is *wakan*, sacred. The process of transforming a generic term into a singular one can be traced in recorded discussions of three generations of Lakota before Black Elk's theological reformulation, from those religious leaders raised prior to the reservations, to those grudgingly adapting to the then new religio-cultural impositions, to those converted to Christianity working for missionaries or the American army as translators.

In summary, a close analysis of the quasi- to fully monotheistic Great Spirit in different cultures indicates parallel processes at work. Either through voluntary adaptation or through forced conversion, the English-language term "Great Spirit" was associated with indigenous concepts or terms that meant something quite different. Nonetheless, the Great Spirit has been a Native religious concept in many traditions for a century or more and is a well-established theological understanding.

Of far more consequence has been the patriarchalization of Native traditional cultures that were either matrifocal or gender egalitarian. The early Christian missionaries were all members of Christian monastic orders, and many were misogynist. Later Protestant missionaries may have been married but often considered females lesser beings. As discussed in Chapter 2, the fur trade had the effect of lowering the value and, hence, the status of women. Even for those who maintained the traditional language along with the rituals, it was modified to reflect the Christian assumption that the deities are necessarily male. In Anishnabe ceremonies in the 1970s and 1980s, although offerings were made equally to Sky and Earth, prayers were addressed exclusively to *mishomis*, Grandfather/the Grandfathers. *Nokomis*, Grandmother/the Grandmothers, was ignored. Generations of daily repetition of the "Lord's Prayer," which begins with "Our Father . . . ," in the schools led to the spirits during traditional rituals being addressed as "Our Father" when English was used. Only among those last to be influenced by Christian culture, in the interior of British Columbia, did I at that time hear prayers addressed to the "Grandfathers and Grandmothers." However, as the revitalization spread and women regained their traditional ritual roles and importance, in the early 1990s I began to hear prayers addressed to "*mishomis, nokomis.*"

In the Spanish Catholic areas, a different mode of adapting to monotheistic domination seems to have taken place: an intertwining of language without changing the Native understanding. The *Popul Vuh* is a rewriting of traditional logographic Maya texts into an alphabetic text after the destruction of the Maya books by the Spanish priests. As is found in the beginning of the *Popul Vuh*, following the translation of Dennis Tedlock (see *Further Reading*): "We shall write about this now amid the preaching of God, in Christendom now. We shall bring it out because there is no longer [the traditional books]."

Throughout the beginning of the *Popul Vuh*, the initial reference to a deity is put in a singular form as in a monotheistic understanding—for example, "Only the Maker, Modeler alone"—but invariably goes on with a list of deities, and the pronoun is always the plural one. Despite some lip service to Genesis—for example, "And then came his word," "Then the mountains were separated from the water"—creation is clearly the result of the combining of female and male spiritual energies: "And then the . . . were told by the Maker, Modeler, Bearer, Begetter [note sequence of four names]. . . . Name now our names, praise us. We are your mother, we are your father. Speak now." In the following we find a full intermingling of Genesis and Maya understanding regarding creation: "Such was the formation of the earth when it was brought forth by the Heart of Sky, Heart of Earth, as they were called, since they were the first to think of it. The sky was set apart and the earth was set apart in the midst of the waters."

This continuation of a Maya polytheistic understanding with but lip service to monotheism is found in the present. In the words of a late-twentieth-century Maya woman: "The one father is the heart of the sky, that is, the sun. The sun is the father and the mother is the moon. . . . They are the pillars of the universe."[2] The rhetoric may be monotheistic in the beginning but quickly switches to the common Native American understanding.

At least one Algonquian-speaking people, the Lenape (Delaware), solved the problem of accommodating the Euro-American expectation of creation by a male monotheistic deity in relation to the aboriginal understanding of re-creation by a culture hero by attaching a creation myth as a prologue to the traditional one. The *Walum Olum* is a Lenape myth cycle of five songs recorded in the early nineteenth century. The first song begins with an account quite similar to Genesis, with the creation of the earth and other *manido* by a male Great Spirit, and ends with a guardian spirit (the missionaries taught that all guardian spirits were the devil) in the form of an evil serpent leading humans astray. The second song begins with Nanabush living on Turtle Island and remedying the problem of the flood caused by the underwater monster (mistranslated as a large snake). The remaining songs concern the migration myth and history of the Lenape. Given that the common number among Native traditions is four, and the first song makes for a cycle of five, the simplest explanation is that the first song is a postcontact addition.[3]

A similar intertwining of monotheism with polytheism as the Maya can be found in another Algonquian-language tradition. The late Art Solomon, an Anishnabe spiritual leader who had devoted his life, often at a great cost to himself, to ministering to the needs of Native urban communities in Ontario, especially women in maximum-security prisons, begins an English-language prayer as follows. It combines the term "Great Spirit" expected by Western language listeners with the more traditional "Grandfather, Grandmother":

> Grandfather, Great Spirit
>   I give you thanks
>   That we can sit here
>   In this circle of Life,
>   We send you our prayers
>   And the very best thoughts
> Grandmother, Great Spirit
>   As we raise this sacred pipe
>   To give thanks to you
>   And to all of your Creation
>   We give thanks
>   To the spirit helpers
>   Who came and sat among us . . .[4]

The concept of "spirit helpers" leads us into the next section.

THE ENVIRONMENT AS NUMINOUS

Just as all the cosmic forces, including the earth itself and weather, are numinous, so are all that surrounds humans: waters, plants, animals, and rocks. But this is neither an animistic nor a pantheistic ideology, both constructs being fantasies of the Western mind regarding primitivism. Although all around one is understood as numinous, far from all are particularly sacred. And even among those who are sacred, some are more powerful than others. Those sacred entities that a traditional individual understands as pertinent to her or his being are invariably limited in number, and those with which one has a particular relationship will commonly be but one or a few. Each relationship has its obligations, and a relationship with many would lead to a most onerous, if not impossible, religious life.

In contemporary North America, most people live in an urban environment, from small towns to megalopolises. We are cut off from the natural world, and all of our senses are blocked from perceiving it by air, sound, scent, and light pollution (with regard to seeing the night sky) as well as distance. In the earliest urban areas, drinking alcoholic beverages changed from a ritual practice to one of daily necessity, as low-alcohol beverages became essential to prevent diseases due to polluted water. Our understanding of nature is not based on our surroundings but on Hollywood images. The prevalent "Bambi syndrome" means we relate to nature on notions of perceived cuteness; for example, it is alright to slaughter cattle but not seals. I have been in poverty-ridden Inuit (Eskimo) villages where large piles of seal hides were rotting because there was no longer a market for them. The Inuit still hunted seals to feed themselves and their dogs, but their only source of cash for the necessities of living in villages, required by the Euro-American governments, had been the sale of furs.

In the dominant society, we do not relate cellophane-covered cuts of meat with living animals nor paper with living trees. Outside national parks, save for the diminishing numbers of hunters, we rarely see nondomesticated animals, and the forests of centuries-old trees are virtually all gone. In my youth, I stalked to within touching distance of deer, and I have walked trails along with black bears. Such experiences leave one understanding animals not as generic but as distinct individuals, not as figments of an urban imagination but as living beings with their own nonhuman natures. One develops a bond with particular animal species, a bond of respect for their own being in relationship to one's own.

In the precontact Native cultures north of the stone and adobe-constructed villages of the Pueblo cultures, people were surrounded by nature. Through a bark-covered wigwam or a hide-covered teepee, one heard the animals, the breezes, all the sounds of nature. And even the larger structures, whether a cedar-planked Northwest Coast or an elm-bark–covered Iroquoian longhouse, made nature omnipresent. Hunted animals were killed, even with the bow, at a very close, often nearly touching, range. Plant foods were handpicked, whether cultivated or wild. People had an intimate understanding of and connection to nonhumans. All were understood as relations. Those necessary for sustenance, shelter, warmth, or healing tended to be understood as female, while those who demonstrated powers useful for hunting or warfare were understood as male; thus, the black bear was commonly perceived as female and the grizzly as male.

The plants and animals on which humans depended were understood as superior to ourselves, for we needed them; they did not need us. We asked them to take pity on us and offer themselves so we might live. When fathers and uncles hunted, many traditions blackened their children's faces with charcoal, the sign of fasting, and sent them into the woods to fast for the day, to help the needed beings to better understand our hunger. When these beings accordingly gave themselves to us, we thanked them with tobacco and other offerings and ritually demonstrated our respect and gratitude. These beings are not simply animals or plants; they are numinous entities.

In horticultural societies, the domesticated plants were not under our control but under the control of Mother of the Garden or the mother of the specific plants, such as the Corn Mother. She was the daughter of Earth, as Demeter, the Grain deity, in Hellenic religion. Some traditions understood corn as growing from the Earth's breasts, and the milky liquid of corn added to the symbolism. In the agricultural traditions, such as the Maya, where males did most of the farming in contrast to women gardening in horticultural societies, Corn was a male deity.

Those plants that had powers beyond feeding or sheltering us, such as those used for purification and medicine (e.g., cedar, sweetgrass, sage, and sweet pine), were deities. Similarly, those animals that exhibited powers that we could but distantly emulate were also deities. Animals that hunted—wolves, foxes, eagles, and owls—had powers that human hunters needed. Animals who could be ferocious in defense—bison bulls and grizzly bears—or animals that knew the healing herbs and brought forth new life from holes in the ground, especially the black bear, again had power essential to human life and were also deities. Thus, humans fasted for four or more days to elucidate visions that engendered connections with these numinous powers. The powers that come may not be animals or plants; they could also be the powerful spirits of the weather, such as Thunder, or other powers.

We asked these powers to become our helping (guardian) spirits. And when they deigned to do so, teaching us special songs and rituals as well as particular behaviors to maintain and signify the relationship, we honored the connection by not speaking directly about them to others, although our neighbors would know these relationships by the symbols we adopted and by our particular ritual behavior. Our ability to be successful was entirely dependent on these personal relationships , which were so important to life that we asked elders to dream of a name for our babies to create such a relationship until they were old enough to fast and develop these relationships on their own.

In Algonquian-language traditions, this special relationship was known as a *dodem* (totem), of which there were two types: clan and personal. All had a clan dodem, for which there might be a clan sacred bundle, but otherwise no special rituals or obligations. A personal dodem was a different type of relationship; it was idiosyncratic, varying from individual to individual. For example, with regard to one of my personal dodems, I am allowed by Her to take Her life if offered by Her for human needs, but I, myself, cannot eat Her. Another person could have the same dodem with an entirely different prohibition.

The concept of dodem in the literature is typical of Western misunderstandings of Native American religion. In Chapter 1, examples of this misunderstanding were presented. Another incorrect assumption is due to Western theorists living in a hierarchical society and religion and assuming that this is the human norm. The dodem is not a hierarchical head of the species, as is usually presented in the literature, for most Native cultures were not hierarchical societies. Leadership, outside the kingdoms, was voluntary. Except for clan heads, leaders were chosen for their abilities with regard to particular enterprises, and one could choose whether or not to follow that leader. Hence, the concept of a head of a species, and only that leader, being numinous made no sense, save for domesticated plants (or in the shift from hunting to herding, as was the case for the Saami and some Siberian traditions).

When one has a relationship with a particular animal, every time one meets an individual of that species, it is a potential meeting with a deity. Not every such encounter is a numinous one, but one never knows in advance. One always treats an individual of that species that one encounters with the greatest respect, calling it Grandmother or Grandfather, never by its species name. Such a meeting is a blessing and leaves one with a spiritual high.

As in the prayer by Art Solomon above, these beings can act as spirit helpers. Having such helpers is essential to life, given that humans are too weak to exist without such help. When a relationship to a spirit comes to one while fasting or performing some other form of vision-questing and offers its help, it is up to the human to use this power wisely. Spiritual assistance can be used for subsistence—hunting and gathering; healing humans, domestic animals as horses, or communities; for controlling the weather when necessary; or for defending one's community or attacking an enemy. The ethics of the situation is dependent on the human; the spirits are morally neutral, since they are not human. In all traditions, it is considered unethical to use these powers for oneself; it must always be used for the benefit of one's community. A person who uses spiritual power to better him or herself is considered a danger to the community, a sorcerer or witch. In traditional times, such a person was liable to be killed, to be excised as though they were a tumor on the social body. Today it is understood that selfish use of spiritual power will lead to the death of the person of someone in his family.

Figure 3 presents two ways in which the same animal can be understood as a deity as well as two ways the animal can be represented. The Pueblo culture figure is of Bear as the great healing deity, and the image is a realistic, lifelike depiction of a bear. The Northwest Coast culture figure is of Bear as a deity who is also a clan ancestor. The figure is depicted as upright and seemingly anthropomorphic, but the short legs indicate that the body is bear like. The head, however, is a stylized mask of Bear used in the potlatch dances (Chapter 7). As well, the image holds a "copper," a large stylized shield made of copper that, in part, symbolizes a clan's wealth and power.

There are many ways in which the spirits can assist a person. Other than when simply assisting in the needs of daily life, this assistance takes place while the person is in a trance, whether light or heavy. One can ask the spirit to come to one or ask the spirit to go somewhere. One can merge with the spirit or bring the spirit into oneself and thus travel and/or act with the powers of the spirit. But in all of these modes, one remains aware of what one is doing. This is different from spirit possession, mentioned below, where the spirit takes over a person's body, the person disappears and has no memory of what took place, and all that happens during the trance is due to the volition of the spirit.

Figure 3: Two diverse miniature images of bear. Left: Mica-infused buff clay tray for burning healing herbs by Crucita of Taos Pueblo (New Mexico). Right: Carved cedar Bear as clan symbol holding a "copper" by Salish youth with rights to design; Vancouver Island (British Columbia). Both in care of the author.

When one becomes an elder, it is at times appropriate to speak directly of one's numinous experience. John Fire Lame Deer, a Lakota ritual leader and healer, told of his first major fasting experience to Richard Erdoes:

Suddenly I felt an overwhelming presence. Down there in my cramped hole was a big bird. The pit was only as wide as myself, and I was a skinny boy, but that huge bird was flying around me as if he had the whole sky to himself. I could hear his cries, sometimes near and sometimes far, far away. I felt feathers or a wing touching my back and head. . . . Slowly I perceived that a voice was trying to tell me something. It was a bird cry, but I tell you, I began to understand some of it. . . . I heard a human voice too, strange and high-pitched, a voice which could not come from an ordinary, living being. All at once, I was way up there with the birds. . . . I could look down. . . . A voice said, "You are sacrificing yourself here to be a medicine man. In time you will be one. You will teach other medicine men. We are the fowl people, the winged ones, the eagles and the owls. We are a nation and you shall be our brother. You will never kill or harm one of us . . .

I felt that these voices were good, and slowly my fear left me. I had lost all sense of time . . . Then I saw a shape before me. It rose from

the darkness and the swirling fog which penetrated my earth hole.
I saw that this was my great-grandfather, Tahca Ushte, Lame Deer . . .
I understood that my great-grandfather wished me to take his name.
This made me glad beyond words.[5]

This leads us to the next section.

ANCESTRAL AND OTHER SPIRITS OF THE DEAD

In gathering–hunting traditions, the tendency is to avoid the dead. In some North American traditions, after a year's mourning, a feast for the deceased was given, and the dead were sent on their way with food and tobacco and asked not to return. Corpses were buried, placed in caves, or put on scaffolds in out-of-the-way places. On the contrary, in horticulture–hunting traditions, with people often living in matrilineal clan longhouses or groups of homes near the gardens, the dead are buried nearby and daily offered food. In the Wyandot and related traditions, in precontact times, the dead were reburied in a communal pit approximately every twelve or sixteen years with a feast and complex rituals. An annual feast for the dead continues to this day. The difference between the two types of religio-ecological circumstances can be seen in the understanding of recipients of daily offerings. Anishnabe elders, among other similar cultures that were originally gathering–hunting, especially if they have a wood stove, will take a small amount of food from their meals and offer it through the fire to the spirit realm (Sky, Earth, Four Directions, and their special spirits), while Zuni traditionalists, among other horticulture–hunting traditions, will do the same, but their offerings are to the dead of the clan.

In agricultural civilizations worldwide, outside the monotheistic traditions, the dead were the focus of sacrificial rituals and were fed daily. It was understood that they were of the greatest importance to the family, serving as intermediaries with the deities, or as the combined clan dead, as deities on their own. While this is the case for the civilizations of sub-Saharan Africa, pre-Aryan South Asia, East Asia, Mesopotamia, and the Mediterranean (Greece and Rome) as well as Polynesian culture, the situation in the Americas in this regard is somewhat different. A major difference is that in all of the listed cultures, mediumism (spirit possession) is an important aspect of ancestral rituals. The dead, beginning with the dead of the family and then other dead who have become deities, possess living humans in order that the family, clan, community, or state can interact with the numinous realm. The example most readers might be familiar with will be found in the Bible (I Sam 28: 3–25). But mediumism seems not to have developed in the Americas.

The closest to this worldwide pattern in the Americas lies outside the area covered by this book, that is, in South America. In the Inca civilization of the

Andes, the ruling brother–sister married couple represented, respectively, Sun and Moon. When the male ruler died, his mummified corpse was placed in the temple to Sun, and when the female ruler died, her mummified corpse was placed in the temple to Moon. All of these mummies were fed daily, along with other offerings, and their advice was sought when needed. But, as far as is known, there was no spirit possession by these dead rulers.

In the Northwest Coast cultures, the dead are spiritually important in at least two regards. First, the originating clan ancestor is often a deity. In the Kwakwaka'wakw culture, the clan originator, such as Orca or Thunderbird, falls from the sky or emerges from the sea or the Underworld. On taking off their masks they become human and thus begin the clan. These sacred beings are found on the "totem" poles and as masked dancers in the pot-latch ceremonies (Chapter 7). Among the Tlingit, when a person dies, a memorial potlatch is given. The matrilineal clan ancestors are present, and the gifts bestowed on the guests are in fact gifts for the ancestors. They are also present when the masks and other dance paraphernalia handed down from the clan ancestors are worn by the living. As the living dance, they are transformed into the clan ancestors who are then present to be with the living members of the clan and to welcome the newly deceased into the realm of the clan dead.

For the Hopi and other Pueblo traditions, the complex of winter ceremonials is the time for the Katsina (Katchina), the deities, to enter the villages. Their presence becomes manifest in the masked dancers who are not possessed by the Katsina, but who are transformed and become the Katsina. The Katsina are not ancestors, yet they invoke memory of the matrilineal clan ancestors. The Katsina, except when they appear in the Hopi villages, live in the realm of Sun after it has set. This is also the realm of the dead. So the appearance of the Katsina vaguely connotes the dead in general but not individually. Some of the Katsina are also the deities of particular clan-origination myths. The dead, living in the Underworld, which is perceived as watery, are understood to have influence over the desperately needed rain, without which agriculture in the semidesert region is impossible. Prayers are directed to both deities and ancestors for the life-giving rain.

Thus, the family and clan dead in the North American horticulture–hunting (or sea mammal hunting–fishing) traditions are spiritually potent yet not deities. They are manifest in the transformed masked dancers but do not possess humans; that is, they do not take over the bodies of the dancers in the mode of typical spirit possession. They can be reached by prayers and rituals, and they can appear in dreams. They can influence the fortunes of the living members of the clan but only subtly. There is a vagueness and ambiguity in these concepts, which is a problem for Euro-Americans trying to understand it, but this is not, of course, a problem for the members of these communities.

Another mode of relationship between the living and the dead is with regard to warfare. In the Iroquoian-speaking traditions preceding the last two centuries, captured enemy warriors could suffer one of two fates. Warfare was usually for revenge, and the women of the family whose dead was being revenged could decide either to adopt the captive, in which case the captive had all the privileges of the dead person, or to torture the prisoner to death. The torture was carried out by the women. Those who demonstrated exceptional bravery were eaten, especially their hearts. This was so the warriors could gain this power. In the Mesoamerican civilization, captured warriors were sacrificed by ripping the beating hearts out of their chests; it was an offering to the deities of life through living blood. The sacrificed prisoners were then also eaten. Thus, the brave dead enemy warriors became part of the living warriors.

North of Mexico, scalps were understood to contain the essence of a slain warrior who then became a protecting spirit of the one who possessed the scalp. (South of Mexico and into the Amazon Basin, it is the heads that were collected rather than just the scalps.) Chona, a Papago (in Arizona) woman whose life spanned the late nineteenth and early twentieth centuries, told her life story to the anthropologist Ruth Underhill in the early 1930s. In her autobiography, she tells of her father bringing home the scalp of an Apache he killed in battle:

> [After] we were purified . . . we could have the Apache scalp in our family to work for us like a relative. All that time that my father was being purified a woman had been making a basket, the kind that we use only for scalps and other sacred things. My father's guardian had taken the Apache hair and made it into a little man. . . . That little man had a buckskin shirt with a fringe, like an Apache, and a feather in its hair and little moccasins. The guardian brought it to my father in the basket. . . . He said to it, "My child." Then he gave it to my mother and she took it in her arms and said, "My child." He gave it to my brothers and sisters and me. We held it and said, "My younger brother." Then it was in our family and it would always help us. My father laid it in the basket and all around it he put eagle feathers which are powerful. He put in tobacco and he said, "This is your house, my child." Then he wrapped that basket in deerskins and hung it in the thatch and we had Power."[6]

Lame Deer, in his first major fast, was visited by the spirit of his great-grandfather. While Lame Deer did not say that his great-grandfather became a helping spirit, he did give Lame Deer his name, and names carry spiritual power. Many contemporary Native people live in urban areas and are far from the gathering–hunting lifestyle. I know of some healers whose helping spirits are dead humans, nonfamily ghosts, rather than animal spirits, as would have been the case in the past. This is yet another way that the dead spiritually assist the living.

CULTURE HEROES AND "TRICKSTERS"

Outside the interrelated monotheistic traditions, among the numinous beings there are those that are mythically understood to have brought to humans the necessities of life. Thus, for gathering–hunting traditions, this would include fire, usually conceived of as stolen from other beings, and the bow or other hunting weapons. For fishing-oriented cultures, this would include nets. And for horticultural traditions, this would be the domesticated plants, especially the primary source of caloric intake: grain or tubers. Often, these numinous beings are understood as semi-deities, that is, half human and half divine. An example was provided in the first part of this chapter: Nanabozho of the Anishnabe traditions. The term generally used in religious studies and folklore studies literature for such beings is "culture hero."

Another type of being found in most traditions is that of a being who is a liminal (a "threshold") figure. It is a deity that exhibits both divine and human characteristics. In central African traditions, such as the Yoruba and related cultures, Exú literally inhabits the threshold between ritual centers and the exterior world, and offerings are made to him at the gate or door-way before ceremonies are begun to elicit his goodwill. Exú is also a joke-ster, a trickster, and it is best to have a sense of humor when involved with him. Such beings are called in the literature "tricksters." This is a term I am uncomfortable with because it ignores the fact that these are numinous beings, if not deities. It is a term applied by cultures who consider them-selves superior to others in order to, in effect, desacralize deities of other religions. But as there is no other term in the literature for such beings, the term will be utilized here.

In the northern traditions of Native North America, the above two roles tend to be concentrated into a single being. This being not only brings to humans the essentials for their life and culture but also figures in stories of trickery. But different from the archetypal model as Exú, the tricks that are played end up as jokes on the trickster himself. Why these two roles become conflated into a single being is unclear. Possibly it is because the animals chosen to symbolize these beings can also be seen to have dual natures.

Raven has these dual roles in the Northwest Coast cultures. On the one hand, Raven is the bringer of such necessities as light and warmth, in that he releases Sun from a bentwood box in which it has been enclosed, and in doing so is burnt black. As other such figures, Raven also steals fire for humans. On the other hand, through greed and other undesirable traits, he is constantly causing harm to himself. If one is familiar with the behavior of ravens, there is a logic to this juxtaposition. Ravens demonstrate consider-able intelligence, especially with regard to novel situations, but they also can be seen to be quite silly as many of their experiments in dealing with novel situations end in failure.

Virtually all of these mythic figures in Native American traditions are shape-shifters or changelings, that is, they can appear in many forms. Often, in their origin myths, they are originally human like. They are mythic beings who exist before the appearance of humans (as Raven) or they may also be human as well as divine. For example, Nanabozho is born of a divine father and a human, or a semidivine, mother. In several versions, his mother dies in childbirth and his grandmother places him on the ground with a bowl over him for protection. Owing to her prolonged grief, she is oblivious to the infant, so Nanabozho changed himself into an animal that could eat the grass under the bowl. When his grandmother comes back to her senses and removes the bowl from the infant, she finds a hare (or a rabbit). And so Nanabozho is portrayed in petroglyphs as a hare, but in the stories he is usually in human form. Figure 4 is a rare anthropomorphic image with rabbit ears. Given that the petroglyph is at the edge of the area in which the Anishnabeg lived before contact, the image surely is Nanabozho and suggests that all of the images were done by Anishnabeg.

For the Lakota, this being is Spider, but the most common symbol throughout the Plains is Coyote. Different from wolves, coyotes do not live in packs, and they do not avoid humans. Often they can be found hanging around hunting camps and from an anthropomorphic perspective seem to be continually smirking if not laughing.

There are more available stories about Coyote than any other similar sacred being. As with the other figures, his exploits serve as a lesson about improper behavior. They are a way of teaching children socially approved behavior in the context of entertainment. The stories are hilarious. And as they are frequently scatological or bawdy, they capture the attention of children and teenagers alike.

Most Native cultures are egalitarian with regard to status and voluntaristic with regard to leadership. Social cohesion and effective action depend on cooperation. Individualism is the norm but only to the extent that it does not impinge on others. The economy is one of sharing, and social prestige is gained by giving away rather than by hoarding. Selfish behavior and hoarding are considered the epitome of evil. The trickster stories teach the folly of greed and selfishness, whether of food or sex. Thus, children are taught in the context of hilarity proper behavior and ethical values. This is also the function of the sacred Clowns during Pueblo ceremonies.

These beings have found their way into the dominant culture of North America. The African slaves brought with them to the southern states of the United States their own trickster in the form of a rabbit, and as they mingled with Algonquian-speaking Native peoples, especially when they escaped in the earlier centuries, their stories merged with the Native ones into those

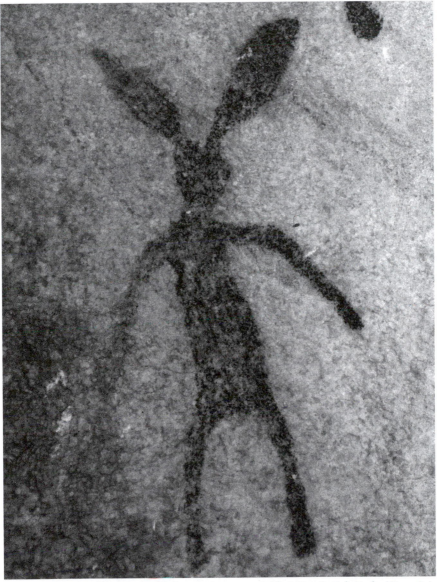

Figure 4:   Nanabozho. Peterborough Petroglyphs Provincial Park (Ontario). Precontact (undetermined date) Anishnabe. Photograph by the author.

about Br'er Rabbit. These stories in turn influenced the development of the irrepressible Bugs Bunny of Hollywood cartoon fame. Similarly, the Coyote stories of the West served as a basis for the animated cartoon figure of Wile E. Coyote. As Coyote of the Native stories, he finds his brilliant but bizarre solutions backfiring on him. Of course, for the dominant culture of North America, neither Bugs Bunny nor Wile E. Coyote is a sacred being.

Thus, as in all other regards, the dominant culture has co-opted aspects of Native religious ideology, just as many Native traditions have integrated aspects of Christianity. Coyote may have been captured on Hollywood celluloid, but, as has been learned from the Christian notion of resurrection, he will be back:

[Old Man:] Coyote and myself, we will not be seen again until Earthwoman is very old. Then we shall return to earth, for it will require a change by that time. Coyote will come along first, and when you see him you will know I am coming. When I come along, all the spirits of the dead will be with me. There will be no more Other Side Camp. All the people will live together. Earthmother will go back to her first shape and live as a mother among her children. Then things will be made right. [Nez Perce tradition][7]

PART 11

CEREMONIES FROM A VARIETY OF TRADITIONS

. 4 .

Great Lakes and Northeast

In the remaining chapters of this book, the focus will be on how Native North American religious traditions adapted to changing circumstances, tracing specific religious ceremonies or modalities into the present where appropriate. While many non-Native people fantasize that Native traditions have maintained some kind of pristine, unchanging purity since the beginning of time, most living facets of human culture are constantly changing, be it spoken languages, the arts, sociopolitical patterns, or religion. The Christianity of today, for example, is quite distant from the Christianity of the past, and the further in time one goes back, the greater are the changes. Christmas was not a Christian celebration until several hundred years after it began, and it was borrowed from Mithraism, as was Sunday as the holy day of the week. The Christmas tree did not become a part of English Christmas celebrations until the mid-nineteenth century. Some Protestant traditions have been around for less than a century. Similarly, we would expect Native religious traditions to be continually evolving as circumstances change. Thus, the subject of this part of this book is not Native traditions of a distant past but, where traditions continue, of the present and the reasons for and the results of change.

ANISHNABE RELIGION: MODERNIZATION OF GATHERING-HUNTING SPIRITUALITY

Anishnabe (Anishnaabe, Nishnabe, "Human Being") is the name by which the Algonquian-speaking people (particularly the dialects of Ojibwe [Chippewa], Odawa [Ottawa], Potawatomi, Menomini, and Algonguin) surrounding the Great Lakes call themselves. Before contact with the expanding European colonies, they lived a life of gathering–hunting, with some having very limited horticulture because of the cold climate and the limited soil on the Canadian Shield, the scoured rocky land whose soil was shoved further south by the glaciers thousands of years ago. They lived in small bands that broke up into family groups during the winter and traded smoked meat and hides for corn with their horticulture–hunting neighbors south of them. They were at the northern fringe of the vast trading network centered on the city of Cahokia.

Their rituals were those to be found throughout northern North America: fasting/vision-questing, menarche and menstruation, hunting/raiding/ gathering, Spirit ("sweat") Lodge, binding rituals (Chapter 8), healing rituals, mourning ceremonies, the Thirst ("sun") Dance among those Anishnabe on the Plains, and any others that might be dreamed. Ritual paraphernalia included the Sacred Pipe, hand-drums (deer rawhide over a hoop frame), and various types of shakers (rattles).

With contact, the Anishnabeg voluntarily involved themselves in the fur trade and involuntarily defended themselves against the expanding Iroquoian-speaking Five Nations seeking hegemony over the fur trade. Their allies and trading partners, the Iroquoian-speaking Wyandot, were wiped out by disease brought by the Jesuits and invasion by the Five Nations, and many of the survivors joined them. Eventually, the Anishnabeg reversed the situation, driving the Five Nations south of the Great Lakes and pushing Siouan-speaking peoples west of the Great Lakes. To do so they needed rituals appropriate to large gatherings of people and that would encourage inter-tribal communication. These factors led to the development of the Midewiwin, a semi-institutionalized set of rituals that cut across Anishnabe tribal lines, in the late seventeenth century.

Euro-Americans have been aware of the Midewiwin since its inception, and all of its elements have a long indigenous past, yet most ethnohistorical analyses understand the tradition to be due, in various ways, to Euro-American influence or to be a nativistic movement. These assumptions follow from a mind-set that perceives Native cultures to be primitive. One of the factors that leads to the assumption of Western influence is the Midewiwin's birchbark scrolls: complex series of symbols with a mnemonic function that assists in the telling of Midewiwin instructional myths and maintaining the complex initiation rituals inscribed on the inner bark of the birch tree. The Great Lakes Anishnabe are not the only North American Natives to have such scrolls; the Algonquian-speaking Lenape (Delaware), originally of the mid-Atlantic coast, also had them. The scrolls also reflect the continuing practice from antiquity of drawing symbols in sand during Midewiwin teachings. In any case, the West did not introduce books to the Americas, the Maya had immense libraries that were destroyed by the Spanish, and the idea of books probably spread up the Mississippi to the mercantile cities and thence northward to the Great Lakes.

The Midewiwin's center is traditionally understood to be at the south-western end of Lake Superior, where by the late seventeenth century, after displacing Siouan-speaking people in the upheavals consequent to the fur trade, an Anishnabe trading town arose. The Midewiwin practices are particularly appropriate for a widespread culture to periodically come together at an established center. This area remains the heartland of the Midewiwin to today.

A second factor in the development of the Midewiwin is the fusion of Wyandot culture with the Anishnabeg at the north end of Lakes Huron and Superior. In this area to today, Anishnabe communities hold an annual Feast for the Dead, a ceremony that reflects Iroquoian rather than Anishnabe practices of the distant past. The Midewiwin ritual structures are Iroquoian-style longhouses; the "Little Boy," the special drum at the heart of the rituals, is the Iroquoian water drum. Presently, there are two types of Midewiwin water drums that differ according to the method of securing the rawhide head to the wooden body, to which water is added when in use. The older, called the "Grandfather Drum," has the head secured in the Iroquoian fashion, by a band around the upper part of the drum. A second type of water drum, which came into use in Midewiwin rituals in the early twentieth century, has its head tied in a manner related to that used by the Native American Church: complex ties around knobs in the head raised by round stones along the sides, which spread among the Great Lakes Anishnabe around the same time that the Native American Church spread into that area.

Midewiwin rituals focus on resurrection. Death and resurrection not only is a prominent theme in circumpolar shamanistic traditions, but would have become of particular importance at a time when most of the population was dying of introduced Western diseases. Hence, the Midewiwin can be understood as an organic development of traditional elements, to which were added aspects brought by the Wyandot when they joined the Anishnabe, forming a highly viable aspect of traditional Anishnabe religion suitable to the changing social circumstances and living patterns because of the fur trade. There is no need to look for Western Christian influence.

The Midewiwin (known as "Medicine Lodge" among the Siouan-speaking Winnebago) is an Anishnabe *cultus* in the original Hellenistic sense of the term: an optional adjunct to the base religion of a culture requiring initiation. A modern example of a *cultus* would be Masonic Lodges in relation to Protestant Christianity. Anishnabeg who are already involved with traditional religion may be invited after nomination by relatives or friends to be initiated into this semi-institutional variant of traditional Anishnabe religion in which the members form a social as well as ritual bond. The initiations, at four sequential levels (eight in some versions), involve teachings and symbolic death and resurrection using cowrie shells and small sacred bundles, made of the skins of a different animal for each level.

Western theorists have commented on a "shamanistic" mind-set in which the initiates actually believed themselves to be killed and resurrected. Had these theorists witnessed initiation rituals, they would have perceived the silliness of such a view. The initiations in this regard are understood symbolically and are a source of merriment. Good acting in pretending to die and then be resurrected is greatly appreciated. And the manipulation of the sacred bags of small mammal skins so that the bags appear to be living animals, when well done, is applauded. Puppetry, acting, illusion, along with actual trance, are all aspects of shamanism worldwide, and those involved know the difference between mimicry and actuality, fully appreciating both.

Aside from initiation rituals, today there are four seasonal rituals of four days' duration, each surrounding a weekend, in which adherents, including initiates and supporters, gather from throughout the area of the Great Lakes. The general ceremonies are held in a longhouse structure of a sapling framework and nowadays canvas covers, except for the winter ceremonial that usually takes place in a suitable building, which is far warmer given the area's very cold winters. The initiation structure has a similar framework, but the lower part is covered with boughs, with the upper part left open. Since only those already initiated to the appropriate degree or the initiates can enter this structure, this allows the other adherents and visitors to observe and enjoy the nominally esoteric initiation rituals from without. A Spirit Lodge will be built in the vicinity for preliminary rituals.

Central to the Midewiwin are the cowrie shell (*megis*), which as in many traditions worldwide, being in the shape of the vagina, symbolizes life, and a water drum called the "Little Boy" in reference to the origin myth of the Midewiwin. All those initiated have the *megis*, but only recognized elders, male and female, will be ritual keepers of these especially sacred drums.

Within a hundred years of establishing hegemony over the northern and western parts of the Great Lakes, and after several wars with the British and the Americans, the Anishnabe found themselves forced onto ever smaller reservations, none large enough to be economically viable. Eventually, even some of these were terminated in the United States. The reserves, especially in Canada, were controlled by Christian priests and ministers. The Anishnabe children were forced into boarding schools often brutally administered by Christian churches, which stripped those who did not die from disease of their language, culture, dignity, and sense of self-worth. Many of these schools' graduates as well as those from terminated reserves ended up on the skid rows of cities from Minneapolis–Saint Paul to Toronto. In the late twentieth century, a revitalized Midewiwin brought to many of the Anishnabeg a renewed sense of positive cultural identification and a meaning to life.

In the late 1960s, after a century of enforced prohibition and mandatory Christianization, a revitalization of Native traditions began in North America. Some Anishnabe leaders of the American Indian Movement (AIM), having been introduced to pan-Indian religious modalities, began to seek among elders specifically Anishnabe traditions. The Midewiwin had continued underground among a few elderly adherents, and they were discovered by this new generation seeking their spiritual roots. Being semi-institutional, the revitalized Midewiwin provided a loose organizational structure, even for those traditionalists who were not initiated per se.

Eddie Benton, from a northern Wisconsin reservation, and one of the early AIM leaders, was among the first of these then young men to be initiated into the Midewiwin and has since become the leading figure in the revitalized movement. He earned a graduate degree in education and, along with others, began a Native-way school based on the Midewiwin teachings, the Red Schoolhouse in Saint Paul, in the late 1960s.

Shortly afterward, Jim Dumont, who had earned a graduate ministerial degree from the University of Toronto, and his then wife, Edna Manitowabi, from the large Wikwemikong Unceded Reserve on Manitoulin Island in Ontario, began to seek their Anishnabe spiritual roots, finding Christianity unsatisfying. They found it with Eddy Benton and the elders who were guiding him and brought the Midewiwin to eastern Ontario. When they sought to hold Midewiwin rituals on the Wikwemikong Reserve, the Catholic priest forced them and their new followers off the reserve, and they purchased land near Sudbury (northern Ontario) to begin a community living by traditional values, free of alcohol and drugs, with their own school. In this, they were assisted by Ed Newberry, a liberal Protestant minister. And both Jim Dumont and Edna Manitowabi were given faculty positions at a new Native Studies program at the Roman Catholic University of Sudbury. Some aspects of Christianity were then changing and, contrary to their past, offering support for the revitalization of Native spirituality rather than seeking to suppress it.

These new, relatively young adherents to the Midewiwin, along with the elder Art Solomon, began an active program of ministering to the acute spiritual needs of Native people in the prisons or suffering from despair, along with the resultant alcoholism and drug addiction, in the cities of Ontario. At the same time, Trent University in eastern Ontario also started a Native Studies program and began to hold "elders conferences," to bring together traditionalist elders, especially those of the Midewiwin and the Six Nations Longhouse Religion, and the young. Elders conferences were to spread to a number of universities and urban Native centers.

Their teachings struck a chord with the youth and spread around the Great Lakes. By the 1980s, Christian clergy lost their control over Native reserves in Canada and the Christian boarding schools closed. Even those Anishnabe traditionalists who will have nothing to do with the Midewiwin were now free to come out into the open and be available for healing and other spiritual activities.

Today, adherents of the Midewiwin seasonally gather four times a year from all over the Great Lakes for ceremonies that rotate widely among Anishnabe reserves in Ontario, Manitoba, Minnesota, Wisconsin, and

Michigan. Members of the ritual society serve as healers and counselors in various urban areas. As the Three Fires Society (Ojibwe, Odawa, and Potawatomi), they sponsor summer music festivals on the larger reservations, especially Wikwemikong, which bring together many Anishnabeg and other Native people.

The Midewiwin is an example of a revised mode of traditional religion first developed in response to the many changes due to the fur trade over three centuries ago and has more recently been successful as the basis of a revitalization of Native religion, not just on reservations but in urban areas, using modern institutions and devices—schools, healing centers, universities, automobiles, telephone, and the Internet—to fill the spiritual vacuum resulting from the boarding schools and, until relatively recently, the persecution of Native religions. Because the Midewiwin offers a ritual structure, including seasonal ceremonies, and because it emphasizes the renewal of life, especially a life that is positive toward self, family, community, and society, it is well suited to modern Anishnabeg, both those living on reserves and those living in cities.

A typical contemporary four-day spring ceremony would begin with people arriving from one to several days before the ceremony begins. After setting up their tents, trailers, or recreational vehicles in the camping area, the men will begin to collect saplings for erecting a Spirit Lodge, the regular Midewiwin lodge, and the initiation lodge. Women will collect cedar boughs for use as flooring in the lodges and pluck the leaves for offerings along with tobacco through fire to the spirit realm. An arbor is built near the main lodge for preparing the daily feasts.

After all the materials are gathered, the lodges are erected and prepared, and male and female Spirit Lodge ceremonies are held at night for first the ritual leaders, then the initiates, and on other evenings, if there is time, for all others. The lighting of the sacred fire at the center of the lodge with flint and steel marks the beginning of the four days. Firetenders will have been chosen, who will take turns to see that the sacred fire is kept burning day and night until the end of the ceremonies. Others will continue to bring wood to the fire in the lodge, to the fires at the Spirit Lodge, to the cooking area, and to the Moon Lodge. It is at this time that the drumkeepers, with their assistants, tie the leather heads onto the wooden bodied water drums using elaborate, symbolic patterns.

The Moon Lodge is usually a nearby house that is volunteered for the use of menstruating women. Women who are menstruating stay away from the ceremonies because at that time of the month their spiritual power is so strong it can overwhelm the power of the ritual leaders and all that is going on. These women take care of the young children, so their parents can take part in the ceremonies without distraction.

The lodge is oriented east to west, with the main opening to the east, in the direction of the rising sun. The sacred fire is in the middle of the large oblong structure, and no one crosses the space between the fire and the eastern doorway. To move about, all circumambulate the interior of the lodge in a sunwise direction. Seating is according to sex, with females sitting along the north wall facing south and males sitting in the south facing north. That way, the two sexes form a complete circle (actually an oval) while facing each other. The Little Boys are in front of those elders who are responsible for them and are placed at the four doorways, both symbolic and actual, of the lodge.

The various rituals that take place during these days are not absolutely fixed. They depend on spiritual inspiration not only from the ritual leaders but for anyone who dreams or has a vision of a ritual. This dream is spoken to an elder. If the elder considers the dream a directive from the spirit realm to the community, it will be carried out sometime during the four days.

Each day usually begins with people gathering for offerings through the fire at sunrise. They then return to their campsites for breakfast. A second gathering will be at mid-day, which will include a feast. The feast consists of whatever traditional foods the women cook. It is first offered to the spirits in an altar before the sacred fire, and then all are served while sitting in the lodge. In the afternoon, there will be teachings, save for the last full day, when the initiations will take place. In the evening, there will be another ritual with a feast. This ritual might be a healing ritual, for the healing of all participants and the earth. It might be a mourning ritual limited to those who have had a death in the family in the past year. In this ritual, those who have lost someone contribute the favorite dish of the deceased to the feast. Before it is offered, the relative will speak about the deceased and their feelings. These are but two of the various types of rituals that might take place.

During a ritual, aside from the feast itself, there will be orations from the elders, prayer offerings with the Sacred Pipe, and songs and dancing in place with the rhythm led by the Little Boys and shakers. After four days of an intense series of rituals as well as several days of preparation, all the participants find themselves in a sacred place in a sacred time. Everyone is sad when it is over and but reluctantly leave, after helping bring the site back to its original state. These rituals not only enhance the well-being of the participants, but promote bonding between the people coming from near and far. All become sisters and brothers and take these relationships with them when they leave to go back to their jobs and homes.

THE HAUDENAUSAUNEE: FROM HORTICULTURE-HUNTING TO AGRICULTURE

Five centuries ago, the five Iroquoian-speaking nations—Seneca, Cayuga, Onondaga, Oneida, and Mohawk—who lived south of Lakes Eire and Ontario, created a political confederation, more highly organized than the other confederations surrounding them. This confederation stemmed from a vision by one who is called Peace Maker. With an oral constitution, called the Great Law of Peace, it became the progenitor of the early United States Confederation. This organization, led by male chiefs chosen and instructed by clan mothers, through military might and skillful diplomacy, successfully gained control over a much larger area around them, giving them dominance over the fur trade with the European colonies. Later, they were joined by another Iroquoian-speaking people, the Tuscarora, when they lost their land in the Southeast to European colonists. The Six Nations called themselves the Haudenausaunee, meaning "People Building an Extensive House" or "People of the Longhouse." Longhouse here did not so much refer to their large clan dwellings as to the understanding that the Six Nations themselves were an extended house, with the Mohawk at the eastern doorway and the Seneca at the western.

As discussed in Chapter 2, they lived a horticulture–hunting lifestyle in matrilineal clan longhouses by the sizeable gardens farmed by the women. The men hunted, raided, traded, and engaged in diplomacy. Horticulture furnished sufficient food resources for the men to go on long raiding and trading trips.

The Haudenausaunee hegemony continued until the American Revolution. The British to keep the Haudenausaunee and others as their allies prevented their colonists from settling west of the Appalachian Mountains. At the time of the Revolution, four of the Six Nations sided with the British and two with the Americans. When the British lost the war, many of the Haudenausaunee fled to Upper Canada (later Ontario) along with the Loyalists, taking up land near present-day Hamilton still called the Six Nations Reserve. For those who remained south of the Great Lakes, their world was turned upside down.

The Americans flooded west of the Appalachians. In what became upstate New York, all of the Haudenausaunee towns were destroyed, and they were left with ever-shrinking land. While the women continued to garden, the men were left with no occupations. The new Euro-American settlers wiped out the deer and other animals hunted for subsistence, raiding and warfare were no longer possible, and diplomacy had become impossible given the Haudenausaunee's weak and fragmented situation.

As often happens under such circumstances, the men gave way to despair, leading to alcoholism and dissolution. The Haudenausaunee were on the verge of collapse. One of the drunkards, a brother of the notable Seneca chief, Cornplanter, with the hereditary name of Ganeodiyo or Handsome Lake, beginning in 1799 while near death after years of debilitating illness had a series of visions. In essence, the visions were that Four Messengers from the Creator were sent to him to instruct him regarding the will of the Creator. He began to preach a new culture and religion for first the Seneca and then all of the Six Nations. At the time, Quaker missionaries were trying to save the Seneca and had befriended Handsome Lake.

This was not a nativistic prophecy. While Handsome Lake preached a return to traditional virtues and the ritual calendar, he was also preaching a radically new way of life. Essentially, it was to turn away from the matrilocal clan longhouses to patrifocal nuclear cabins, with men farming and women keeping the home. The longhouse, now built as a European-style rectangular structure, was to be, in effect, a church, where the rituals would take place at stated times. Powerful women were declared to be witches and killed. The men were to adopt the Protestant work ethic and become farmers, eschewing alcohol, gambling, and music. He recommended that the children be sent to the Quaker schools.

Theologically, Handsome Lake moved away from the general traditional theology of his culture described in Chapter 3 and focused on a semi-monotheistic male deity named the Creator, the Great Ruler who lived above. In effect, Sky was excised from the Sky–Earth complementary duality, and became a single deity. The Creator struggled with an evil spirit for the souls of people. It was a struggle between Heaven and Hell, between goodness and sin. If humans continued as they were, the apocalypse would arrive, and the world would be destroyed by fire. But if all repented of their sin, the world would be reborn anew. It was a theology closer to Christianity than that of traditional Haudenausaunee religion.

Handsome Lake's prophecies were embraced by many of the Haudenausaunee, for it was clear that if they did not change, they had nowhere to go but down to oblivion. After he died, his prophecies were embodied in a long oral text, the "Code of Handsome Lake," that was recited at ritual gatherings. But his theology and teachings were modified to bring them back to more traditional ways and understandings; it became what is called the Longhouse Religion.

Handsome Lake's teachings were instrumental in the survival of the Haudenausaunee. It eased the transition from horticulture–hunting to agriculture already mandated by both the Americans and the British in Canada. It encouraged a Western education and a lifestyle little different from poor Euro-Americans, but far better than for those on many other reservations. Some Haudenausaunee became well educated and were able to work for the welfare of their people. Handsome Lake's modified teachings also allowed the survival of the traditional religion, the Haudenausaunee languages, and a matrifocal society to the present day. If one removes the slight Christian theological overlay and the church-like appearance to some degree of the longhouses, there remains the traditional religion. Because the "Code of Handsome Lake" was recited in the indigenous languages, along with the long Thanksgiving Prayer, a number of times throughout the year, the languages were preserved. While the men took up farming, carpentry, and other trades, the Longhouse Religion was based on matrilineal clan identity, and the clan mothers kept their traditional role of choosing and instructing both political and ritual leaders, the latter called Faithkeepers. Even the nuclear family residences often maintained a matrifocal ambiance. So despite the insistence by the dominant cultures of legally only recognizing patrilineal descent, the religion mandated identification by matrilineal descent, thus preserving the Haudenausaunee social order.

While some of the rituals take place in the home, the longhouse functions as the primary ritual center. They are framed wooden rectangular single-room buildings, with benches along the sides, two wood stoves toward each of the long ends, benches in the middle for the drummers and those with shakers, and two doors at the narrow ends. The building is oriented in an east–west direction; thus, there are eastern and western doorways. The clans are divided into two groupings (moieties), with each group using a different doorway and stove. As with the Midewiwin lodges, women sit on the northern side and men on the southern side with their clans.

There is a yearly cycle of rituals combining gathering and horticultural foci. The seasonal round begins with the Midwinter Ceremony, a yearly renewal ritual. It is followed by a dance in honor of the dead, a Maple Dance, Thunder Dance, Planting Dance, Moon Dance, Strawberry Dance, Green Bean Dance, Green Corn Dance, and Harvest Dance. The seasonal dances vary to some extent from one Longhouse community to another.

The following description of the day-to-day events of the Midwinter Ceremonial is general, as details vary from one Longhouse to another. It is but meant to give an idea of the many dances and healing events that take place. Even the count of days varies, depending on which is considered the actual first day.

The day before the Ceremony begins, a ceremony is held in which all the infants born since the last Green Corn Ceremony are publicly named. Boiled corn mush is eaten in honor of the new members of the community. Early the next day, the actual first day of the Ceremony, two persons, one from each moiety called Bigheads, go among the homes announcing the New Year. When everyone is in the longhouse, the Bigheads reveal their dreams. Members of the False Face Society go to each house and stir the ashes in the stoves while singing a thanksgiving song. They return to the longhouse and dance, blowing the ashes on the sick of the village. The following day, groups of people go from house to house, stirring up the ashes while singing the thanksgiving song, and asking people to guess their dreams (a very old custom attested to in the sixteenth-century Jesuit Relations). The next day, all perform the Feather Dance, and the women alone, the Women's Dance. Afterward the various secret medicine societies (membership is by invitation and initiation) perform healing rituals.

In the past, on the fourth day was the White Dog Sacrifice. Many Native traditions considered the sacrifice of a dog, especially a white dog, the greatest sacrifice of all. Given how people feel about dogs, one can understand this sacrifice to be in lieu of a human sacrifice. But given the attitude of modern Western society toward eating dogs, this is now done symbolically. The

Thanksgiving Dance is performed, and the medicine societies continue their curing rituals. On the following day, teams travel from house to house playing the sacred Bowl Game, the medicine societies dance for the welfare of the sick, the False Faces dance for gifts of tobacco, the Husk Faces dance in honor of the Three Sisters (corn, beans, and squash), and there are social dances in the evening. On the sixth day, the Faithkeepers gather the people in the longhouse and recite the long Thanksgiving Prayer to the deities, the cosmic forces, and all the animals and plants on the earth. The next day is a continuation of past events: people sing their personal thanksgiving songs, tell their dreams and feast, and the medicine societies continue to heal. On the final day, new longhouse officers are inaugurated, there is a final performance of the sacred Feather Dance, and feasting and social dancing continue into the evening.

Until the 1960s, the Longhouse Religion was attracting fewer and fewer Haudenausaunee; on some reservations, the Longhouse itself became defunct. Many considered the Longhouse Religion old fashioned, and the majority were Christians. Beginning in the late 1960s, with a reawakening of interest and pride in Native identity, the Longhouses became a source of cultural revitalization and political assertion. It was members of the Longhouse who were behind the border bridge blockage at Akwesasne (discussed in Chapter 2), the formation of a Mohawk language school, and political activism for independence from the dominant culture. The administration recognized by the U.S. and Canadian governments, elected chiefs and councils, were seen as subservient to the dominant society. Young people began to become active in the Longhouses.

But in the 1980s, the introduction of casinos led to factionalism and eventually violence: two Mohawks were killed because of this struggle in 1990. The Longhouse people were opposed to the building of a large gambling hall, rather than to gambling itself, because they feared the influence of organized crime in the running of the gambling establishments, which would then lead to further criminal activities. Indeed, smuggling of cigarettes, liquor, guns, and people did become a major source of income at Akwesasne. Those in favor of the casinos as a source of employment—often as armed guards—and community income saw the Longhouse people as conservative obstructionists. The traditionalists split among themselves, especially the youths, into pacifist members of the Longhouse and Warrior Societies who wanted to fight for land and other rights through armed struggle. Service in Vietnam and the influence of the more personal religious practices of the AIM (fasting and "sweat" lodges, although before Handsome Lake these were aspects of Haudenausaunee religion), along with employment in the casinos, were among the motivating factors for the members of the Warrior Societies.

As mentioned in Chapter 2, some of the Longhouse members left Akwesasne, but there remain problems regarding the continuation of the

Longhouse Religion there and elsewhere. First, Handsome Lake's reforms were based on a small-scale farming economy, but this economy is no longer viable in the United States or Canada. Second, the revitalization of Native traditions led more and more to see the Christian overlay that Handsome Lake placed on traditional religion, seen, for example, in the words of a member of the Warrior Society:

> [T]he Handsome Lake Code; a lot of us view it as being a code that's a mixture of Christianity and traditionalism. And the reason why that was used, [it's] another way of assimilating our people and so many of us . . . refused to accept the Handsome Lake Code.[1]

One can but wait and see if the Longhouse Religion will again change to meet new circumstances and remain the traditional religion of the Haudenausaunee or become stagnant and slowly fade away as tradition-oriented youth turn from it.

· **5** ·

Southwest and Southeast

DINÉ MENARCHE RITUALS: CELEBRATING FEMALE SPIRITUAL POWER

Western traditions are to a large degree misogynist. In Christianity, with the doctrine of original sin, women were understood to be the source of human evil. This understanding was applied to female physiology; menstruation came to be considered unclean and shameful, to be either hidden or ignored. This attitude was also employed in the Western understanding of non-Western traditions. Native American rituals regarding menarche and menstruation, particularly the sequestering of females, was understood to be practiced because women at that time were considered dirty and impure. Nothing could be further from reality.

In most human cultures, blood is understood as the essence of life and symbolically to be a sacred color. In China, religious structures are painted red, because the color of blood is considered sacred. Both men and women traditionally wore red at weddings, because it was the color of life and fecundity. The symbolic opposite to the color red is white, the color of death, of the human corpse drained of blood. Thus, unbleached cloth is worn by the immediate family at Chinese funerals.

In virtually all Native North American traditions, menstruating women sequestered themselves to varying degrees, usually for four days. This is because it is understood that at the time of flowing blood women are particularly sacred. Sacredness is coterminous with spiritual power, and their power at this time could overwhelm male power, which would be detrimental to all.

Also, as I have been told by an Anishnabe woman, women at this time avoid the sacred objects of males because their overwhelming power at that time could draw the male power into themselves, which they neither want nor need. Other Anishnabe women told me that it was a monthly four-day vacation from all work. In the traditional culture, women's work was continuous, while male work was sporadic. Males had periodic time-offs; this custom of sequestering ensured that women had it also.

It was particularly at menarche, at the first menses, that female spiritual power was considered particularly dangerous, because the young women had not yet learned how to control and utilize it. So at menarche, women fasted to gain spirit helpers and learn to control their spiritual power. It was also a time when they bonded to Earth and Moon. As Verna Johnston, an Anishnabe woman, put it in the title used for her biography, *I Am Nokomis, Too*—Nokomis meaning Grandmother but specifically Grandmother Moon. Because the menses occur according to the cycle of the moon, it is understood that women have a special relationship with Moon.

In northeastern Iowa, there is a cave resembling a vagina, with regard to both the form of the opening and the shape of the cave itself, close by a flowing stream. On the sandstone walls is inscribed over and over again the sign for the vagina, which is also the sign for Earth. There had been a village in the vicinity. Given nearby Native practices that continued well into the twentieth century, it can be safely assumed that this is where young women came during their menarche to fast. They sat on the earthen floor, their blood flowing and merging with Mother Earth, in a vagina-like hole within Earth's body while they could hear the flow of Her blood from the stream but a few meters away. Each young woman scratched the vagina sign onto the wall in a sacred commemoration of coming into her maturity, both physically and spiritually.

The most elaborate menarche rituals are found among the Athapaskan-speaking Dené and Diné. The Dené live in present-day Yukon and Northwest Territories. Rather than speak of individual spirits with regard to the spirit realm, they speak of Power in general. Women are understood to be spiritually more powerful than men. Vital Thomas (d. 1990), a Dogrib (one of the Dené tribes), told the anthropologist June Helm the following:

> They say a woman's *ink'on* (spiritual power) is stronger than a man's . . . some women cure with it . . . A woman gets *ink'on* same way as a man does. When a young girl has her first monthlies, got to build a little spruce tipi. . . . Out of the camp. Nobody should see her . . . The girl lives by herself until she get's older. And if she's lucky she going to get *ink'on*. That's the time.[1]

After the first menstrual seclusion, young Dené women wore a beaded veil and only drank from a swan- or goose-bone drinking tube, among other ritual behaviors, for a year.

The Dené were the last to migrate from northeastern Asia to the Americas, and some kept moving south. A few groups moved to the coast and adopted Northwest Coast cultural patterns. Some moved onto the Plains, where some remained in present-day southern Alberta. And some continued to the southern reaches of the Plains (New Mexico and Arizona), arriving about five hundred years ago. There they are known by the southern Athapaskan dialect pronunciation of Diné. They were nomads, hunting bison, and carrying their possessions by dog travois. They began to trade with the Pueblo peoples of the Southwest and, when horses became available, began to raid as well.

In 1680, the Pueblos revolted against the Spanish colonists and drove them out of the Southwest. In 1696, the Spanish retook the area, and many of the Pueblo people fled and joined the Diné. Intermarriage took place, and there was a fusion of the traditions. One group of Diné, known as the Navajo, adopted horticulture and sheep raising, becoming semisedentary. Another group, known as the Apache (including the Chiricahua, Jicarilla, and Mescalero), continued a foraging–raiding lifestyle. They first raided the Spanish and then the Mexicans and Americans. These were the last group to be conquered by the U.S. Army. A Chiricahua band under the great war spiritual leader, Geronimo, did not surrender until 1886. The Navajo reservation is the largest in the United States and has the largest indigenous population north of Mexico. The Apache have several reservations scattered throughout southern Arizona and New Mexico.

Fusing the Dené focus on female spiritual power, particularly at the time of menarche, and the matrilineal, matrilocal, matrifocal Pueblo elaborate ceremonialism, replete with masked dancers embodying the deities, the Diné have created the most powerful menarche rituals in the world, which are ongoing to today. For in these rituals, the girl becoming a young woman does not just merge with or embody the Earth Mother; for a short period of time, she *is* Changing Woman/White Shell Woman, the Earth Mother (Chapter 3). The menarche rituals do not in fact take place during the first menses, as they require much time for preparation as well as to accumulate the necessary wealth to pay for ritual specialists and the feasts and gifts for all who honor the young woman by coming to the ceremony.

These are the most important ceremonies of these cultures. No man who has taken part can possibly disrespect a woman who has undergone these rituals, and no girl who has endured the ceremony can ever lose her empowerment in being a woman, for during the time of the ceremony, the young woman becomes a deity.[2]

Navajo Kinaaldá

The Kinaaldá is part of the great Blessingway, the Navajo ceremonial that celebrates creation and life. The Navajo female puberty ceremony involves four days of public ritual, followed by a further four days of private teachings and rituals.

On the first day, the girl's hair is combed, and she is dressed in typical modern Navajo finery—velvet blouse and turquoise jewelry—by a relative who then "molds" the initiate as she lies on a Pendleton blanket with her head to the west. This is on top of a pile of blankets lent by those who want special blessings. The massaging follows the Navajo creation myth in which Changing Woman is molded into her perfect shape. After the molding, she ritually returns the blankets to those who lent them, who then thank her, calling her Changing Woman. The girl then stands in the center of the blanket facing east, while those in attendance circle the fire in the center of the hogan—the traditional log and earth Navajo dwelling—and form a line before her. Each turns their back toward her, and she puts her hands on the back of the neck and lifts upward. Having the power of Changing Woman, the girl thus promotes the health of those she lifts.

When the healings are completed, the girl begins the first of a series of runs, always toward the east—running being the means of inducing trance in Southwestern Native traditions. During the ceremonial, each run must be longer than the previous one. The longer the runs, the longer will be her life. Anyone may run with her, but most who do are children and young teenagers.

In the evening, she grinds corn with a mano and metate, the traditional Southwestern and Mexican stone roller and stone rolling tray for grinding corn. Grinding corn is one of the major tasks in the Pueblo menarche rituals. When finished, she is allowed to sleep.

At dawn of the second day, the girl runs the first race of the day. She runs a second race at noon and a third toward sunset. During the day, she grinds corn.

On the third day, she again runs at dawn. Male and female ritual specialists prepare a pit for baking a special cornbread. During the day, while the runs continue, a fire is lit in the pit and the batter prepared. A feast is served to all present. Toward the end of the day, the fire is removed from the pit, it is laid with cornhusks, and the many buckets of batter made from the cornmeal ground by the girl are poured into the pit. The female ritualist blesses the batter with sacred cornmeal, it is covered with layers of cornhusks, newspapers, and earth, and the coals are raked on top. Men keep a fire burning on top of this large earthen oven throughout the night.

Toward midnight, the hogan is prepared for a sing (the term used for Navajo religious ceremonies). A blanket with sacred ritual objects is placed at the back of the hogan, facing the eastern entrance, with the male ritualist at one end and the girl at the other end. As in other traditions, women sit on the north side of the hogan and men on the south side. The hogan is blessed with corn pollen—the most common means of blessing in Pueblo cultures—followed by blessing the girl, and each person blesses themselves with the sacred pollen. Ritual singing starts and continues until dawn.

Just before dawn, the girl's hair is ritually shampooed, as is the jewelry, lent by holy persons, she has been wearing, while songs of purification are sung. At the dawn of the fourth day, she races for the last time. While she is running, racing songs are sung, and the pit is uncovered for the bread to cool. When the girl returns from her run, a final song is sung, and pollen pouches are again passed around for blessings and purification. Everyone gathers around the fire pit. The bread is cut according to the sacred directions and passed around. A meal of traditional foods is served to all but the girl, who does not eat.

After the meal, the girl's hair is combed while combing songs are sung. She is ritually painted with a special white clay that has been prepared by a female elder. The girl then stands facing east and puts a dab of paint on all those who want a blessing. A final molding takes place on a pile of blankets outside the hogan. Afterwards, she again returns the blankets, each again thanking Changing Woman as they receive their blanket. This brings to a close the public part of the ceremonial.

The effect of the ritual lasts a lifetime; it influences every aspect of a woman's life, for a ceremony that ensures a positive understanding of oneself—physically, spiritually, socially, and mentally—is empowering and timeless. For example, research on menopausal women indicates that the Navajo women's puberty ceremony leads to far fewer menopausal symptoms than those Navajo women who have not undergone it:

> The most traditional Navajo women who had Kinaaldá reported few or no [menopausal] symptoms, even after hysterectomy. The less traditional Navajo women who had Kinaaldá reported few or no symptoms, even after hysterectomy. The less traditional women, who did not have Kinaaldá, experienced menopausal symptoms much like non-Navajo women—especially "sweats," feeling tired, "waist pain," moodiness and frequent trips to the bathroom.[3]

Apache Sunset Dance

The Apache maintained a nomadic lifestyle until the late nineteenth century; a Chiricahua band was the last Native American group forced onto reservations when Geronimo surrendered in 1886. The males raided into Mexico well into the twentieth century. They remain a matrifocal tradition, whose single traditional ceremony that brings the community together is the one that celebrates a girl's menarche, for it is the ritual that brings the presence of a major deity, Changing Woman (also called White Shell Woman/White Clay Woman in some Apache traditions), into the community to heal the sick and renew social harmony. Now commonly called the Sunset Dance, it has different traditional names among the Apache tribes. Several call it Na'ii'ees ("preparing her").

Because the ceremony requires considerable preparation—the girl's dress alone needs to be sung over for several months—and considerable expense—payment for the singers and other ritual specialists, food for several feasts for all who come, gifts for all—the ceremony rarely takes place at the time of the first menses. Instead, in traditional families, a truncated version of the ceremony will be performed, with the actual ceremony taking place up to a year later. Nowadays, schooling also has to be taken into account, so the ceremony is usually held when the school term is over.

Two elders will be asked to lead the ritual: a woman, who dresses, leads and sings over the girl, called "she who makes the sound," and a man who sings the public songs and supervises the construction of the Gowa'a. The Gowa'a is a structure of four poles tied at the top, each leg aligned with one of the four directions, to which eagle feathers and other sacred objects are attached, creating a sacred space. In choosing elders to lead the ritual, a woman who learned the ritual directly from Moon or had a vision of Changing Woman is preferred, as is a man who sang for women-to-be who subsequently led a good life. A third ritual leader will prepare and arrange for the Ga'an (Crowndancers), the masked and headdressed dancers who, when costumed, take on the power of the Mountain Spirits. A fourth participant to support the pubescent girl is a friend who has already completed the ceremony. This friend will support the girl by dancing with her and encouraging her as she carries out the arduous tasks.

The Na'ii'ees takes place over four days, with four further days of private reflection for the girl-changed-into-woman. The following description, as with Kinaaldá, is but a brief outline and generalized from several sources and several of the Apache traditions. It is intended to present the spirit of the ceremony only. What happens on which day is not fixed and can vary from one Apache tribe to another.

The ceremony begins with a Spirit Lodge for the male ritualists, the raising of the Gowa'a, and the making of the ritual items for the girl. These include a scratching stick, as the girl is not to touch herself with her fingernails during the eight days, and a reed drinking tube, from which the girl will drink for the eight days. Both of these ritual paraphernalia survived the migration from the far Northwest to the Southwest. On the evening of the first day, the ritual items are brought to the girl, prayers are sung, and she is instructed on their use.

Before sunrise on the second day, the female ritualist places pollen on the girl as a blessing and prays for her. She arranges the girl's hair and dresses her. The girl, now Changing Woman, faces the rising sun (Sun is the husband of Changing Woman), while the men sing over her. These are the songs of Changing Woman, and she begins to dance facing Sun (constant dancing facing the sun is reminiscent of the Plains Thirst Dance; see Chapter 8). While theoretically she dances alone, often she dances with the friend mentioned above. She dances for several hours to four sets of four songs. She must not waver or show any signs of fatigue, for she is becoming an Apache woman. Any deviation from proper form will lead to correction by the ritualist or any of the women present. She can then sit or kneel on a deerskin placed over several blankets, but she will sway with hand movements to the continuing songs. After several more hours, she lays down on the deerskin and is "molded," as was Changing Woman in the origin myth, into the proper shape, while further sets of songs are chanted.

A prepared sacred cane is placed to the east, and after the molding she races to it and back. The cane is then moved to each of the other four directions. After each set of races, the canes are moved further and further away. Young boys and old men run behind her, praying for long life and good health, but she must stay ahead of them. Those who tire of chasing her are replaced by others, but she must continually run.

At the end of the runs, gifts for the crowd are poured from baskets over her, while all rush in to grab them. Food is placed along the ground of the run toward the east, which is eaten by the crowd while she continues to dance in place. Then while she is dancing, the ritualist and all attending one by one bless her with pollen and pray over her. While they are praying for her, she, Changing Woman, is healing them, all the time dancing in place.

Toward the evening, a fire is lit in a traditional way in the Gowa'a, which will be kept burning through the remaining days of the ceremony. When the sun sets, the Ga'an arrive, appearing with the sound of a bullroarer and frightening away all negative energy. The Ga'an are treated in a most reverential manner as they embody, although do not actually become, the Mountain Spirits. They then dance around the fire in the Gowa'a four times. During the dancing, men beat the rhythm on rawhide skins as is done on the Plains or with pottery water drums, as used in the Pueblos. Later, people retire to their campsites where they engage in social dancing, gambling, and otherwise having a good time.

Before dawn of the third day, the ritualist mixes a special clay paint, praying all the while. At sunrise, Changing Woman will again be found dancing facing the sun. But this time, the Ga'an reappear and, after banishing all negativity, dance facing her. Everyone lines up to bless the Ga'an with pollen and be healed by them in turn. After further dance rituals and when the Ga'an conclude that all has been purified, the painting begins.

The paint is thickly applied all over the girl by the ritualists, the singers, and the Ga'an. The girl then walks through the crowd carrying the bowl of paint while the ritualist dabs and sprays it on everyone. When the paint is used up, the onlookers line up behind Changing Woman, the Ga'an, the sponsor, and the singers, and all dance through each of the four doorways, the sacred directions, of the Gowa'a. The final act is for Changing Woman to throw the blankets on which she lay toward each of the four directions. The onlookers then return to their campsites for more dancing and fun.

On the fourth day, Changing Woman remains available for all those who need healing; this concludes the ceremony. Two years later, the young woman will hold a ceremony in which she will present gifts to her sponsor and all those who assisted her in her Na'ii'ees.

For those women who went through the ceremony, it remains the most important and empowering event of their lives. Elbys Naiche Hugar, a Chiricahua elder, nearly a half century later, still clearly recalled her menarche ritual:

> I had mine back in 1944 at the old ceremonial grounds. It's something good that a girl goes through. The parents and the godmother and god-father [sponsors] talk with the young girl before the puberty ceremony. The girl will know what to do and she'll know about it before she can enter the ritual. . . . It's for four days and nights. A girl has to fast, and sometimes you lose weight. That's what I experienced. It's still part of me and it's going to be that way for the rest of my life. I'll never forget the good it did for me and how it helped me over the hardships.[4]

The ritual benefits not only the young women and their families but the entire community. It is the occasion for the appearance of Changing Woman and the Ga'an, for the community to come into contact with the deities and be blessed and healed by them. It is, moreover, a means to continue tradition and for the community to reaffirm its solidarity in the presence of the sacred.

But the ritual is becoming increasingly infrequent. Those who become Christians do not hold this ritual for their daughters. Modern education tends to trivialize traditional religion, and the school year makes holding it difficult. Fewer families are willing to undergo the considerable expense of the ritual. As well, according to Apache traditionalists, the Bureau of Indian Affairs, along with their elected tribal governments and the Christian churches, do all they can to hinder holding the rituals. But without the Na'ii'ees, Apache traditional religion and culture cannot survive, for it is the center of their ceremonial life.

MUSKOGEE GREEN CORN CEREMONY: CONTINUING AN AGRICULTURAL TRADITION[5]

When the Cherokee, Chickasaw, Choctaw, Muskogee (Creek), and other peoples were forcibly marched by the U.S. Army during the 1830s from the Southeast to the newly declared Indian Territory (now Oklahoma), they were devastated. Many died en route, and they were moved to an area already occupied, of course, by other Native peoples who were hardly happy about this de facto invasion. Perhaps even more important, they were forced from their fertile farms in a climate most amenable to agriculture to a drier, harsher climate with poorer soil. Their way of life was shattered. Yet they have been able to hold on to central aspects of their religious traditions into the present.

Most religious traditions, not only in the Americas but worldwide, celebrate the renewal of life, the new year, either at the time of the winter solstice (e.g., the Christian Christmas/New Year's celebrations) or at the full moon thereafter (e.g., the Chinese Spring Festival). It is at this time that the days begin to lengthen with the promise of spring and the renewal of life. But the Southeastern Native traditions celebrated the New Year with the first harvest of their most important crop: corn. Corn has two stages of harvesting: in July, when the ears are in their "milk stage" and can be eaten after cooking, and in the autumn, when the ears have dried on the stalk and can be stored as well as ground into meal. Thus, many Native North American traditions have a Green Corn Ceremony, as do the Haudenausaunee. But for the Southeastern traditions, the ability to eat the fresh new corn instead of the dried old corn from the previous autumn harvest marked the turning of the seasons, of the New Year.

Held in July, the ceremony is called *Ahgawela Seluutsi* (Old Woman Corn Mother) by the Cherokee; the Chickasaw call it the Renewal Festival, and the Muskogee call it *Posketv* ("Busk" in the literature), meaning "to fast." Fasting in this regard has two meanings: first, to refrain from eating the fresh new corn until the celebration is held, and second, that the participants refrain from eating during the ceremony until the feast of the "green" corn at its climax. This discussion focuses on the Green Corn Ceremony of the Muskogee.

The Oklahoma Muskogee originally lived in present-day Georgia and Alabama and named their present towns in Oklahoma after their original towns in the Southeast. Their language is part of the Muskhogean language family, which also includes Chickasaw, Choctaw, Tuskegee, Alabama, Natchez, Miccosukee, and Seminole, comprising the major languages of the Southeast, save for the Iroquoian-speaking Cherokee, originally from, with some still remaining in, North Carolina. Typical of many reservations, the Muskogee are divided into traditional and Christian factions. It is the former, of course, that celebrate the Green Corn Ceremony.

Before describing the four-day ceremony, it is necessary to understand some of its constituent parts. These include stomp dances, the "stick-ball" game, the importance of fire, and the special herbal medicine.

The stomp dance is unique to the Muskogee and related Southeastern cultures; the Oklahoma Cherokee learned it from them. It is a dance of a spiraling line of alternating women and men. The women wear leggings over their calves, on which are sewn tortoise shell rattles—nowadays some use tin cans. As the women stomp their feet in the dance, they create a distinctive sound which beats out the dance rhythm. Stomp dances are a central feature of the Green Corn Ceremony, but they are also done alone as social dances, although even then the dance never loses its religious aspect:

> "We dance on Saturday night. Our tribe [Chickasaw] dances from midnight 'til dawn, other tribes have different times to dance," [dance leader Larry] Seawright said. "We dance around the fire and some consider us to be paganists or devil worshippers, but we are really thanking our Creator. Each dance has different significance."[6]

The stick-ball game, played by many eastern cultures from the Haudenausaunee in the Northeast to the Muskogee in the far Southeast, is the forerunner of lacrosse. During the Green Corn Ceremony of the Muskogee, men play against women. The men are not allowed to touch the ball with their hands, but each uses two sticks a little over a meter in length with a small pocket at one end, while the women use their hands. The object is to hit a cow's skull or an image of a fish on a pole with the ball. There is also a version played during other ceremonies of male teams using the sticks where the points are scored by throwing or carrying the ball between two goal posts.

Fire was considered especially sacred; a major feature of the Green Corn Ceremony is the lighting of a new fire on the ashes of the old, as with the Haudenausaunee Midwinter Ceremony. Traditionally, people put out the fires in their homes and started a new fire with the newly started fire from the ceremonial ground. In traditional times, the Muskogee also burned their furniture at this time and replaced it with new furniture. Of course, before domination by the United States, the furniture was relatively simple and made from natural materials readily at hand.

During the Green Corn Ceremony, a special herbal drink, *passv*, is prepared by persons imbued with sacredness. In the literature it is called, from its color, the "black drink," but for the Muskogee it is a "white drink," as it purifies the person. It is a purgative and emetic, and it was drunk while fasting in order to clean one's insides, bringing out all that is old and making one's digestive tract new again. It is also used as a kind of vaccination; the skin is scratched with thorns and the liquid brushed over the scratches.

Traditionally, the Green Corn Ceremony was held on the full moon after the green corn harvest, but given the modern work week, it now begins on the Thursday after the new moon following the ripening of the green corn and lasts through the weekend. Some towns hold the ceremony on a fixed weekend in July.

On the first day, people set up their campsites on one of the square ceremonial grounds. In the afternoon, there will usually be a stick-ball game between men and women, followed by a feast of last year's corn. After this feast, all will abstain from food and water until they feast on the new corn on the third day. In the evening there will be a social stomp dance.

Early on the second day, four brush-covered arbors will be built on the edges of the ceremonial grounds, one in each of the sacred directions. The arbors are made from willow boughs, and benches are placed underneath for the elders. Willow is often used in making sacred structures, such as the Spirit Lodge, because it is understood to have a special relationship with water, the lifeblood of the Earth Mother.

The first dance of the day is the women's Ribbon Dance. The women wear dresses decorated with ribbons and their shaker leggings. They carry willow branches in their hands to gather up the prayers of the people. This dance is to purify and make ready the grounds for the new sacred fire through the life-giving and nourishing power of the women. The new fire is started in a traditional way on the ashes of the old, to which is offered the willow branches that have gathered up the prayers, the first ears of the new corn, and other sacred items. This fire will be kept alive until the following year's Green Corn Ceremony.

The second day focuses on the women's dance, and the third day is for the men's dance. But first, in the morning, women and children line up to be scratched and treated with the special herbal preparation that a holy man has been preparing since dawn. Then the women leave the ceremonial square. The men now drink the herbal preparation until they vomit, thus purifying themselves. The men are then scratched. Afterwards, all bath in a nearby stream or, nowadays, in showers built by the ceremonial grounds. After all are purified, the men do the Feather Dance for healing the community. The day ends with a feast of the new corn and other traditional foods. Stomp dances will then go on for the rest of the night.

On the fourth day, there are friendship dances at dawn. In the morning, there will be another stick-ball game between men and women. Afterwards, people pack up and return home. They go home purified of old ills. All resentments have been pushed away as misdeeds have been forgiven. All are renewed in spirit and in their tradition.

One of the many means the dominant culture has used to eradicate traditional Native religion is to secularize it. As this book is being written, the town of Bixby, Oklahoma, is advertising its "Green Corn Festival" to be held on June 22–24, 2006, in the town park. According to their advertisement, the Green Corn Festival is a "Community festival that is pure Americana. Festivities include a carnival, crafts, food, multiple states of live entertainment, parade, games, frog jumping, turtle races, and an amateur talent show."

But despite repeated attempts to stifle Muskogee religion, there are still fourteen active ceremonial grounds, each maintaining a sacred fire, some of which are a continuation of the fire the Muskogee brought with them during the "Removal." As Kenneth McIntosh, a Muskogee scholar, has written:

> At this gathering [Green Corn Ceremony] the Muskogee language is spoken in its different dialects. Men and women share traditional communal duties. Fasting and stickball play remain import elements of the ceremonials. Ceremonial fires burn atop ceremonial ashes carried from the homeland during the removal. Stomp dances, particularly the Green Corn Ceremonial, continue to keep Muskogee culture and identity intact despite two centuries of pressures to assimilate.[7]

· 6 ·

Plains

MISSOURI BASIN HORTICULTURE–HUNTING COMPLEX: TWINNING CORN AND BISON[1]

Many of the Native cultures that moved onto the Plains after horses became available did not originally live on the Plains. For example, the Lakota were a horticulture–hunting culture in Minnesota before being forced westward by the expanding Anishnabeg and the competition for fur trade territory. Once on the Plains, the horse allowed for following the enormous bison herds as they slowly migrated north in the spring and south in the autumn. In the winter, small groups sought valleys sheltered from the fierce winter winds with adequate firewood for warmth and protected pasturage for the horses. Only in late spring, when the grass was lush and before it dried in the summer, could whole tribes come together for ceremonies, particularly the Thirst Dance (Chapter 8).

Cultures that lived along the Missouri and its tributaries had a Plains lifestyle that preceded the adaptation to the horse. Owing to the mud left behind by spring flooding, the river valleys were quite fertile and readily supported horticulture. Thus, the peoples living there practiced horticulture and only hunted the bison in the summer and late autumn as they passed by on their seasonal migration. The amount of meat that could be brought back was limited by the amount that dogs could pull on travois (two poles slung over a dog or horse's back that dragged behind on the ground to which parcels could be tied). When horses became available, loads that could be carried were significantly larger, and the hunt could take place further from the large villages of matrilineal–matrilocal log and earthen dwellings built on the bluffs above the valleys. This led to a culture that was half bison hunting and half corn-based horticulture and a remarkable intertwining of both lifestyles' rituals.

The two major traditions living in this mode were the Pawnee and the Mandan. Both were seriously impacted by smallpox after contact with Euro-Americans, and the Mandans nearly disappeared in the first part of the eighteenth century. This section focuses on the interrelated bison and corn rituals of the Caddoan-speaking Pawnee, but it should be understood that there were many other important aspects of their religious gestalt, especially the ceremonies of the healing and other societies held during a great winter ceremonial. Not only were the different subsistence rituals intertwined, but the rituals also demonstrate an intertwining of visions and calendrical rituals. Different from all other discussions in Part II of this book, the discussion focuses on the mid-nineteenth century, the period just before the Pawnee were forced onto reservations. The lifestyle depicted ceased with reservation life; it was impossible to continue because of the deliberate near extermination of the bison and the forced relocation of the people away from their fertile valleys.

Pawnee oral history speaks of their coming from the south in the distant past. Given that their ritual life was determined by the movement of the stars more so than any other northern North American traditions—they had elaborate star maps—and that they were the only tradition north of central Mexico to have practiced very limited human sacrifice (for fertility), this oral tradition seems quite reliable. Archeology places them in present-day Nebraska and Kansas several centuries before the arrival of the Spanish. The Pawnee became aware of horses in the late seventeenth or early eighteenth century.

The ceremonial year began with a renewal of the tribal sacred bundles (see *Nitsitapi Bundle Ceremonies: The Effects of Horse Nomadism*), particularly the Evening Star Bundle. The timing for this round of rituals was based on both the movement of certain stars and the appearance of the first spring thunderstorms, usually in March. Subsequent ceremonies involved the spring planting.

The planting rituals began not in the spring but during the winter bison hunt when a highly respected woman had a vision that she was to sponsor the planting ritual. This was the essential beginning. She then asked one of her brothers to kill a special bison; the meat was dried and stored for use during the spring planting ritual. She invited four elders to a feast and informed them of her vision.

The planting rituals were based on star patterns and the appearance of willow buds in late April or early May; seeds were placed in the ground on the New Moon. It was under the aegis of the Skull Bundle and used items from the Evening Star Bundle and other sacred bundles. The ritual involved four male and four female elders as well as the woman sponsor. The ritual was highly elaborate and involved both esoteric and public aspects. The public aspect included a dance in which women pantomimed hoeing the ground with sacred bison scapula hoes from the sacred bundles, followed by a great feast. The dance also included warriors with bows, rubbing against the women as did male bison with female bison. This involvement of warriors in fertility rituals, especially the paralleling of male warrior roles with female sustenance roles, is ubiquitous throughout Mexico and Mesoamerica. After the completion of the four-day ceremony, the fields could be cleared and prepared, and first the corn, followed by beans, squashes, including pumpkins, and watermelons, were planted. Before the ordinary varieties of corn were planted, a sacred corn, which was not eaten but whose ears were kept with the sacred bundles, was planted.

The second fertility ritual for corn also began during the winter bison hunt. A man who was a successful bison hunter and eagle trapper had a vision that he was to sponsor this ritual. He then killed a special bison for the ritual. The meat from this bison was dried and stored for the feast at the end of the ritual to which would be added boiled dried corn by his wife. During the ritual and thereafter, the hunter who had the vision was spiritually connected to the Thunder deity, who is essential for the rains to nourish the plants.

This ceremony, the ritual of the Young Mother Corn, took place when the special sacred corn had sprouted four leaves. The elaborate ritual symbolized the birth and growth of the young corn plant to become the Mother of the People. After preliminary rituals, the hunter pushed pellets made of heart, tongue, and fat from the bison he had especially killed into the hilled-up sacred corn in each of the four directions. A bundle-keeper then eased the infant plant from out of the ground, symbolizing its birth, wrapped it in bison wool, and gave it to the hunter, who carried it on his back in a bison robe just as human infants were carried. A special arrow shaft was made, straightened, painted, and otherwise decorated with special symbols and anointed with human breast milk from a nursing woman. The baby plant was then tied to the shaft and dressed. The hunter who had the vision then carried this holy plant from that time until the end of the summer bison hunt when all returned to the village. Only after the ritual of the Young Mother Corn was completed were the corn plants weeded and hilled up. Subsequently, the preliminary rituals for the summer bison hunt took place.

The primary preliminary ritual for the summer bison hunt involved bringing all of the sacred bundles together and for those who had visions of special powers from various animal spirits dancing their spirits. This was followed by offerings to both the corn and animal spirits. A symbolic search for the bison herds took place using sacred stones from the bundles. On the fourth day, there was a symbolic washing in the river of all the sacred items in the Black Meteorite Star Bundle, followed by a purifying bath in the river and Spirit Lodges for the elders.

The hunter who carried the Young Mother Corn had many obligations, including constantly wearing a buffalo robe, even in the heat of summer, and never being able to bathe until the end of the hunt. He was treated by all as a holy person and was always the first to be given food. When the bison herd was reached and throughout the hunt, he faced the herd and constantly prayed for the success of the hunt. If anything went wrong, blame would accrue to him. During the hunt, there were a number of rituals, one of the most important being the taking of a special bison for the sacred bundles. At the end of the hunt and on the return to the village, the hunter who carried the Young Mother Corn was released from his many onerous obligations and could finally bathe.

After the hunt, a young man was sent back to the village ahead of the main group to push strips of bison heart and tongue into the four sides of the corn hills as a thanks offering. On the return from the summer bison hunt, it was time for the harvest. As with all the corn horticultural traditions, there was a green corn and a mature corn harvest rituals. Both were connected with sacred bundles. During the mature corn harvest rituals, the sacred ears of corn in the bundles were replaced with the now-ripened ears from the plots of sacred corn. These rituals involved symbolic decorations to bring all the powers into the sacred ears. The old ears from the bundles were given to warriors or traders to spiritually assist them in their endeavors.

After the completion of the harvest and the storage of the various foods, other ceremonies were held until it was time for the winter bison hunt. During this hunt, again meat was set aside for the various bundles in preparation for the spring rituals, and a vision was had by a woman and a man to begin again the corn planting cycle.

The above ceremonies but briefly outline the complex relationship between bison hunting and corn horticulture in pre-reservation Pawnee religion and life. The planting ceremony began during the winter bison hunt, and a sacred corn plant supported the summer bison hunt. Bison meat was offered to corn, and corn was brought to the bison. All of these ceremonies were regulated by the pattern of the stars, yet they required a woman or a man to have a vision for the central ritual roles.

In each bundle, there were two ears of the special sacred corn sewn into bison skin covers: an ear for winter in a tanned hide and an ear for summer in the skin surrounding the heart. At every meal, the woman of the lodge spoke to the ears in thanks for the food. Bison meat was dedicated to the ears of sacred corn, and corn was offered to the bison skull on the altar below the hanging sacred bundle. Leaders of raids wore an ear of the sacred corn from a bundle on their left shoulders so that she, the sacred ear of corn, could aid in the battle. A leader of a trading or diplomatic mission, besides carrying two sacred pipes, similarly carried an ear of the sacred corn to assist in the success of the mission. Thus, the two modes of subsistence, one the domain of women and the other the domain of men, were thoroughly intertwined.

While the above rituals have been lost, and most of the Pawnee sacred bundles are in museum collections, a few of the traditional ritual dances of the medicine societies are still occasionally performed. Other traditions continue—clothing, rituals, and songs—within dominant culture festivals, such as during Memorial Day and Christmas celebrations.

The virtual uniqueness of pairing and intertwining two sustenance deities—Corn and Bison—can be understood when compared with other Plains traditions, where the focus is entirely on Bison, with regard to the fertility aspects of major rituals. In comparison, for the Algonquian-speaking Plains people, the Tsistsistas ("People") known in the literature as the Cheyenne, their major renewal ritual, as the other Plains traditions, is—what in many Plains traditions is known as—the Thirst Dance ("Sun Dance," see Chapter 8). The Tsistsistas call this ceremony Oxheheom ("New Life Lodge," the meaning of the Anishnabe Midewiwin; see Chapter 4). As with the Pawnee and the Nitsitapi, the ceremony must be sponsored by a woman who has a vision to do so and is subsequently called the "Sacred Woman." She is the center of the complex ritual which focuses on Bison and leads the processions of sacred objects and dancers. In the past, as part of the Oxheheom, she had ritual intercourse in private with a male elder chosen by her. This was the sacred act which led to the renewal of life, particularly of the primary source of food, shelter, robes, and tools: Bison.

NITSITAPI BUNDLE CEREMONIES: THE EFFECTS OF HORSE NOMADISM[2]

On the eastern slopes of the Rocky Mountains in present-day southern Alberta and northern Montana are the reservations of three Algonquian-speaking interconnected tribes collectively named Nitsitapi: the Apikuni, Kainai, and Siksika (known in English as the Peigan, Blood, and Blackfoot, respectively). Before being forced on reservations, they lived a nomadic life following the bison herds within a large defined range. In the late eighteenth century, elderly Apikuni people spoke of living near the Eagle hills of present-day Saskatchewan before the adaptation to a horse-centered life and of hunting the bison on foot. The Nitsitapi are among the few Plains cultures to have lived full-time on the Plains before the adaptation to the horse. Typical of the equestrian Plains cultures, Nitsitapi tribes have a rich ceremonial life focusing on large-bundle complexes, age-graded ritual societies, and a yearly renewal ritual, Okan (the Thirst Dance discussed in Chapter 8).

Ritual bundles are a collection of related sacred items that are wrapped in skins and/or cloth. They are common among the Native traditions of northern North America. Most ritual bundles are personal or for a family and relatively small, thus easily carried. Before the use of horses, ritual bundles had to be small enough to be carried by a person, as the only mode of transport was the dog travois. With the shift to horse nomadism, much larger parcels could be carried, including large ritual bundles. With large bundles now being practical, there developed an understanding of tribal bundles for major rituals. These could be up to a meter and a half in length and a meter in diameter. Often there are many coverings, new ones being added every time the keeping of the bundle is transferred. These bundles can include pipes, dance wands, and shakers as well as items specific to particular rituals such as headdresses.

These large ritual bundles are the most precious possessions of the Plains cultures, in the sense of both cultural importance—the lives of the people are based on the care of these sacred items—and material value—as a sign of their importance, those to whom their keeping is transferred pay a large sum in the currency of the day (horses and robes in the past) for the privilege. Of special interest with regard to the Nitsitapi is that the bundle complexes, which include the associated rituals and songs, are held by a married couple, the daily care usually provided by the woman. The rituals of opening the bundles as well as transferring them require the leadership and participation of female–male pairs. That the keeping and rituals associated with the great tribal bundles require a married couple is a prime example in Native North American traditions of the complementarity of the genders in religion.

George Bird Grinnell quotes an 1879 description of a healing ceremony that involved the opening of a sacred pipe bundle. After purifying themselves,

> The man and woman [the keepers of the bundle] now faced each other and again began the buffalo song, keeping time by touching with the clenched hands–the right and left alternately–the wrapping of the pipe, occasionally making the sign for buffalo . . . After singing this song for about ten minutes, it was changed to the antelope song . . .

Following further purification, both wife and husband, separately and alternately, undertook healing rituals, the woman with the special pipestem of the bundle and the man with a general-use sacred pipe.

Walter McClintock presents detailed descriptions of bundle ceremonies and transfers. In all cases, males and females have equal and indispensable roles, paralleling the relationship between male Sky and female Earth. One of the introductory songs of the major Beaver Bundle ceremony includes the verses:

> Sky provides us with food.
> Sky is glad to behold us.
> ....
> Earth loves us.

Earth is glad to hear us sing.
Earth provides us with food.

Two Beaver songs maintain this balance:

The Old Man (chief male Beaver) is coming in.
The Old Man has come in.
He sits down besides his medicine.
It is very strong medicine.

The Old Woman (chief female Beaver) is coming in.
The Old Woman has come in.
She sits down and takes the medicine.
It is very strong medicine.[3]

Throughout these songs and the various lifting of the bundles and their components, husbands and wives sit facing each other and hold the sacred items together, or the woman might sing while the male performs ritual gestures and vice versa. There are also women's songs and dances, along with men's songs and dances. When there is a pipe smoked by men in a bundle, there is usually also a second pipe smoked by the women, a fact which androcentric writers almost invariably ignore.

The necessity for couples in these rituals is not a dispensable feature. In the 1960s, when traditional Native religions were at their lowest point, it was difficult to find couples willing to take on the onerous burden of caring for sacred bundles as well as having the resources for their transfer. To save the bundles, some of the Nitsitapi ritual bundles were ritually transferred to the Alberta Provincial Museum in Edmonton. The Museum has honored the sacred nature of bundles obtained in this way, as only a museum curator initiated in the rituals of the bundle is allowed to handle it. At other times, they are kept in a locked cabinet, and they are not put on display. When the major Beaver Bundle was ritually transferred to Museum, as documented in the film *Iyahknix: Blackfoot Bundle Ceremony*, a woman had to stand in as wife for the curator, John Hellson, who was not at the time married. When Mrs. Rides-At-The-Door's husband died (see below), she engaged in rituals with her brother as her "partner."

Many important bundles are associated with the secret ritual societies. These societies tended to function in pairs, male and female. For example, the male Horn Society is paralleled by the female Motokiks Society. Paula Weasel Head, a Kainai elder, told Beverly Hungry Wolf that when she was an advisor for newer members of the Motokiks Society, her husband, Mokakin, was doing the same for the Horn society. Both societies put up their own lodges during the annual Okan ceremony, which brings the tribe together once a year. For four days, the Motokiks have initiations and ritual dances, many of which are private and esoteric. Within the Motokiks, there are four subgroups, each with its own ritual bundle, songs, and dances.

Okan (the Nitsitapi "Sun Dance"; see Chapter 8) is the major community ritual of the Nitsitapi tribes and intimately connected with the sacred bundles. In early summer, when there is sufficient grass for the large gathering of people and their horses, the tribes come together for this ritual and the subsidiary rituals of the various ritual societies. All the societies have important roles as well as the keepers of the major sacred bundles and pipes.[4]

The origin myth of Okan found in the literature is based on the story of Scarface, a poor young man with a scar on his face (who in some versions is the Morning Star). He was in love with a beautiful young woman from an important family. He went on a journey to find Sun and seek his aid. After a series of adventures, he achieved his goal and was given the ritual and many presents. He returned without the scar and married the girl, and they carried out the first Okan together.

George First Rider, a Kainai elder who was initiated into the tradition when a youth, told a different origin myth in 1974, when he was seventy. This myth, with the length and details of ritually told myths (seventeen typescript pages of translation for the first part alone), covers all the major ritual features of the Okan. Briefly, the story begins with a poor young woman who married an older man, who in misplaced jealousy repeatedly abused her. She attempted to hang herself but the rope broke; she fell asleep and had the first of a series of powerful dreams. She tried to tell her husband, but he beat her again. "This time a woman came in to help her. This woman grabbed the man by the hair and threw him all over the place." She listened to the young woman's dream and told her own husband, who notified the people. The sacrificial ritual of the young woman's dream was carried out at the tree from which she tried to hang herself. In a series of visions, she learned further details of the ritual, including the center pole, the lodge, the buffalo tongues, and the self-inflicted flesh offerings. Her husband reformed and assisted her with carrying out the rituals.

Ben Calf Robe, a Siksika elder, tells part of another Okan origin myth, the story of a young woman who marries Sun. Transported to the sky world, she gathers prairie turnips but is told not to dig an especially large one. Eventually, out of curiosity, she does. When she gets it out of the ground, she finds a hole through which she can see the earth (this relates to the Iroquoian creation myth). Because of her act, she must return home to earth, but she is given the Okan to take back with her.

As with the Tsistsistas, central to the Okan is the Sacred Woman, the term for a woman who vows to Sun to put on the ceremony sometime in the preceding year. Only a woman who has the respect of her community can make such a vow, and only if a woman makes this vow can the ceremony be held. In the past, the vow was often taken during a request to Sun to aid a husband or son away on a raid; in modern times, the vow is usually given when requesting Sun's aid for a seriously ill member of the family. From the time the vow is taken until the completion of the Okan, the woman and her husband live a ritually prescribed life. Traditionally, the woman's family would gather a hundred dried buffalo tongues as a food offering for Sun, to be shared by the people during the Okan. (To try and stop the Okan, the government once forbade Native people from gathering buffalo tongues!)

When all the people gather at the Okan grounds, the Sacred Woman's lodge is put up, where she will fast during the four days of the ceremony. This lodge, which only the ritual leaders enter, along with the four Spirit Lodges and the main Medicine Lodge, is the focus of the Okan. Meanwhile, the Sacred Woman's husband will engage in a series of sweat rituals. The Sacred Woman will wear the Natoas (Sacred Turnip) headdress, kept with the important Beaver bundle (the keepers of the Beaver bundles function as the head priests in the ritual). The Sacred Woman and her husband will request the ritual passing of instructions for carrying out the ceremony from a couple experienced in this ritual; this couple will serve as their ritual grandparents. The Okan is rich and complex, and a proper description would take many pages; moreover, there are several detailed descriptions in the literature.

Beverly Hungry Wolf recorded the words of several elders, which helps understand what these rituals meant to the bundle-keepers. The following is from the thoughts of the Sacred Woman, Mrs. Rides-At-The-Door:

My Husband and I lived by our Indian religion through all our many years together, and I am still living by it today. We went through many ceremonial transfers. We were given a medicine pipe bundle which we took care of for many years. . . .

I have had a beaver bundle for many years. It is the biggest medicine bundle of all the ones among our people. There is a very long ceremony for its opening and they used to sing several hundred songs during it. The men and women all join together to sing these songs and dance with the different parts of the bundle. We used to have a really happy time with this beaver ceremony, but now there is no one left who can lead it. . . .

I was very young when I first started with this holy business, and now I am an old woman [had been given a very long life], on account of it. It has been a very trying life, especially during the medicine lodge ceremonies [Okan]. Sometimes when I had to go out [from the Sacred Woman's lodge] during the four days of rituals my assistants would have to hold me up, I would be so weak [from fasting]. I have always been devoted to my religious duties to help my family and people. All the younger people are like my children.[5]

From Paula Weasel Head, Beverly Hungry Wolf received the story of her initiations, from which the following is extracted:

> I was also initiated to join with a medicine pipe bundle when I was very small. Each of those bundles has a man and a wife for an owner, and a child goes with them to wear the special topknot wrapping and fur headband that is kept with the bundle. That is what they transferred to me, and I sat right up front with the main people, each time the bundle's opening ceremony was held. . . .
>
> Mokakin and I got married in 1921. . . . We were still very young when we made a pledge to take that bundle called Backside-to-the-Fire Medicine Pipe. We treated it very well. I was very scared to do something wrong to it, there are so many rules and regulations to follow. The ones who initiated us for it were the real old-time people, so we were initiated in the old-time way. The ceremony took a couple of days. . . .
>
> We lived very good by that medicine pipe bundle. I used to take it outside every morning, before the sun came up, as was the custom. I always had to start a fire in the stove so that I could make incense before I took the bundle out. I watched it during the day so that nothing would happen to it while it hung outside. . . . Then I made incense again before the sun went down, and I would bring the bundle back inside. I made incense once more before we lay down to sleep. That is when we really learned to pray. . . . Since then I have been praying steadily, and up to this day I am still praying. . . .
>
> Mokakin and I joined the Horns Society several times. First, we had that membership called Has-a-Rattle, which is one of the leading ones. These membership bundles come from long ago. We went around with this bundle for several years, and I treated it good, too, just like our pipe.[6]

These are remarkable couples. I feel privileged to have been a guest in the home of the Apikuni Sacred Woman, Josephine Crow Shoe, and her husband Joe, who have lived through virtually the entire twentieth century. They have kept important bundles since 1934 and have worked for most of their lives to keep the traditions of their people alive and to stop the desecration of their sacred Old Man River by damming. In 1992, they were both awarded the Order of Canada, Canada's highest honor. This indicated unexpected insight on the part of the Canadian government in recognizing that all of their work was as a couple. And it is ironic, because they were given the award for preserving Apikuni culture, when the government had been trying for over a century to destroy it!

Josephine and Joe Crow Shoe were keepers of the Thunder Bundle among others. At the time I visited them in late spring, there had been a drought for a couple of months, and there was considerable concern about sufficient pasture for the cattle and horses, the Nitsitapi often being ranchers. While I was there, the Thunder Bundle was opened to pray for rain. The next day, there were severe thunder storms and heavy downpours. As I was due back in Toronto, where I then lived, in a few days, I could not delay my parting. Each day, as I drove through Montana, North Dakota, and Minnesota on the way back, I would drive fast to get past the eastward moving storm front, only to find that it caught up to me while I was sleeping at night. Thus, the next day, I would have to drive through the heavy winds, dark skies, many lightening flashes, and sheeting rain all over again. Fortunately, the Thunder Bundle is not opened often.

· 7 ·

Northwest Coast

POTLATCH: RELIGIOUS HEART OF COASTAL TRADITIONS

Giving gifts, commonly called "giveaways" by Natives, is an essential aspect of Native social life and religion. Prestige leading to traditional leadership positions comes from having the resources to sponsor feasts and to give gifts, which in the past meant being a very successful hunter or raider. When a young boy killed his first bird or rabbit, he would bring it to his mother or sister who would cook it and tell him to invite all the elders. When the elders arrived, the boy would serve them portions, often tiny, of the little animal he killed but eat none himself. This was the beginning of his training to hunt and raid not for himself but for others.

In the various ceremonies described in the preceding chapters, putting on feasts is a common element. Each time I completed a traditional fast, my wife or a female friend would cook a feast with food that I donated for my coming-out ceremony. At the feast, I gave gifts to all those who assisted me. There are other reasons for giveaways. For example, when a person dies, it is common to give away all that person's possessions. Once I was at a seasonal ceremonial when the sister of a highly respected woman elder who had recently died went around the circle with a huge bag of her sister's clothes. Everyone, male or female, was given an article of her clothing.

Giving away is the traditional norm; accumulating wealth is perceived not just as antisocial, but as the mark of a dangerous person and, in at least some traditions, as evidence of evil sorcery. Thus, there is an essential conflict between the Western value of accumulating wealth as a good and the

Native value of giving away wealth as a good. This at times causes Native-run businesses to fail. Relatives and friends may expect not to have to pay for items, and it is at times expected that any profits will be given away rather than reinvested. To most missionaries, this value of giving rather than receiving was an indication of barbarism.

On the Northwest Coast, the tradition of giving away combined with feasting, dancing, dramatic performances, and oratory to create one of the most elaborate ceremonies to be developed in Native North American traditions, on a par with the elaborate dance dramas of the Hopi and Zuni of the Southwest. These ceremonies tend to take place in the winter, the season for long, elaborate ceremonies throughout the temperate and northern zones of the world. Aside from the usual human need for occasional festivities and ritual renewal, the Northwest ceremonies served as the means of continuing tribal and clan memory and their oral histories, and they were used to validate the transfer of names, of social status, of subsistence rights, and of ritual prerogatives such as masks, songs, dances, and precedence. Gift-giving was at the center of the ceremony, and the rich maritime and rainforest environment allowed for an enormous outflowing of gifts. Those who received the gifts, heard the oratory, and observed the dances were forever witnesses of the clan history to that point in time.

The name for this ritual, "potlatch," comes from Chinook Jargon (not to be confused with the language of the Chinook people), the trade language (or pidgin) of the Pacific Northwest, which spread up the Northwest coast from Oregon to Alaska in the nineteenth century. Potlatch means "to give" or "gift." It was this word that was used to label the Canadian law that prohibited Native dancing, gift-giving, and ceremonies in 1884 (the potlatch was made illegal in the United States in the early twentieth century). Since then, all the peoples of the Northwest Coast have used the word "potlatch" to describe their primary ceremonial when talking in English.

The first major description and analysis of the potlatch was by the seminal anthropologist Franz Boas. In a letter published in the Victoria *Province* 11 February, 1897, in which he defended the potlatch, Boas writes of the potlatch primarily as a means of economic exchange, as a way of accumulating and distributing wealth, and as a means for competition (through gift-giving) that had come to replace warfare. Since then, primarily based on Boas's ethnology of the Kwakwaka'wakw (Kwakiutl), the potlatch, more so than any other Native American tradition, has been used by anthropologists to create grand theories. Abraham Rosman and Paula Rubel used the potlatch to relate ceremonial structure to social structure in *Feasting With Mine Enemy: Rank and Exchange among Northwest Coast Societies* (1971); Claude Lévi-Strauss used the potlatch as an example of his structuralism in *La voie des masques suivie de Trois excursions* (two volumes, 1975 and 1979); Irving Goldman, using a structuralist approach, pointed to metaphoric equivalences in the nature of Kwakwaka'wakw cognitive processes, understanding the potlatch to be essentially religious, in *The Mouth of Heaven: An Introduction to Kwakiutl Religious Thought* (1975); and Stanley Walens used the potlatch to argue that the Kwakwaka'wakw visualize the world as a place of mouths and stomachs, of eaters and eaten in *Feasting with Cannibals: An Essay on Kwakiutl Cosmology* (1981). All of these and other analyses, some bizarre, were based on earlier ethnological texts, not on what the people whose ceremonies these are said.

Traditionally, potlatches were put on for many reasons, which varied from one Northwest Coast traditions to another. These included funerals and later memorials honoring the dead, payment of debt witnessed by all the invitees, the erection of a "totem pole," the completion of a house, a wedding, a menarche, and so forth. The houses of the villages were very large, accommodating an entire clan, and the potlatches were usually put on in these structures. When Captain Vancouver visited 'Namgis village of the Kwakwaka'wakw in 1792, he noted that there were thirty-four of these large, rectangular plank structures. (See Figure 5a for the present state of totem poles in front of collapsed houses at the Haida village of Nan Sidens, abandoned because of smallpox in the late nineteenth century.) It could take years for the head of a clan to accumulate enough of the clan's wealth to put on a major potlatch, but such an event would become part of the tribal oral history, validating and perpetuating all of the names, titles, social positions, and ritual prerogatives orated during the potlatch.

The ritual costumes have changed over time. Originally, aside from the elaborate carved masks, dancers wore Chilkat and Raven's Tail robes and skirts. The former were woven from mountain goat wool and cedar and the latter entirely of mountain goat wool. While a few of these types of time-consuming costumes are still made, most wear blankets made from navy blue and red trade wool decorated with the inherited traditional designs outlined by mother-of-pearl shell buttons, called "button blankets."

The first potlatch after they were decriminalized in Canada in 1951, put on by the famous traditional carver Mongo Martin in 1952, took place in a replica traditional house, now called a "big house"; he had been commissioned to construct on the grounds of the Royal British Columbia Museum in Victoria. The Kwakwaka'wakw of Alert Bay (on Cormorant Island off of northern Vancouver Island), who were forcibly moved there from their village of 'Namgis in the late eighteenth century to work in a fish canning factory, built their first new big house purposely for the holding of the potlatch in 1963. Following this, big houses were built at many Northwest Coast Native communities. Communities that do not have big houses use community halls for potlatches, but everyone agrees that there is no comparison with the grandeur of the big house as well as the importance of the traditional dirt floor, which keeps one in contact with the Earth Mother,

Figure 5:   Northwest Coast—from old to new. (a) Haida clan poles by collapsed big houses at Nan Sidins (Haida Guai, British Columbia). The village was abandoned late nineteenth century because of smallpox. United Nations Educational, Scientific, and Cultural Organization (UNESCO) World Heritage Site. (b) Late-twentieth-century Kwakwaka'wakw big house at Alert Bay (British Columbia). Note large parking lot. Both photographs by the author.

and the central fire pit, the fire representing the Sun Father. Big houses, with their tall ceilings, large insides unbroken by central supports, massive carved pillars, and magnificent painted designs, are as awe-inspiring as European cathedrals.

This big house at Alert Bay eventually proved too small, and it was used as a museum to house the return of the confiscated masks mentioned in Chapters 1 and 2. A new house was built in 1990 that can hold over seven hundred people (Figure 5b). The following is a description of a typical potlatch that can take place at the Alert Bay big house; it should be understood that the order of events and the like will vary not only from tradition to tradition, but from clan to clan.

Invitations to a potlatch are often made at a preceding potlatch. A few days before the potlatch, members of the family will travel by boat and ferry to various communities inviting the members of the tribe. While potlatches in the traditional times would last for up to eight days, with people arriving by canoe after paddling for many days, contemporary potlatches are kept to a weekend, with people arriving up to a few days beforehand. Relatives and friends will come early to help prepare the big house, collect firewood, gather hemlock branches for decoration, and help cook the huge amounts of food for the feast. As well, the gifts have to be trucked over to the big house and the ritual items prepared and properly placed.

In the past, entry and seating at the potlatch was by rank invested by a potlatch and only those with a name certified at a potlatch could enter. Now seating is random, except for the host family and the singers and drummers. Often there will be, preferably invited, non-Natives in attendance.

The potlatch begins with oratory, a welcome speech from the host family. Then women from mourning families are called to sit in front of the singers wearing button blankets. On the completion of the mourning songs, the women dance in place, shaking off their sadness. If it is after the death of a high-ranked person, that person's ritual regalia will be danced and then at that time or later transferred with the deceased's rights and privileges. If a "copper" (a shield-shaped large piece of copper signifying a clan's wealth) is to be sold or transferred, it would be done at this time. Should the potlatch include a wedding or recognition of a girl's menarche, there will be special rituals, dances, songs, and gift-giving in that regard. At this point in the ceremony, the feast usually takes place. As in Native feasts in most traditions, young people first serve the elders and those leading or facilitating the rituals. At the end of the feast, feast songs are sung.

A ritual which often follows at this point is the cedar bark ceremony. A highly ranked woman of the host family enters with a large circle of cedar bark dyed red held by four chiefs. One who has inherited the right cuts the cedar on the fourth attempt. The bark cut into lengths is torn into strips and distributed, according to precedence, to everyone present. They fashion it into a headband which is worn during the Red Cedar Bark Dances of the Winter Ceremony.

This is followed by the appearance of the *hamat'sa* (Cannibal Dancer), which in the past fascinated anthropologists and horrified missionaries and government officials, who seemed not to appreciate that symbolic cannibalism is as much a part of Christianity as it is of Kwakwaka'wakw religion. Hamat'sa dancers are males who must both inherit the rights to the ritual and spend time alone in the forest to turn into a Hamat'sa. When they come out of the woods to a potlatch for the first time, they may enter from the smoke hole in the roof and, as wild humans, go around the big house trying to bite the participants while four people try to restrain them. Slowly they are tamed through the dances of a woman, symbolizing the making of a proper human being. At this time, the Hamat'sa dancer and the female who tames him will receive a new name. The Hamat'sa dances symbolize in complex rituals the movement from wild to tame in a series of ceremonial actions and dances. For the Kwakwaka'wakw, the Hamat'sa dance is the most important of the potlatch dances. Gloria Cranmer Webster expresses the feeling of the Kwakwaka'wakw toward this ritual:

> Women in the audience stand and dance in place, honoring the *hamat'sa*. For many of us, this is the proudest moment of the whole potlatch. The floor is filled with dancers, the singing is powerful, and there is such an intense feeling of pride and belonging that it is hard to describe to those who have not been part of something so vibrantly alive.[1]

This dance is followed by others, as decided by the elders, with a lighter meal served late in the night. Toward the end, the formal ritual dances give way to more social dances and fun dances for the children. Then the piles of gifts are brought out. While this is done, money is distributed to everyone, the amount depending on precedence. It takes a long time to distribute all of the gifts, and while this is being done, various visiting chiefs give speeches regarding the evening and the host family. This brings to an end the potlatch.

The potlatch is the means to continue tradition, to use the Native language, to legitimize people's names, to bring into memory the ancestors, and to bring people into direct contact with the divine through their dancing of their spirits and through the presence of the spirits in the masked dances of others. The potlatch is the heart and soul of these traditions. I have often heard young people speak of how the potlatch makes them happy not only because it provides a sense of personal and cultural identity but because it is in itself an ecstatic experience. Agnes Alfred, an elder at Alert Bay, said in 1980,

> When one's heart is glad, he gives away gifts. It was given to us by our creator, to be our way of doing things, to be our way of rejoicing, we who are Indian. The potlatch was given to us to be our way of expressing joy.[2]

MAKAH WHALE HUNT: CONTINUING PERSECUTION OF NATIVE RELIGION

In the middle of May 1999, an unprecedented public furor arose to stop the revitalization of a Native spiritual tradition. The Qwiqwidicciat (People Who Live By the Rocks and Seagulls) are officially known by the name the Salish people use for them, Makah. They have lived for many thousands of years at the westernmost part of mainland United States, at the junction of the Straight of Juan de Fuca and the Pacific Ocean in present-day Washington State. The Makah are closely related to the Nuu'chah'nulth (All Along the Mountains and Seas), called the Nootka because of a mistake by the first Europeans to come across them. The Nuu'chah'nulth live along the Pacific coast of Vancouver Island in British Columbia just north of the Makah, and their archeological record also goes back many thousands of years.

The subsistence and religion of these people had been based on hunting whales. This can be traced back archeologically a thousand years, but undoubtedly the practice is considerably older. Whales were not understood primarily as an economic resource; rather, as for all Native American hunting cultures (Chapter 3), Whale was a deity who in her mercy offered her body so the people may live. In turn, the people offered Whale the greatest respect and spent months spiritually preparing themselves with elaborate rituals for the hunt.

Hudson Webster, a Nuu'chah'nulth elder, has said:

Our people were very spiritual people. They prayed before they did anything. When they went sperm whale hunting for example, our people would prepare for that hunt with prayer and ceremony. These whales were the main source of dietary food. When a whale was caught and brought home to the people, before distribution and feasting, there was a chant to give thanks. The people were very excited as they knew that they would be fed and not go hungry.[3]

The Makah have elaborated this understanding on their Web site:

More than anything else, whaling represents the spiritual and technological preparedness of the Makah people and the wealth of culture.

To get ready for the hunt, whalers went off by themselves to pray, fast and bathe ceremonially. Each man had his own place, followed his own ritual and sought his own power. Weeks or months went into this special preparation beginning in winter [the whales migrate from Baja California to Alaska passing by the Makah in the spring] and whalers devoted their whole lives to spiritual readiness.

The next step was to tow the whale home–a distance of only a few miles if its spirit had heeded prayers to swim for the beach, perhaps

10 miles or more if not. Songs eased the paddling. Songs welcomed the whale to the village; welcomed the returning hunters and praised the power that made it all possible.[4]

One piece of evidence for the supreme religious importance of the hunting of Whale to these people is the shrine that was taken in 1905 from near the village of Yuquot, at the mouth of Nootka Sound in the middle of Vancouver Island's west coast. The shrine was a small house built on an island which was visited only by those who led the whale hunts. In it were eighty skulls of great whale hunters, forty on each side, along with the skeletons and cradles of those who had died in infancy. Over time, many carved wooden human figures were added to the shrine. Those who led the hunts came to the shrine to fast and washed in the lake by the shrine four times a day over four days, rubbing their skin with many branches of hemlock. The purpose was to purify themselves for the spiritual endeavor of the hunt and to gain the power of those many spiritually powerful persons whose skulls or wooden images were in the shrine.

At the beginning of the nineteenth century, the foremost anthropologist Franz Boas learned of the shrine from his informant George Hunt and commissioned him to obtain it. Hunt was part Kwakwaka'wakw and thus distantly related to the Nuu'chah'nulth, which gave him access to the shrine. He tried to purchase the shrine for two years, but it would have been the equivalent of trying to buy the Vatican from the Catholic Church. When most of the people were away hunting, Hunt slipped an enormous sum of money in those days, $500, to a chief who claimed he owned it—no one owned the shrine but certain clan leaders and whale hunters had rights to it—and surreptitiously stole it. By the time it arrived at the Museum of Natural History in New York, Boas had left the museum. The Whale Shrine has since sat in drawers and on top of cabinets for a century in the Museum storage area (where I saw it while doing research there in the mid-1980s).

In the late 1990s, Nuu'chah'nulth elders visited the shrine in New York, and this has led to a cultural rebirth. As this book is being written in 2006, negotiations have been going on for several years to repatriate the shrine.

The Makah began their own cultural rebirth two decades earlier with the discovery of an old village site at Ozette that had been lived in for thousands of years until it was covered by a mudslide three centuries ago; it was the Northwest Coast equivalent of Pompeii. In 1970, unusual high tides washed some of the mud away and revealed many artifacts. An archeological dig by the Makah with University of Washington archeologists continued until 1981. More than 55,000 artifacts were uncovered, one of the richest archeological resources found in North America. The Makah built a large museum to house and display the pieces and gained a renewed interest in their heritage and traditions, much having been lost when their religion was made illegal a century ago.

This cultural renaissance increased a desire to bring back their spiritual traditions. The whale hunt had ended in the 1920s because the grey whales had been brought close to extinction because of non-Native commercial whaling. In 1994, the grey whale was removed from the endangered species list, and the Makah sought to return to their right under the 1855 Treaty of Neah Bay to again hunt a whale for religious purposes. With the support of the U.S. government, permission was granted by the International Whaling Commission. After seven months of preparation, the Makah began the hunt from traditional canoes in the spring of 1999. This led to an uproar in the public media pushed by animal rights groups. The hunt could not be delayed because there were few remaining persons who had been alive when whaling ended seventy years earlier, and all knowledge of the hunt would soon be lost.

By happenstance, or so I then thought, I took a slight detour to Neah Bay to visit the Makah museum while driving from Toronto to Victoria, Neah Bay being a relatively short distance from Port Angeles where one takes the ferry to Victoria. It was during the whale hunt, which at the time I knew nothing about. The vociferousness of the protest I saw just outside the reserve was something I mistakenly assumed could no longer take place at the very end of the twentieth century. A few days later, I was to fly off to a conference on religion and animals at Harvard University, organized by animal rights scholars. From a Native perspective, important events do not happen by chance. I realized that Whale had brought me to Neah Bay to bear witness at the conference and elsewhere to the Native perspective on what was taking place.

Non-Natives did everything they could to interfere with the hunt, including attempting to ram and sink the canoes with power boats, thus endangering the lives of the Native people in the rough seas and strong currents of the Straight. I understand that at least one of the boats, in their frenzy to interfere with the hunt, ran over a whale, seriously injuring it. Apparently it was alright for the protestors to kill a whale for no reason but not for the Makah for whom it was a religious imperative. Despite the hysteria on the waters, the Makah succeeded in taking a whale on May 19, 1999. To my mind, this confirms that Whale truly wanted to offer itself to the Makah.

For the Makah, the hunt was indispensable for a revitalization of their rituals and conception of self-worth. Whale is a major deity, a spirit which offers itself to the Makah so that they may live, not just physically but spiritually. For contemporary, urban Western culture in general, having a contrary perspective, the hunt was an unjustifiable and intolerable abomination, the Makah hunters placing themselves outside the bounds of humaneness. Hence, protesters could comfortably shout: "Save the whales; kill the Indians," reminding one of the nineteenth-century Euro-American adage that "the only good Indian is a dead Indian." I saw another protester crying and mumbling that "Indian" culture had to disappear to save the animals. There was no indication that most of the protesters were vegetarians; rather, this was a religious clash between contemporary, secularized Western Christianity and Native religions, continuing a long history of religious intolerance and attempted cultural genocide in the Americas.

The Makah were seeking to reestablish their traditional communion with their deity, Whale. The protestors seemed to have forgotten that Christianity too seeks a communion between humans and a sacrificed deity, a communion celebrated in the Eucharist. The difference is that for the Makah their deity is an animal and for Christians it is a being that is both human and divine. I have yet to see protestors outside a Catholic church, or any other Christian church with the doctrine of transubstantiation, because the congregation was eating human flesh.

In an editorial published in Canada's premier national newspaper less than a week after the event, there was the statement, "There may have been a time, oh, several hundred years ago, when the Makah needed to kill whales for food and fuel. But now there are alternatives–like McDonald's."[5] Obviously, the statement could not hold if prepackaged, frozen hamburgers were understood to come from living animals.

The opponents of the hunt cited several reasons why the hunt should be banned. None hold up to logical scrutiny. First, it was argued that the hunt would lead to commercial whaling. But the request to the International Whaling Commission and the permission given was limited to a few whales for ceremonial purposes. Second, it was argued that this would set precedent for limited whaling by other indigenous groups, but this is already taking place in the Arctic, the Caribbean, and elsewhere. Finally, it was argued that the Makah were using modern technology, that after the whale was harpooned, rather than using a lance, the whale was put out of its agony with a high-powered rifle, and the Makah towed the dead whale to shore with a powerboat. So the animal rights opponents of the Makah were arguing, in effect, that the Makah should have prolonged the whale's suffering. They also refrained from pointing out that it would have been difficult to dispatch the whale with a lance or tow the whale to shore with canoes because of their own harassment of the Makah's canoes.

The successful hunt was celebrated in a potlatch:

In the presence of over 2000 guests, the Makah people of Neah Bay, Washington, celebrated their successful hunt of a gray whale, the first taken in over 70 years. Amidst the drums and songs of their neighbouring tribes in Washington State and the Nuu-chah-nulth peoples of Vancouver Island and in the presence of the whalers and their traditional cedar canoe "Hummingbird", the Makah and their guests sat down to a traditional feast of blubber and whale meat. As the crowd of young, old, native and non-native people eagerly lined up for second and third helpings, the successful whalers looked on with a pride only their grandfathers had known. With a single thrust of a harpoon, and two quick shots of a rifle, an entire community had been fed.

The celebration lasted through the night, and into the dawn of the following day. Throughout the proceedings, respect was paid to the spirit of the whale which had so willingly given itself to the hunters; of all the guests present, the whale was the most honored. As the celebration continued, time and again its presence was acknowledged: speakers made mention of the fact that "the whale's spirit is here, among us, watching and listening . . . it is happy." Elders and chiefs spoke of the tradition that has once again come to life and paid respect to the whalers for their poise, grace, and focus in the face of extremely hostile opposition.[6]

But afterwards, the opponents of the Native people were able to gain a local court injunction to stop future hunts. In 2004, the Ninth Circuit Court ruled that for the Makah to pursue their treaty rights, despite authorization by the international body which controls whaling, to which the United States is a signatory, they must go through the process prescribed by the Marine Mammal Protection Act, a costly and time-consuming process. The Makah applied for such permission in 2005 and, as of this writing in 2006, are still awaiting a response. Thus, despite laws in the United States specifically allowing freedom of religion for Native peoples, this freedom is frequently denied them by the courts.

Interestingly, I have been to Inuit (Eskimo) communities in the United States, Canada, Greenland, and Russia, and limited whaling continues in each of them. In none of these places have there been the same protests. Clearly, the protestors choose places they can drive to near comfortable hotels, where they can indulge in restaurant meals, if not McDonald's hamburgers.

Several years later, a similar religio-cultural clash occurred with the Mowachaht/Muchalaht community of the Nuu'chah'nulth. The same community whose sacred whale shrine was stolen in 1905.

A few days before he died in July 2001, Chief Ambrose Maquinna of the above community said he had a vision that he would come back as a *kakawin* (an orca or killer whale)—Northwest Coast cultures have a fluid concept of reincarnation. Four days after he died, a two-year-old orca swam into Nootka Sound to stay. For the local Native community, and for anyone who takes Native religious traditions seriously, that orca was their Chief who had come back home.

The orca, named Tsux'iit in honor of the late Chief, was numbered L98 by whale researchers and outside the Native community was known as Luna, a name given by a Seattle newspaper. Tsux'iit entered Nootka Sound voluntarily and could, of course, have left anytime he wished; he was not being held captive nor was he being fed. Tsux'iit adopted the people and boats of the area and was happy to be with them. This is not unprecedented. There are stories from late-nineteenth-century non-Native whaling communities along the Northwest Coast from Oregon northwards, as well as Australia, of an orca adopting a community and leading the oar-driven whale boats to grey and other whales, the orca sharing in the rewards of the hunt.

Two years after Tsux'iit arrived and before a public furor again arose, I traveled to the area, knowing nothing of the orca, to sail around the Nuu'chah'nulth territory on a small freighter. I encountered Tsux'iit when returning on the vessel. When it was tied up at the dock, Tsux'iit swam over to the boat to be sprayed with fresh water from a hose, an activity in which he delighted. I was within a couple of feet of him, and he clearly was a happy orca. The people of the local community delight in him, although they do not approach him, but only interact if he approaches them.

Nonetheless, people hundreds of miles away decided that he should be returned to his pod, whether he wanted to or not. He was to be captured and transported on a ship to the Straight of Juan de Fuca, a risky procedure which could cause him harm, if not kill him. There he was to be penned up until, it was said, he joined his maternal pod. But documents released under the Canadian Access to Information Program indicate that discussions about him had taken place with aquariums in Ontario and California. The attempt at capture was made in 2004, but the Native people came out in their traditional canoes and Tsux'iit followed them away from the trap.

Urban people, who at best have seen orcas on whale-watching boats, somehow assumed they knew better than the local people what was good for Tsux'iit. Indeed, they assumed that they knew what was good for the orca contrary to the orca's own wishes. The argument was made by people at a distance that Tsux'iit was a danger to local boats. But most of the local people were happy to put up with a minor nuisance to have him around. The many articles, especially in Seattle newspapers, that urged for the capture of Tsux'iit and his transfer to the Seattle area seemed not to care that this would have been an attack on Native spiritual sensibilities. The Native community made it very clear that they would not tolerate the capture of Tsux'iit. They readily agreed, however, to lead him out of the sound into the ocean if his pod passed by, so he could choose to join them or not.

Afterwards, the authorities decided not to again try to capture him. In any case, he was becoming far too large to transport; by 2006, he was seventeen feet long. Sadly, Tsux'iit was killed by a very large tugboat in March 2006. The tugboat, pulling a string of barges, entered the narrow Nootka Sound from the ocean to take shelter from an unusually late winter storm. The orca apparently was caught under the boat and sucked into its huge six-foot propeller which tore him apart; it was a propeller far larger than any he was used to encountering in the sound.

Ben Jack, a Mowachaht band council member during the confrontation over Tsux'iit, on the day the orca was killed spoke of the sadness in his community and of Tsux'iit: "He brought a lot of inspiration to our people. It just brought your whole spirit alive. You wanted to be there with him and have him around all the time."[7] The Native community held a memorial ceremony on the shore of the sound for him, their dead chief and their ancestors, singing and dancing the passing song to the beat of traditional drums. Later there will be a memorial potlatch in his honor.

· 8 ·

Pan-Indian Rituals

Until the latter part of the twentieth century, anthropologists tended to take proprietary interest in particular Native North American traditions. Often a few weeks of ethnographic research spread over a couple of summers with a Christian Native interpreter led to a lifelong reputation of expertise in that tradition. Some anthropologists jealously guarded this reputation, claiming, in effect, ownership of a Native people. A half century ago, I heard anthropologists speaking of "my" and then the name of a tribe. This alleged specialization often led to a view that Native traditions were utterly distinct and shared no cultural features. In turn, this led U.S. and Canadian courts to take the position that rituals that crossed cultural lines were ipso facto modern and for that reason, inexplicably, were inauthentic and had no legal protection—an utterly bizarre understanding that was not applied to any other group of people.

But as pointed out in Chapter 1, Native American traditions shared many common features. Furthermore, many of the most important rituals have always been cross-cultural or were created to be so, some at least a couple of thousand years ago. By convention, these rituals are termed "pan-Indian."

CIRCUMPOLAR RITUALS

Among the oldest rituals are those that are circumpolar, rituals that are found throughout far northern Eurasia and North America, some being mentioned in Chapter 1. The two circumpolar rituals described in this section are clearly connected with Eurasian shamanism and may be among the oldest human religious rituals. A third circumpolar ritual, a bear sacrifice with particular features, is no longer practiced in North America, although it continues in parts of Siberia and among the Ainu in northern Japan. This sacrifice involves raising a bear, in some traditions having it nurse at a human breast, bestowing it with honors, and then killing it, often with arrows. The body is treated with respectful rituals and then is feasted upon by the community. It seems to be a substitute for human sacrifice, bears and humans being similar in many regards, such as being omnivorous and appearing human-like, especially as skeletons. Rituals regarding bears are among the oldest of human rituals, as is evidenced in Paleolithic finds in European caves. The sacrifice relates to the dog sacrifice which is not just circumpolar but global, as it is also important in central Africa and East Asia. The dog, which is often treated as family, is probably a human substitute when sacrificed.

Spirit ("Sweat") Lodge[1]

Of Native North American rituals, the most pervasive are tobacco offerings to spiritual powers, including tobacco smoked in a pipe (see next section), and the complex commonly termed in the literature, "sweat lodge." Most ethnographic descriptions until recently, because of familiarity with the secularized sauna, which was a religious ritual in Scandinavia before it became Christian, misunderstand the sweat lodge to be primarily a hygienic practice. They failed to understand that it is primarily a potent ritual of confession, catharsis, decision-making, and direct communication with sacred beings. Thus, the Western term for the ritual complex has an entirely secular connotation, while its name in the various Native American languages has an explicit religious connotation. From the Native perspective, the ritual creates an opportunity to offer oneself through suffering to the spirits. It is also a potent means of purification in preparation for major ceremonies, purification not only of body but of the mind and soul. Thus, in most traditions, the ritual is preliminary to major ceremonies, but it also takes place on its own. Possessing many functions, including healing, the sweat lodge also serves to induce light-to-medium trance, usually in a communal context.

Native North American structures for heat rituals vary, including rooms dug from the earth (Southeast), parts of longhouses or special plank structures (Northwest), mud-covered domes (Southwest), stone structures (Mexico), and skin- or bark-, now canvas- or blanket-, covered domes (North central, Northeast, and Plains). The latter structure is essentially the traditional Northern Woodland dwelling or "wigwam" in Algonquian languages.

The following description of the Anishnabe lodge, symbolism, and ritual is given as an example of one tradition's version. Major aspects are ubiquitous throughout North American traditions, while other aspects are specific to the Anishnabe ceremony. The description is not meant to provide directions for putting on such a ritual. To do so one must have received the right from the spirits and acknowledgment of that right from the elders of a community.

The Anishnabe sweat lodge is called *madodoswun*, "Spirit Lodge," and is constructed with four pairs of poles, preferably willow, forming four doorways in the cardinal directions. The poles are driven butt-end into the earth at the circumference of the structure; opposing poles are bent and twisted around each other to form arches. The length of the poles varies with the size of the structure, which depends on the number of expected participants. Thinner poles are tied around the bent uprights with basswood roots or hemp twine, forming four concentric, horizontal rings, except the lower two do not cross the eastern, physical doorway.

A round pit is dug in the center of the cleared earthen floor and the excavated earth added to the moon-shaped altar east of the structure. The fire for heating the rocks is laid within the altar's crescent. The lodge framework is covered with sufficient layers of material to ensure a completely lighttight interior. The floor, excluding the center pit, is covered with cedar boughs, and a line of cedar foliage is laid between the fire pit and the altar.

The dark hemispherical interior of the structure reproduces the night sky; the doors, the Four Directions, three being symbolic rather than actual. The horizontal support rings symbolize the four levels of Sky knowledge, mirroring the unseen four levels of Earth knowledge below; these levels represent the Midewiwin degrees, for those following the Midewiwin tradition (Chapter 4). The physical entrance opens eastward, the direction of the rising Sun, the source of knowledge, of beginnings. In some contiguous cultures, the physical openings are differently oriented, but with related symbolic understanding: the Cree opening is to the south, symbolizing life, and to the west for some Lakota, the direction of life's path. The floor of the structure is the surface of the Earth Mother; the pit dug in its center, her vagina. Hence, it should be completed, as the earthen altar in the shape of Grandmother Moon, by women.

Cedar is the major traditional Anishnabe purifying plant, similar to sweetgrass, sage, and juniper for other cultures. Cedar represents the healing and life-giving power of nature and is linked to Grandmother Bear, the primary theriomorphic spirit of regeneration and healing. The line of cedar foliage to the altar, the entrance to the spirit realm, symbolizes the path of life and the umbilical cord of the newborn. The cedar too is gathered and laid by women. The willow branches for the structure's framework relate to water and the blood of the Earth Mother and signifies growth.

The fire in which the rocks are heated, burning to the east of the lodge, represents Grandfather Sun, the most potent power of the male Sky. As the female rocks become red-hot in the fire, they are transformed into Grandfathers, the male sacred persons. When they enter the lodge's pit, Earth's vagina, under the canopy of the dark night, the female Sky, cosmogony, is recapitulated. As the glowing red Grandfathers are sprinkled with water, the fluid of life, hissing steam shoots forth, surrounding the act of cosmic coition with hot vapor. The lodge dome becomes a womb in which grows the seed of new life. Both the cosmos and the participants are re-created.

As with all Native ceremonies, sweat lodge ritual begins with the collection of needed materials in a sacred manner. Each plant removed, each rock is offered tobacco and asked to give itself in order that the people may live. Usually males collect the branches and build the structure; females prepare the pit and the altar. Males collect the wood and tend the fire, which, once lit, is never left unattended. Women gather the water and prepare and place the cedar.

Two people take the roles of ritual leader and fire-tender; the latter does not enter the lodge during the ritual. If there are a number of participants, four others are designated doorkeepers, through whom the Spirits enter the lodge. For male ceremonies, Doorman cares for the eastern, physical opening, the doorway of life; Birdman, Cedarman, and Bearman, respectively, guard the west, south, and north doorways.

When the fire, which is laid in a symbolic pattern, has heated the rocks sufficiently, the participants strip themselves of clothes and other possessions. Before entering the lodge, each prayerfully places a handful of cedar foliage, for purification, and a handful of tobacco, as offering, on the fire.

Except for the fire-tender, because of practical necessity, no one crosses the line of cedar foliage from the fire to the lodge. All others circumambulate the lodge and fire following the path of Sun. Hence, the light from Fire, the representative of Sun, shines unbroken on the lodge entrance.

The leader enters the lodge first, turns south, crawls around the pit, following the direction of Sun's journey, and sits on the north side of the opening. The fire-tender passes in the ritual paraphernalia: a water container with a dipper and a brush of cedar leaves or sweetgrass to sprinkle the rocks, forked sticks to manipulate the hot rocks, sometimes a filled Sacred Pipe, and a shaker or drum, to bring forth the heartbeat of the cosmos. Individuals may also bring appropriate shakers with them into the lodge. After the leader is settled, the other participants enter in the order of seating to the right of the leader, the last being Doorman.

When everyone has entered, the fire-tender will carry the Grandfathers, one at a time from the fire to the lodge. The Grandfathers will be manipulated into their proper places with forked sticks by Doorman. Embers will be brushed from each Grandfather with cedar leaves by Cedarman, and each is vocally greeted by the congregation. The Grandfathers enter in a symbolic series of numbers, first four, representing the sacred directions, then other series of numbers depending on the nature of the ceremony and the size of the lodge. When the last of the Grandfathers enters, the flaps are closed by the fire-tender, who ensures that no light enters the lodge. A shaker is shaken or a drum is struck four times to begin the session.

From this point, the proceedings are flexible and vary according to the purpose of the particular sweat lodge ritual and the specific procedures of the ritual leader and experienced participants. Sacred songs will be chanted by the ritual leader. The drum or shaker may travel sunwise among the participants, each in turn, speaking or singing from the depths of their feelings to the Grandfathers, Mother Earth, other spirits who may be summoned to the lodge, and the participants, who become brothers or sisters, bonded by the powerful ritual. Crying under these circumstances is not unusual.

At times, the Grandfathers are sprinkled with water to create live steam, the fire-tender is asked to offer tobacco through the fire, a ladle of life-giving water is passed around and each takes a few sips, and the fire tender may be asked to pass a lit Sacred Pipe into the lodge. There are normally four rounds, punctuated by the temporary raising of the flaps at the eastern doorway for relief. The ritual may last from one to four or more hours, depending on the number and needs of the participants.

At the conclusion of the ritual, the various paraphernalia are passed out of the lodge to the fire-tender. The participants then crawl out of the lodge, beginning with the ritual leader, completing the sunwise circle about the pit begun when entering the lodge. Each greets the fire-tender and those who have stood by the lodge during the ritual, supporting the participants in their sacred act, with his or her name. As renewed beings, they must reintroduce themselves. Again they place cedar foliage and tobacco on the fire, expressing gratitude for the gift and wonder of new life.

The physical and ritual features of the sweat lodge engender common physiological effects. The intense heat affects the metabolism, and sweat pours off the participants, leading to dehydration. The increased metabolism of the participants in the small sealed structure reduces the oxygen and carbon dioxide builds up, causing hypoxemia. The total darkness of the lodge engenders partial sensory deprivation. The scalding steam is at times painful, and the hours spent tightly confined in the tiny space and unmoving, because of the danger of burns from the hot rocks, create discomfort, possibly leading to the production of endorphins. Drumming and chanting with the use of shakers may lead to auditory driving.

The combination of some or all of these potent neurophysiological factors induces the participants, experienced in ecstasy from fasting and other rituals, to enter a light trance. In trance, one is still constantly aware of all the other participants, not only those pressed to one's body on each side, but those normally unfelt and unseen. One is intensely conscious of powerful spiritual presences, those present at all sweat lodge rituals and those called to the lodge by individual participants, to whom one's suffering is an offering. One makes oneself pitiable to elicit their aid for the people and oneself.

The shared physical experiences combined with the collective experience of the numinous among the participants create communal bonding. Strangers become immediate brothers or sisters; any potential hostility evaporates in the union of common, intense, spiritual experience. When a participant speaks or sings, that person receives the total focus of the others. If confession takes place, it often leads to immediate catharsis. In a shared trance, individuals join their thoughts and reach consensus.

Decisions made under these circumstances are fully accepted by all; they become the decision of each and remain after the conclusion of the ritual. Such a decision-making process voids controversy and division. A larger consensus is ensured when many of the community spend hours outside the sweat lodge to encourage the sweat lodge participants in their endeavors. This is why the sweat lodge ritual normally precedes all other rituals: it enables the community and ritual leaders to reach consensus in a sacred context on the procedures for the rituals to follow.

In trance, time disappears. One is at no-time or the beginning of time, the time of cosmic creation. In this timeless, spaceless moment, having undergone the catharsis of confession or speaking one's inmost feelings, the participants, shorn of past ills and regenerated, are purified. At the end of the ritual, one crawls from Earth's dark womb, through the small birth canal, toward the light, hot, wet, cramped, yet exhilarated, a new person born into a new world.

The importance of sweat lodge rituals has been ignored by many scholars of Native American traditions, either because sweat lodge precedes and is at times at a distance from the major rituals or because of its affinity with the long secularized north European sauna or eastern Mediterranean sweat bath. This dismissal of a common major ritual has blinded scholarship to the use and importance of communal shamanic trance in Native North American cultures, while it is recognized in the entheogenic substance using cultures of Mesoamerica and South America. Indeed, it is particularly in the northern nomadic and seminomadic cultures that mechanisms for the creation of community are essential.

Even fixed settlement cultures, where males may leave the communities for long periods of time, required means to reestablish community and create consensus. Both of the pervasive rituals, tobacco offerings with the Sacred Pipe and the Spirit Lodge, had important functions in these regards. Both continue into the present as major preliminary rituals, especially when so many Native communities have been fragmented, and in modern pan-Indian contexts, including nontraditional Native situations: urban settings, ecumenical gatherings, universities, prisons, and so on. Moreover, Roman Catholic churches that minister to Natives have begun to utilize the sweat lodge ritual as preliminary to Christian rituals in the post–Vatican II climate.

The pervasiveness of the Spirit Lodge throughout North America allows insight into traditions that otherwise seem vastly different from those with which one might be familiar. When I was touring Maya archeological sights in Yucatan and came across three ruins of sweat lodges built in typical Maya stone architectural style, it was a revelation (Figure 6a,b). As soon as I saw the low entrances, through which one had to crawl, I realized that Maya religion had direct connections with northern North American traditions,

Figure 6: Mayan sweat lodges. Chichen Itza (Yucatan). (a) Exterior of one of three sweat lodges. Note small entryway, which all have. (b) Small plunge pool by another sweat lodge. Photographs by the author.

and I was able to begin to understand other aspects of the religion. Thus, from Alaska to southern Mexico, there is the commonality of at least one complex ritual with similar symbolism.

Sweat lodges were repressed along with all other forms of Native religion, but they continued underground in many areas to come to the fore again when overt repression ended. It is now common to see sweat lodge frameworks at the rear of homes on reservations on the Plains, and it is ubiquitous to all ceremonies in the Great Lakes area. In Oklahoma, the Southeast version continues to be practiced by spiritual leaders of those traditions. On the Navajo reservation, ceremonies called sings are still preceded by sweat rituals. On both coasts though, save for northern California, the ritual slowly became lost.

With the revitalization in the late twentieth century, young Lakota or Native youth trained in the Lakota way brought this mode of the sweat lodge to the reserves of the Atlantic Provinces of Canada and the reservations of the New England states, along with the new Native Bible, the Catholic–Lakota *The Sacred Pipe* of Black Elk. In the book, the *inipi* (sweat lodge) is the second of the seven sacraments and fits well with the Christian culture of those reserves where the traditional religion has been completely lost. (For a full description of the modern Oglala Lakota sweat lodge, see Powers, 1982 in *Further Reading*.) Similarly, on the Northwest Coast, people had forgotten that sweats traditionally had been held in temporary or permanent structures within their big houses. I have heard Native youths on the Northwest Coast complain of sweats beginning to be held on their reserves as not being part of their tradition—not that the Plains form of the ritual was foreign, but that sweat rituals in themselves were foreign. Thus, in those areas where the ritual had been fully repressed by missionaries and even the memory of them has been lost, the sweat lodge now has come to be understood by many as a Lakota tradition.

In Mexican Native villages, one can still see the stone Mexican forms of the Spirit Lodges behind the homes, not the large ones of the Maya ceremonial complexes, but small ones suitable for one or two persons. In Oaxaca, where there are many Native villages in the vicinity, some of the luxury tourist hotels have built small stone sweat lodges as an enhancement to their spa facilities, using the Aztec name for them: *temazcal*. The following is a blurb from such a hotel's Web site:

> Therapeutic Temazcal (Traditional indigenous steam bath), The Natural, Traditional and Cultural generator of energy and well-being: Our program is directed and guided by . . . a [Native] doctor of traditional and natural medicine. The temezcal is universally recognized as the place of ceremonial ritual that improves spiritual, mental and emotional health. The traditional Native American steam bath assists in the detoxification and purification of the body whilst enhancing the relaxation of the mind. . . . The purpose of the process is to enable

participants to experience direct contact with nature. Instrumental sounds and songs help to unblock the natural creativity within, to liberate the senses and emotions, enhancing the focus of one's spirituality. Leaving the steam bath is a symbolic representation of the rejuvenation of the body and soul by Mother Earth.[2]

So Native sweat lodges not only have been taken up—stolen from the standpoint of most Native traditionalists—by the New Age, but have become an expensive commercial commodity for well-off tourists.

Binding Rituals: "Shaking Tent" and Yuwipi

Binding rituals are those rituals which have the following characteristics: (1) The specialist with considerable spiritual power, female or male, called in the earlier literature the "conjurer" (a term as good as any, as it here means to conjure up particular spirits during the ritual) is completely bound. In particular, their fingers are tied together. (2) The conjurer is then placed in a special tiny tent or an enclosure within a tent, building, or large igloo, to the end that the conjurer cannot be seen by observers and is in a completely dark space. (3) The conjurer will sing to summon the spirits or will have assistants who drum and sing outside the special lodge. (4) Within a short time, the conjurer is freed from the bonds by the spirits. The bonds may be tossed out of the enclosure. (5) When the spirits arrive, they can be heard, and the tent or enclosure shakes, often indicated by rattles attached to the framework, hence the oft-used name "shaking tent" for the ritual. (6) The conjurer and the spirits speak to each other, which can be heard by the congregants outside the lodge. The spirits then go off to gather the needed information and then return. (7) Tobacco is offered in Native North American traditions, and a feast is laid. (8) The spirits may be seen as tiny points of bright light. (9) The purpose of the ritual includes the finding of needed animals for food and the success of those who hunt them, the recovery of the sick, and the finding of lost people or objects.

In North America, the ritual takes place among the Inuit and throughout the sub-boreal forest or slightly further south, from Labrador to eastern Washington State. Two complete early descriptions are offered here: one from the late eighteenth century among the Nitsitapi and one from the early nineteenth century among the Cree.

Peter Fidler, a Hudson's Bay surveyor, wrote of a ritual he observed in January 1793. Some young Peigan had gone to the territory of the Lakota several weeks before, and as they had not returned, their relatives were concerned and asked a Blood conjurer to determine how they were and when they could be expected to return. He described the ritual as follows:

[The specialist] was laid upon his back in the Tent and all his toes upon both feet was tyed together with strong sinnew. His arms was

then put before him & all his fingers tyed together in the same
manner. He was then sewed up in a Buffalo robe & after this above
40 fathoms of strong line was folded about him in every part to
secure him—not a part was to be seen but his head & it appeared
impossible that he could never extricate himself from all these band-
ages that confined him. A little square house or rather 4 strong
upright stakes has been drove into the ground within the Tent opposite the Door & dressed moose, Buffalo skins, etc. covered it up
impervious to the Day. This building was about $5\frac{1}{2}$ feet high & 6 foot
long by 3 wide, all hung round on the outside with a great number of
the dryed hoofs of [bison] calves, strung together in several bundles of
100 or more each which make a rattling noise when shook. The necromancer was lifted by 4 men & put inside this House all alone & the
skins covered securely again over the part that he went in at. A rattle
composed of the dry cod of a buffalo, with a few small stones within,
was put in along with him. All was quite mute & all attention in the
Tent, surprising to relate that he alone in 20 minutes time had one or
both of his hands at liberty & began to rattle; in 15 minutes more he
appeared to have extricated himself entirely as by his voice he
appeared to be standing upright & now began to shake the little con-
juring house of his as if he was determined to shake it all to pieces.
The rattling of the dry hoofs made a very loud noise, the man now
began to speak in a particular kind of manner & continued so 2 minutes, then again shaking vehemently his enclosure & continued in this
manner alternately speaking in unknown jargon & rattling his little
house for about 10 minutes, when he at that time announced that the
Spirit has condescended to favour him with what answers he required
to demand. He then told in a particular tone so as to be understood,
that the Young Men would arrive in 2 days & that we must pitch away
directly to the Spitcheyee where they would join us, that they would
have been here sooner but that the legs of some of them was sore &
unfit for walking. This ceremony occupied from the space from $1\frac{1}{4}$ to
$4\frac{1}{3}$ PM, when every person retired from the Tent for a few Minutes
while the necromancer clothed himself. We had then a sumptuous
supper of several dishes of meat on the happiness of soon seeing the
safe return of the Young Men. . . . On the third day . . . the Young
Men returned safely, but some had legs swelled with walking.[3]

George Nelson became a fur trade clerk in 1802, serving the various fur
trade corporations as they merged until he was a factor for the Hudson Bay
Company from 1821 to 1823. During his sojourns with Ojibwe and Cree,
he took a Native wife, became fascinated with Native culture, and wrote
detailed letters of his experiences. In his journals, he describes two Cree
shaking tent rituals, both at Lac La Ronge in northern Saskatchewan, held

in 1819 and 1823. He wrote several pages regarding the latter, which though partial are still too lengthy to provide verbatim.[4]

He first describes a typical Woodland shaking tent built at a distance from the dwellings at night: eight poles of human height put in the ground in a circle a little over a meter in diameter. Two or four hoops tie the poles together, the whole covered with hides (now canvas). The conjurer began by singing with his hand-drum for the spirits to take pity on him and assist him. He was then joined by others with drums and shakers to sing the songs of the various spirits that are invited to come. He then removed his clothing save for his breechclout and asked to be tied. Nelson provided the twine and assisted in tying him, particularly noting the strength of the knots. His fingers were tightly tied together under his legs, and then he was wrapped in a blanket which was tied in all directions. Nelson tied the knots of the rope around the blanket and certifies that they were good knots. Nelson with another forced his body through the small opening of the shaking tent and then covered the opening with a blanket.

Others outside the shaking tent, using the conjurer's drum, began to again sing. Nelson sees the first spirit conjured enter the lodge: ". . . and the man [the spirit] entered in an instant. I was struck dumb with astonishment; for he appeared to me to *slide* in by something that was neither invisible nor discernable–I heard something that for the life of me I cannot account for . . ." (original italics). But a few minutes after the conjurer was put in the lodge, the twine that bound his fingers as well as the blanket and rope is tossed out of the tent; Nelson notes with astonishment that none of the knots are untied. Nelson goes on to describe the entry of many spirits, and the talk of the conjurer with them. Among them is Turtle, the most important spirit of the shaking tent ritual for the Cree and Ojibwe. Some of them made jokes and amused the onlookers. While the ritual was a serious undertaking, there was also laughter, one of the characteristics of traditional Native rituals.

In the middle of the night, Nelson was asked by the conjurer if we would like to see the spirits. Nelson lies on his back and put his head under the blanket of the doorway. "I looked up and near the top observed a light as of a Star in a Cloudy night about $1\frac{1}{2}$ inches long and 1 broad., tho' dim, yet perfectly distinct. Tho' *they all* appear as lights, some larger and others smaller" (original italics).

Nelson was a hardheaded Euro-American businessman, as a successful Hudson Bay Company factor had to be. Thus, it is remarkable that his experience led him to take Native religion quite seriously: "I am fully convinced, as much so as that I am in existence, that Spirits of some kind did really and virtually enter, some truly terrific, but others again quite of a different character." Nelson was a rarity among Euro-Americans involved with Native people in the sub-boreal forest, as he commissioned shaking tents to determine the location of missing employees and supplies.

Among the Anishnabe Ojibwe, the conjurer is called a *djiskiu* and the shaking tent, a *djiskan*. As with the Cree, the *djiskiu* is considered the most powerful of those who can act with the support of potent spirits. Usually the vision to do the shaking tent ritual is received in adolescence, but the vision is not effectuated until later in life. The *djiskiu* can not only ascertain information and effect healing but produce material goods. The ethnologist Diamond Jenness obtained this story in 1929 from Jonas King of Parry Island (in Georgian Bay of eastern Ontario):

> Before there was a settlement at Parry Sound, Bill King and two or three other Indians exhausted their supply of flour and bacon; but they had four marten skins. One of the Indians was a conjurer, so Bill and his companions erected a *djiskan* for him. They passed the four marten skins inside the lodge, and within a few minutes the conjuror produced in exchange for them a 50-pound sack of flour which his *medewadji* [*manido* of the *djiskan*] had brought from Penetanguishene 100 miles away.[5]

The last shaking tent ritual among the Algonquian-speaking Innu in Labrador took place in 1973. But shaking tent rituals are now taking place on Anishnabe and Cree reserves, pretty much as described for the early-nineteenth-century Cree, without being hidden. Those who can perform them are highly respected. Turtle remains a revered deity with particular powers for healing through the shaking tent.

Similarly, the modern Plains version is little different from that described for the late eighteenth century, save for that people now live in houses rather than tipis, except when camping at Sun Dances and powwows. William Powers in his *Yuwipi*[6] (the Lakota term for the binding ritual) describes in detail a typical Lakota ceremony as it is now practiced on the northern Plains reservations. The following is but a brief synopsis; readers should refer to Powers' book listed in *Further Reading* for the full, rich description.

The preparations begin as cars arrive at the house where the ceremony will take place, with people bringing blankets and tarpaulins. All the furniture and furnishings of the house were removed—as the spirits do not like the things of the white man and to make room for all those who will attend—and what cannot be removed, such as a stove, is covered with blankets. Blankets and tarps were nailed over the windows, the purpose being to make the room lighttight. Rolled-up blankets and cushions were then placed around the walls of the room for people to sit on. Blankets were then nailed atop the doorway, which opened to the east, so they could be pulled aside for the people to enter. The people then entered in a clockwise direction, with the men sitting on the south side, the women sitting on the north side, and the singers, entering last, sitting on the west side.

The Yuwipi man's wife then entered the room carrying tobacco offerings tied into small bundles in the Lakota fashion and six flags of the colors for the Four Direction, the Zenith and the Nadir. Behind her came an assistant with seven large coffee tins filled with earth, followed by the Yuwipi man with a suitcase containing his ritual paraphernalia. The Yuwipi man placed the cans of earth into a special pattern in the center of the room and then put the flags tied to willow wands into the cans along with the tobacco offerings. He then creates a complex traditional Yuwipi altar that also has aspects particular to his own sacred relationships. Two special shakers are placed by the altar with their handles crossed. The assistant now brings in a large bunch of sage (this is not the alien tumbleweed but the indigenous smaller sage). A large bed is made for the Yuwipi man and a smaller one for the Sacred Pipe. Sage is passed around to the congregants who place a spring behind their right ears so that the spirits will know them as participants. A braid of sweetgrass was then lit and taken around the room to purify it and for the participants to purify themselves. By now, the only light is a kerosene lamp on the floor near the door.

The Yuwipi man now puts his pipe together in the ritual way praying as he did so (see *The Sacred Pipe: Ritual of Adoption*). As he ritually filled the pipe, the singers began the song he was given in a vision. He then ordered the kerosene lamp to be blown out. He stood and recited his vision granting him the right and rituals to heal. He then ordered the lamp lit and put the filled pipe on the bed of sage prepared for it. Ordering the lamp put out again, he sat in the center of the sacred space created by the tins of earth and flags and spoke of why they were here and the healing work that needed to be done. He took off his shoes and placed them outside the sacred space. An assistant now moved a tin of earth that would close the circle around him. The main part of the ceremony could now begin.

Two assistants brought a star quilt to the center of the sacred area. The Yuwipi man stands up and the fingers of his hands are tied together. The quilt was placed completely over him and tied around him seven times. He was then placed face down on the bed of sage prepared for him. The assistants closed off the sacred space with a string of tobacco ties and returned to their seats, and the lamp was again put out. The singers with their hand-drums now began the songs to summon the spirits taught to them by the Yuwipi man, which he had learned in his visions.

As the special songs were sung, the shakers placed by the altars began to be heard. The rattles moved around the room, and tiny sparks were seen whenever the shakers hit the floor. The spirits had arrived; the singers sing a final song. The Yuwipi man begins his dialogue with the spirits, his voice muffled by the quilt. The Yuwipi man's wife now begs the spirits to help, as does a close relative of the person to be healed. As each finished an utterance, the participants say *"hau"* in agreement.

If the person to be healed is not present, the spirits go off to the one who is sick. All wait until the spirits return, announced by the shakers. The Yuwipi man reports to the congregants what the spirits tell him about their visit to the sick person. The spirits, who are now hungry, are offered a dog feast, and then the singers sing dance songs for them. The spirits are now ready to cure all those present who have illness, who stand up and, if they have not already done so, announce to the Yuwipi man their problems.

A powerful spirit visits each in turn, although the spirit may make some jokes for all to hear before beginning. Only each sick person in turn hears what the spirit says to her or him, while the rattles dance around the patient in time with the healing songs sung by the singers. The patients may feel the spirits touch them in various places or smell the soothing smell of burning sweetgrass. After each healing, the patient sits down.

The spirits now move the rattles around the room with sparks again appearing. They are asked to take the tobacco offerings with them as they leave to return to their homes. The singing ends; all is quiet. The lamp is lit. The room is completely disordered. The Yuwipi man is sitting quietly, the quilt neatly folded, with the thongs on top. The tobacco strings are neatly rolled up next to him. He now lights the Sacred Pipe, and it is ritually passed around the room.

The curtains are removed from the doorway so the women can bring in the food, and the Yuwipi man packs up his ritual paraphernalia. A bowl of water is ritually passed around the room. The room is cleaned up. The feast of traditional foods is now brought in and placed in the center of the room. After the feast, the curtains are removed from the windows and the furnishings brought back in, and all is put back the way it was before. The ceremony is over.

These rituals are taking place on reservations throughout the Plains. Raymond Harris, discussed in Chapter 2, was a practitioner of this healing ritual.

REGIONAL PAN-INDIAN RITUALS

Different from circumpolar rituals, some pan-Indian rituals developed in response to the particular nature of a region and its ecology, such as the Sun Dance on the Plains. Other pan-Indian rituals developed locally, such as the Dream Dance and its special drum, which then generalized into drum groups, connected to the wide-spreading powwow phenomenon.

Thirst ("Sun") Dance

Horse nomadism was most effective in relatively small groups, due in part to the limitations of pasture for the herds of horses and of firewood when sheltering in small valleys during the fierce winters. But when the grass was lush in late spring before the summer drought, there was sufficient pasturage for many horses (the only wealth was in the number of horses), allowing an entire tribe to come together once a year. This was the occasion for the Thirst Dance (the most common term, but Sun Dance is invariably used in the literature because of the usual Western misunderstanding), which became the major seasonal ritual, replacing the winter rituals of more settled cultures. It was at this gathering that young women and men could meet each other, that old friends and distant relatives could again come together, that initiations into the age-graded ritual societies could take place along with the dances of these societies, and that all could take part in one of the most intense rituals to be found in North America.

Seemingly, the elements of the Thirst Dance were already present among the Missouri Basin cultures before many traditions moved to living on the Plains full-time. When George Catlin (see *Further Reading*) visited the Mandan in 1832, seven years before they were virtually wiped out by smallpox, he was able to witness the *O-kee-pa*, which, save for it taking place inside a large lodge, had most of the elements of the Thirst Dance as it exists today. The ritual had two purposes: fertility of the bison and attaining warrior spiritual power. The latter remained the motivation for thirst dancing and ritual self-sacrifice until the late nineteenth century.

Most males were warriors as well as hunters; there were also a few women who had a vision related to warrior power, demonstrated this to the satisfaction of their tradition, and became warriors. The adoption of the horse but added to this predilection, for now warriors raided to demonstrate their power not only by touching, not necessarily killing, a ritual enemy, but by stealing the enemy's horses. Thirst Dances were undertaken to have visions leading to the gaining of enhanced warrior power.[7]

With the onset of reservation life, raiding had come to an end and Native males lost their warrior roles as well as their major reason for living, leading to the well-known problems due to despair and ennui. Of course, the Thirst Dance was prohibited along with all other Native rituals. When it slowly came back in the mid-twentieth century, it did so with changed motivation and/or theological understanding.

The Thirst Dance underwent revitalization and adaptation to the changed circumstances in the reservation period. Beginning with the Shoshone at the turn of the century—see Jorgenson in *Further Reading*— a moderately modified Sun Dance spread to the Bannocks, Ute, Crow, and Arapaho. The motivation for thirst dancing became that of reforming oneself so that one could serve one's people. Through the powerful spiritual experience engendered by the ritual, the participants gained the strength to continue to resist alcoholism and other forms of negative behavior, which they already had begun to do in order to take part, and gain the spiritual strength to rededicate one's life for the benefit of others, the traditional Native ethic.

A second motivation for putting on the ritual was the encouragement by local chambers of commerce to hold the ritual as a tourist attraction, thus desacralizing the ceremony. Elsewhere, a change in ideology could be found in missionary, especially Jesuit, encouragement to create a Christian form of the ritual. Thus, among the Wind River Shoshone and Arapaho, we find a Christian theological framework, with,

> . . . great attention paid to God as personal Creator and Father. Arapaho Offerings Lodge [Thirst Dance] worshipers can be seen to wear scapulars, rosaries, and medals about their necks, and Christian symbols on their beaded aprons. Recent tradition says that each participant over the three-day period should dance to each one of the twelve side poles, which now represent the apostles in their positions around the Center, Christ.[8]

With the resurgence of Native religion since the 1970s, the numbers of Thirst Dances held during the summer have increased geometrically. The Web site in 2006 of a single reservation, the Rosebud Sioux Reservation in South Dakota, mentions thirteen regular Sun Dances each season. Aside from more regular tribal rituals, individuals may have a vision to sponsor Thirst Dances, sometimes of a form from a neighboring rather than their own tradition. I was once at a Thirst Dance put on by a Pikuni who had a vision that he should sponsor the Cree version of the ceremony. Relatives and friends supported him in putting on the ritual, and many people from several traditions came to take part. Throughout the summer, many Thirst dances are now taking place on the Plains.

Tourists are no longer welcome. Most Thirst Dances are open to sincere non-Native observers who can treat the ritual with respect, but because of a history of abuses others are off limits to non-Native persons. In all cases, alcohol and drugs are not allowed on the grounds, and intoxicated persons will be removed.

The following is a general outline of the Thirst Dance as it takes place today based on those I have observed. Of course, the details will vary from one tradition to another, even from one vision to another. *Further Reading* provides recommended works that have more complete descriptions of particular tribal ceremonies.

Those taking part, or supporting those who will take part—family members and friends—will arrive several days before the ceremony itself begins. First they will set up their own camps and then begin to prepare the ceremonial grounds. If Thirst Dances had been held on the grounds previously, the framework of the previous lodges can be seen as they are left in place for nature to take its course. In virtually all North American traditions, major ceremonies begin with the Spirit Lodge. For the Thirst Dance, the ritual will take place for the sponsor, in many traditions, a respected elder woman; the ritual leaders, usually male; and the men and women who have pledged to dance. Separate female and male Lodges will be held. And as with all traditionally semi- and fully nomadic traditions, even though the people today will live in permanent dwellings, the next procedure would be to build the temporary ceremonial structure (as the Midewiwin ceremonies discussed in Chapter 4). This differs from the Mandan version, perhaps the original one, which was held within a permanent structure.

The dance arbor is relatively simple: a center pole, an outer circle of poles, usually twelve in number, poles to join the center pole to the tops of the outer poles, and a woven wall of leaved branches around the outer poles. The top is not enclosed, so that the dancers can see and feel the heat of the sun; the only shade is around the outer wall, depending on the time of day. Although the structure is simple, the meaning is not. A colleague of mine, back in the late 1960s when elders feared the demise of their traditions, collected thirty-five hours of taped interviews on the symbolism of the ceremony of one tradition—seventeen hours were on the center pole alone!

The poles are of cottonwood. As they grow by the banks of streams, they symbolize the life-giving waters, which the pledgers will voluntarily do without during the four days of the Dance. The center pole is treated as an honored enemy. First a scout is sent out to find a suitable one: a tree that is tall and straight. The tree, approached by many of the congregants, will first be touched by a noted warrior or a virgin maiden, depending on the tradi- tion. The tree is then chopped down and the branches loped off. It is then carried, as a fallen hero, by an honor guard to the camp grounds (or nowa- days, to the truck that will transport it to the camp). I will never forget the feeling of awe and honor I felt when I was selected to be one of those carrying the pole.

Before the pole is placed into the pit to receive it in which tobacco is placed, offerings from the participants are tied to its top. Special ritual items may be placed there, again depending on the tradition. Also, thongs used during the last day are attached to the top. The pole is then ritually raised and the rest of the arbor constructed. The next day, the Dance begins, following further preliminary rituals. The participants consist (this varies to a degree according to the different traditions) of the sponsor, who fasts the entire time in a small hut outside the arbor; one or more eld- ers who lead the ritual; drummers and singers who sit around the drum— often a complete, stiff, rawhide bison skin—throughout the four days; the pledgers, who will abstain from food and water for the entire four days and dance in place throughout the long daylight hours while blowing on eagle- bone whistles and facing the sun, except for short breaks; and the rest of the community, who will go in and out of the arbor, sitting along its perimeter, supporting the dancers with their good thoughts and prayers.

Much goes on that will not be readily apparent as friends and relatives strive to support the pledgers and the ceremony. For example, I am aware of a supporter noticing a small thunderstorm off in the distance and heading toward the lodge. While it is considered good fortune if it rains at the completion of the Thirst Dance, rain during the ceremony is not a good omen. This supporter, who had Thunder power, danced in place outside the lodge facing the storm. The storm slowly veered around the ceremonial grounds returning to its original course. Then, well over an hour later, the supporter ceased dancing in place. The supporter told no one there of what had been done.

On the fourth day, depending on the pledge, some dancers will be either attached to the thong hanging from the pole with a skewer thrust through their breasts or attached by thongs to one to four bison skulls by skewers thrust through their backs. Female dancers, however, are not pierced (as far as I am aware). The former will dance facing the pole and leaning against the thongs until the skewers are torn from their chests; the latter will dance around the perimeter of the arbor dragging the bison skulls behind them until the skewers are torn from their backs. After their wounds are ritually treated by the elders, these dancers are placed on their backs on a blanket in the arbor; hopefully, they enter a trance state and have the sought-after vision giving special powers from the spirits. Most pledgers dance four times over a period of years, as will be evidenced by the scars on the bare-chested men. Such persons are invariably highly respected.

That evening there will be a grand feast, and after a final sweat ritual on the next day, this once-a-year gathering will break up, as family groups go off in all directions. The arbor is left in place to slowly decay.

The above synopsis, of course, does not begin to do justice to a very powerful religious experience for all those present, for these rituals bring the participants into an even more immediate presence of the spirits than is the case in ordinary life or daily rituals. Such rituals create a sacred place and time that separates all present from mundane existence; and all are sad when the ritual is completed and the sacred time—a time out of time—reaches its end.

Dance Drums and the Powwow

Another ceremony has roots in the Plains, spread to the Great Lakes area, and then became a continent-wide phenomenon that is the most common Native ceremony to be found in North America. Its origin is in the development of a large drum that is played by from four to eight persons at the same time. The typical North American drums are of two types. The most common is of an animal skin tightly drawn over a wooden hoop. These can be of varying sizes so long as they can be held by one hand. The skin can be on one side or both sides, and there may be additional pieces that rattle or buzz with the vibration of the drum. The drum can be held by the inside thongs that stretch the hide over the frame on single-sided drums, by a stick attached to the frame on large single-sided drums or by a leather handle on two-sided drums. All Native American drums are played with a drumstick, never by hand as are African drums, so they must be able to be held by one hand.

The second type of drum is a water drum, whose base can be wood (Northeast) or pottery (Southwest); more recently, with the Native American Church [see *Native American Church (Peyote Religion)*], the base can be a small cast-iron pot. The skin head can be stretched and held over the base in several ways, such as a hoop or ties that go around the bottom and attach to round stones placed on the parts of the head that go over the sides. The head is wetted before being stretched and some water is poured into the base, which when shaken keeps the head wet. The wet head gives a distinctive sound. Water drums may be small, so they can be held under one arm while dancing, or larger and placed on the ground in front of the drummer.

A large drum played by several persons in the Plains is one of the earliest drums used by humans. It is simply a full-sized bison rawhide which is laid on the ground during the Thirst Dance and other Plains dances and pounded with drumsticks by as many as can sit around the hide.

No matter what type of drum is used, the drummers are also singers. When four drums of the first type are used in ceremonies or when the full-sized hide is beaten with a number of drummers, all sing in unison. Sometime in the middle of the nineteenth century, a hide drum on a large wooden frame played by several drummers evolved from the full-sized bison rawhide drum.

There are several origin myths regarding this drum and various theories as to where and when it began. In the Plains, this drum became attached to the Grass Dance, originally a warrior dance of the Omaha. The dance was so named because the dancers, as part of their dance costume, wore a long bunch of grass symbolizing scalps attached to the back of their belts. Two to four singers playing a single large drum became a definitive aspect of the Grass Dance, and it spread throughout the Plains from around 1860 through the 1880s. Drum Dance societies evolved on the model of the warrior society that was at the basis of the Grass Dance using the large drum.

This drum led to a different relationship of the singers during ceremonies. With the individual hand-held drums, generally held vertically close to the head, the drummers faced the dancers or ritual activity. With the large drum held horizontally by four stakes and the dancers kneeling or sitting around it, the drummer–singers now faced each other, and this led to greater musical interaction among them.

The Drum Dance spread eastward and was adopted by the Anishnabe by the turn of the century. Among the Anishnabe, the drum was connected to certain dreams and elaborately decorated accordingly. Except for a woman's Drum Dance drum, the drums were played by men—the drum itself conceived of as representing the female Earth—surrounded by eight women at the cardinal and semicardinal directions singing in harmony an octave above the men, a custom that precedes the adoption of the large drum. The Drum Dance societies on the Plains and among the Great Lakes Anishnabe began to fade throughout the early decades of the twentieth century; they had always been resisted by the missionaries.

But while the Drum Dance societies were fading, another related phenomenon was expanding to become the most widespread and common Native ceremony in North America. This is the powwow. The word probably comes from an eastern Algonquian-language term *pauau*, which meant a gathering of persons with spiritual power for a healing ceremony, but came to be applied by Euro-Americans to any gathering of Native people. As Native people began to use English, they adopted this new meaning of the term cross-culturally.

By the end of the nineteenth century, Native dancing was illegal in Canada and the United States, although it continued surreptitiously. Some Native communities, possibly the first in Montana, began to hold the equivalent of the Drum Dance openly on July 4 as purportedly a secular celebration. It was hard for the authorities to stop an overtly patriotic festivity. Thus, powwows began to be held throughout the United States, slowly replacing the Drum Dance. The process took a half century.

By the second half of the twentieth century, powwows came to be held in community centers and special grounds throughout the United States and Canada. Where there are special grounds, they tend to be a large cleared circle, often with an arbor around it with benches for the dancers, and smaller covered arbors within for the leaders and drum groups. In community centers, they tend to be part of a feast that could be put on for any number of reasons. Slowly, local chambers of commerce began to perceive powwows as being financially beneficial to the larger community as a tourist attraction. The larger powwows attracted vendors from a distance, and the selling of Native crafts and foods became part of the powwow itself. All of this was perceived as nonthreatening to the dominant culture as the powwow was assumed to be entirely secular.

Young men organized themselves into drum groups and traveled from powwow to powwow. The powwow drum was nothing other than the Dance Drum, either completely made from wood for the frame and hide for the drumhead or a purchased bass drum that was decorated in a modern Native fashion. These drum groups became the equivalent of the warrior societies of old and competed with each other, not with weapons, but with singing and drumming.

By the 1980s, large intertribal powwows began to be held, attracting dancers from all over North America to compete for prizes of large sums of money. By this time, the types of dances were regularized and the dance costumes became quite flamboyant. In urban areas, coliseums and exposition buildings were used for huge powwows run by professional convention organization companies. But smaller ones were held by more and more communities as a way for everyone to come together for a summer celebration in what was now understood to be the most predominant mode of expressing Native culture.

With the resurgence of Native spirituality in the latter part of the twentieth century, the powwows were no longer perceived by the participants and communities as secular. More and more a spiritual aura came to the fore, and for many Native people the powwow became the only form of Native spirituality available. In outdoor powwows, Spirit Lodges began to be held in conjunction with them. The powwow grounds were purified as would be religious ceremonial grounds. It is expected that the grounds will be treated with respect and people will act accordingly while they are there. Drum groups indicated sacred drumming by hanging eagle feathers from the drum supports, removing them for purely secular dancing. Before drumming, tobacco was placed on the drum head, and the drum was purified with the smoke of sacred herbs. Eagle feathers began to be added to dance regalia, and the whole outfit then became holy and was treated accordingly. People began to use the powwow as an opportunity for giveaways, as they did traditional ceremonials. One of the most recent recognized dances is the women's Jingle Dress dance. The dance itself arose from a vision, and only those who have dreamed of dancing it and their costumes take part. Clearly, this dance is a traditional sacred ritual in every aspect of Native religion.

Thus, what developed as a secular dance from a religious dance so the dominant society would not suppress it has come full circle and is again, to varying degrees from powwow to powwow, a religious ceremony. It is a ceremony that includes all of the traditional general features of Native religion: purification, sacred items, oratory, feasting, honoring warriors—now veterans—drums and drum societies, socializing, feasting, and, most important of all, dancing. Dancing is done for joy, to exhibit one's skill and stamina, for beauty, and primarily because dancing is how one expresses one relationship with the divine in Native traditions. This can be best understood in the beautiful words of a longtime powwow dancer, the same person who wrote the poetic statement which begins this book:

> American Indian dance is not a form of mindless amusement. It is a form of praise, worship, and a way to experience interconnectedness through motion. Dancing is an art that was here before the conception of art ever existed. It is a necessity for Indian people. A necessary spiritual action requiring dedication and a devout sense of reverence.
>
> When American Indians dance, whether it is at powwows or other gatherings, all senses become heightened as cultural chants, drumming and songs fill the air. These haunting, mystical sounds transport the imagination to other times and places. The drum – its round form

representing the shape of the sacred universe – emits strong, steady heartbeats that bring entrancement through repetition. This enables the dancers to put to rest the distractions of worries and cares of everyday life so that they may become one with all. Dancers from different nations in splendorous regalia dance the spirituality of their cultures into being as they pay homage to an ancestral tradition as sacred and important as rain. Agile and full of purpose, their artistic movements bring chills to the soul.

Serious dance is prayer that can open a doorway to a connection with the total universe. A way to find that "inner being" who recognizes and appreciates the spiritual essence of interdependence and gratefully ask Creator for recognition of the needs of his or her people in return. . . .

Those who dance as an offering to Creator are keeping traditions alive and setting reverent examples for the young people of their nations. They are the ones who realize that to dance is to pray; to pray is to heal, to heal is to give, to give is to live, and to live is to dance. To these dancers, I say, "Dance on and on and on . . . we need your rhythmic, heartfelt prayers."[9]

THE SACRED PIPE: RITUAL OF ADOPTION

In most Native American languages, the word for a people simply means "human being." By implication, everyone not of one's tribe is not. Most of the common names for Native tribes used by Euro-Americans are not the names that Native people use for themselves; often they are the pejorative names given to them by their enemies. Thus, the word "Sioux" is an Algonquian word for "snake." This is why, in this book, these types of names have been avoided as much as possible. All the traditions were warrior ones; thus, strangers were likely to be killed as an enemy. For long-distance travel to take place, for trade or diplomacy, there needed to be rituals to allow persons from afar to be accepted. These were rituals of adoption. With these rituals, strangers could be made relatives.

In 1673, Father Marquette, seeking a route to China, reached the Mississippi River from the Wisconsin River and began to travel down it. According to Lafitou, writing in 1724:

It was the 25th of June the Indians, having recognized them as Europeans, sent four old men to speak with them. Two of them carried pipes to smoke tobacco in; they were highly ornamented and adorned with feathers of different sorts. They walked solemnly and raised their pipes toward the sun; they appeared to present it to him to smoke [i.e., stem first] without, however, saying a word . . . they were Illinois, and to guarantee peace they presented their pipes to smoke; then they invited him to enter their village. . . . It is sufficient if one carries the calumet with him to show it, by which means they may walk in safety among enemies who, in the midst of fighting, will lower their arms to one who shows it. It was for this reason the Illinois gave this pipe as a safeguard among the nations through which they had to journey. There is a calumet for peace and one for war. They use them to end their differences, for strengthening their alliances, and to communicate with strangers.

It is made of a red stone polished like marble, and pierced so that one end serves to receive the tobacco, and the other has a socket for a handle, which is a stick two feet long . . . and pieced through in the middle. It is ornamented with the head and neck of different birds of the most beautiful plumage, to which they add also red, green, and other colored feathers. They regard it as coming from the sun, to whom it is offered to smoke when they want calm or rain or sunshine.[10]

Thus, the early English and French explorers of North America quickly learned that they could travel with impunity by carrying with them the Sacred Pipe. What the Native people they encountered did not understand is that these Europeans were using the pipe deceitfully. To them the pipe was not holy but merely an instrument by which they could travel with the ultimate aim of wresting the land from their inhabitants.

Well over 2,200 years ago, Native North Americans, as discussed in Chapter 2, used a pipe of a particular shape, with a shared ritual and common theology, to enable long-distance travel. A unique pipe, often termed the Sacred Pipe, that replaced the earlier pipe shape with an unknown ritual began to be used at least 1,500 years ago.

What is particular to the Sacred Pipe is that it is of two parts: a bowl, usually of stone, and a stem, usually of wood. The bowl can be of several shapes and the stem can be of different lengths and be plain or decorated in many ways. What is significant is that the two parts are kept separate until ritually used. During a pipe ceremony or when the pipe is used as part of a larger ceremony, the circle of participants will be talking and enjoying each other's company while the pipe-keeper arranges the ritual elements in front of her or him. When the congregants note that the pipe is about to be joined together, a hush ensues, for when the two parts are brought together the pipe becomes spiritually potent; a sacred time and space has come into existence. Not until the pipe is separated into its two parts does one again reenter mundane existence.

The ritual of smoking the pipe is invariably the same from the earliest European recordings from the mid-seventeenth century to today. Given its accordance with the basic theological commonality (Chapter 3) of Native American traditions, one can assume that it is the same ritual since the Sacred Pipe began to be used between 1500 and 2000 years ago. The following brief synopsis of the ritual passes over several minor details.

Before the pipe is joined together, the parts and all other ritual items involved are purified with sacred fumigants. After the pipe is joined together, it is filled with tobacco (Chapter 1), a pinch for each of the Four Directions, Sky and Earth as well as for any other special recipients of the particular ceremony. Each pinch will be spoken over as it is placed in the bowl. When the pipe is lit, preferably with a coal or a smoldering braid of sweetgrass, a puff is offered to each of the Four Directions, Sky and Earth, and possibly other spirits. Either before or after the pipe is lit, it is offered stem first to the spiritual recipients while prayers are said, whether spoken or silent. The pipe is then passed around the congregants in a sunwise direction. Each congregant usually takes four puffs and may, if they have the right, perform their own minor ritual as they may have been taught by their spirits. When the pipe returns to the ritualist, if there is any tobacco left, he or she will finish smoking it. If the circle is large and the tobacco is finished before it completes the circle, it will continue around the circle with each person putting their lips to the pipe until it returns to the pipe-keeper. The pipe will even be brought to the mouths of infants who are in the circle, although children are not expected to actually smoke it.

The ritual creates a double communion. By offering tobacco smoke in a vessel from which both the offerer and the recipient both smoke, the smoke creates a communion between the spirits and the person. Second, as the pipe circulates around the circle from which all smoke, it creates a communion among the smokers. This is how the Sacred Pipe can make relationships not only with the spirits but with humans. Thus, strangers on sharing the Sacred Pipe become relations, no longer enemies. Nonetheless, this communion can be used for several functions, not only for making peace, but, for example, for making war.

The significance of the two parts to the Sacred Pipe can be found in the meaning of its symbolism. The bowl of the Sacred Pipe is in itself of major symbolic significance. Both hollows symbolize the female. The smoking end is a vessel for offering tobacco and is symbolically parallel with food vessels, usually made and used by women. The hole for receiving the stem symbolizes the vagina, which is symbolically (and linguistically in some languages) equated with Earth. The most awesome part of pipe ceremonies is when the two parts of the pipe are joined, when the male stem is inserted into the female bowl, at which time ritually significant pipes become potent. The predominant colors of stone pipe bowls also relate to female symbolism. Red catlanite bowls, although mythic details vary from culture to culture, as red ochre, symbolizes blood, the body's life fluid, or life itself. Life comes from the female, Earth or woman, and is visible, respectively, in water and menstrual blood. Black pipe bowls symbolize Earth itself. As well, stone or clay, the predominant substance of Sacred Pipe bowls, is of the Earth. Red and black bowls are approximately equal in number among traditional Sacred Pipes still extant.

Most Sacred Pipe bowls are plain. Where there is decoration, it tends to be limited to circular ridges and incised circles, holes on flanges or keels, and cutouts on flanges. The symbolic significance often lies in the numbers, usually four or its double eight, representing the Four Directions. Also of importance are the numbers six, representing the Four Direction, Earth and Sky, and, especially among the Lakota, the number seven, having several associations, including the Pleiades and the Big Dipper.

Among the most interesting pipes from a sculptural perspective are those of animals or humans, and these have engendered major misunderstandings, particularly in regard to their placement and function. In Sacred Pipe ritual, the pipe is offered stem first to the spirits and then circulated among the ritual participants until the tobacco is exhausted. In virtually all the hundreds of premodern Sacred Pipes I have studied with a ritual context, those with such effigies are oriented opposite the direction of the stem. They face the person praying with the pipe as the stem is offered toward the spiritual recipient. This is not the case with one-piece pipes, where the effigy invariably faces the smoker.

The symbolic significance of the stem is multiple. When married to the bowl for ritual use, it symbolizes male energy and creative potential. As the channel for the smoke offering, the stem represents our voice and, as in Pawnee culture, may be decorated with black circular lines along the entire stem, making the stem symbolic of the trachea. The stem also represents the journey of life and may so be symbolized by a red line the length of the stem along its top. Representing life itself, the stem may be rubbed with red ochre mixed with bear-grease, each symbolic of life-giving forces.

Most pipestems are plain, but depending on the ritual and individual spiritual inspiration, there are decorated pipestems exhibiting a rich symbolic world. Except for intricate decorative piercing and cutouts or simple repeated incised lines, there are relatively few carved pipestems, but these can have several different carved symbols.

More common are stem coverings. The simplest covering, aside from an ochre–bear-grease mixture, is paint. The most common decorative covering in older pipes is quillwork. Of significance are the bird heads and feathers wrapped around some stems. Common are the duck, which may symbolize the re-creation of the world after the great flood, the horned owl, and the red scalp of the ivory-billed woodpecker. A few pipestems are wrapped with fur, probably of significance to the individual who made the stem or to the particular bundle of which it is a part.

The most common addition to hang from a pipestem are feathers, particularly those of the golden eagle, usually in a set of four, seven, or eight (Figure 7). Eagle has varying symbolic functions that differ from culture to culture but invariably is a major spirit. Eagle may represent Sun or West Wind. Also Eagle represents the sending of our messages to the Spirits, a meaning related to the trachea decor. The eagle feathers may have eagle

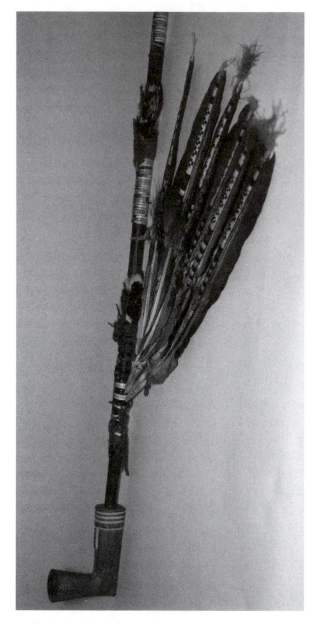

Figure 7:   Anishnabe Sacred Pipe. Early nineteenth century. Grey stone bowl; quill-wrapped reed stem with six quilled pendant eagle feathers. National Museum of Civilization (Ottawa) III-G-826ab. Photograph by the author. First published in author's *Offering Smoke: The Sacred Pipe and Native American Religion* (see *Further Reading*).

down appended to it and may be decorated along the shaft with quillwork. The pendant feathers may hang separately or be arranged in the fashion of a spread fan. In the East, turkey feathers shared some of the symbolism of Eagle, and in the Southeast, flamingo feathers were used. Owl feathers were also hung from pipestems in a number of cultures, before the Christian impact made all female theriomorphic spirits a symbol of evil.

Also common are ribbons of varying colors, the colors signifying the Directions and particular spirits. The ribbons may be changed from ceremony to ceremony to indicate differing symbolism by the colors. Horsehair, often dyed, usually red, is a frequent addition to stems. War pipes may have pieces of scalps or full scalp locks tied to the stems. The possibilities of bowl and stem decorations are considerable as there are cultural variations and all are subject to individual vision experiences. Hence, the above discussion is but suggestive of the rich symbolic world of Native religion.

For at least the last thousand years, the Sacred Pipe has been the most common item of ritual paraphernalia. In many respects it in itself represents Native North American religion as a macrotradition, although it must be understood that the Sacred Pipe was not part of Southwestern or Northwest Coast traditions, except as they may be used in greeting those from the Sacred Pipe using traditions. In California and the Pueblo traditions, the most common pipe shape is the one-piece tubular pipe. Everywhere else, the Sacred Pipe was used not only in pan-Indian situations but as well in tribal, clan, family, and personal rituals. Along with dancing, it is the most common means of praying. In itself, the Sacred Pipe is holy, and those who understand and use it do so not only with great reverence but with exceeding awe. It is also a sacred item that has, as the Spirit Lodge, been much abused by non-Natives playing at being Indian.

Father Marquette, quoted at the beginning of this section, came to understand that the Sacred Pipe was far more than a cart de passage; it was the holiest item they had, as he writes in his own words:

[The Sacred Pipe] is the most mysterious thing in the World. The Scepters of our Kings are not as much respected; for the Savages have such a Deference for this Pipe, that one may call it the God of Peace and War, and the Arbiter of Life and Death.

From the Native perspective, the understanding is summed up in an Osage ritual song:

The holy Pipe,
Holy, I say
Now it appears before you
The holy Pipe, behold you.

NATIVE AMERICAN CHURCH (PEYOTE RELIGION)

Of the many pan-Indian religious developments that took place in response to Native people being forced onto reservations, those that sought to return to the past before the deleterious impact of Euro-Americans proved to be unviable, while those that sought to accommodate to the new circumstances had a better chance of enduring. The most successful development was that of the Native American Church, which today has perhaps a quarter of a million adherents to varying degrees and involves, by some estimates, one out of every four Native persons in the United States.

The Native American Church is based on the ingestion of peyote, in itself understood to be holy, as a sacrament. Peyote is an entheogenic (psychoactive) small, low-lying cactus (*Lophophora williamsii*) that, among other effects, causes one to see, when the eyelids are closed, a kaleidoscope-like flowing pattern of dots of vivid primary colors. In an appropriate ritual setting with a shared symbolic–mythic substrate, these dots come to form meaningful visions. [In Peru, the related but larger San Pedro cactus, which contains similar entheogens, is used by *curanderos* (indigenous healers).]

The use of peyote in North America is different from the use of other powerful psychoactive substances as it is ingested by all the congregants, not just religious specialists, such as the use of *Datura*. A second major feature of peyote is that it is not simply nonaddictive; it is anti-addictive. Peyote is so incredibly vile tasting that one has to have a strong spiritual need to ingest it, and after the first experience, the body so dislikes it that again one has to have a spiritual need rather than a physical one to force it down one's gullet. I have never come across anyone who has ever taken peyote for recreational (in the common meaning of the word) purposes, at least more than once.

Yet peyote, along with every sacred substance, except tobacco (so far), used in Native traditions throughout the Americas, in effect, is listed on the U.N. Convention on Psychotropic Substances (1971), even though none meets the primary requirement of creating "a state of dependence." What is striking is that alcohol is not on the list, even though it does meet the requirements for being listed. The Convention criminalizes virtually every Native traditionalist from Mexico through South America and many Native Americans north of Mexico. It functions as an attack on indigenous religions worldwide in support of the major proselytizing religions—Christianity, Islam, and Buddhism—as well as in support of the alcohol industry. Peyote used in a ritual setting has been proven to be highly effective at removing a desire for alcohol and as a cure for alcoholism.

From the archeological standpoint, based on findings in caves and rock shelters in Texas, peyote has been used in a ritual setting for over three thousand years. Undoubtedly, its use would go back even further in time. The traditional religious use of peyote was briefly discussed in Chapter 2 with regard to the Cora, Huichol, and Tarahumara traditions of northern Mexico, all of which ritually dance after ingesting peyote, either fresh or grated and made into a beverage. Their rituals using peyote are probably of considerable antiquity.

Reservation life in conjunction with the near extermination of the bison was particularly onerous to Plains traditions. Hunting the bison, along with raiding, was central to male occupations and essential to the major ceremonies. Native people, if they wish to be employed on ranches and elsewhere, were required to adopt the Western week and calendar, and this considerably impinged on the nature of traditional ceremonies. Native leaders were searching for new ways to maintain their cultural identity and spiritual needs.

Peyote is indigenous to the Rio Grande valley, and the Comanche and the Kiowa may have been aware of its ritual use in northern Mexico before being restricted to reservations. Of the two persons most responsible for the early development of Peyote Religion among Native peoples in North America north of the Rio Grande River, one had already taken peyote in Mexico in the 1880s for medicinal purpose. Quanah Parker, a Comanche leader, whose mother was Euro-American, was responsible for developing and spreading Peyote rituals among tribes in Oklahoma. Second in importance was the Caddo, John Wilson, also of mixed heritage, who developed his own version of Peyote ritual as early as the late 1880s and also attracted many adherents. The religion rapidly spread to reservations throughout the United States and Canada.

Factors involved in the spread include the greater communication among Native leaders due to the mixing of peoples from different traditions at the boarding schools. Particularly important in the early years was the Carlisle Indian School at Carlisle, Pennsylvania, and the Haskell Institute in Lawrence, Kansas. Modern forms of communication and travel, particularly the postal service, the telegraph, and the railroads also enhanced the spread of Peyote Religion.

The different versions of Peyote Religion reflect a mixture of traditional and Christian elements that varies from one version to another. Quanah Parker's version is called the Half Moon ceremony, based on the shape of the altar, or Tipi way (because it is held in tipis). It is the least Christian and the Bible is not used. The theological focus is on the traditional Native deities with an emphasis on Mother Earth. The version of John Wilson, who was a Catholic, is called the Big Moon or Cross Fire ceremony and, varying from one ritual leader to another, has invocations to Jesus, has baptism, and uses the Bible as a sacred artifact in its rituals. Members of either tradition, if they wish, will also take part in more traditional Native ceremonies or more normative forms of Christianity. The most Christian version, which spread among the Winnebago, first in Minnesota and then Wisconsin, was that of John Rave. Following the usual Christian intolerance for other traditions at that time, those who followed this version were required to give up their sacred bundles and all participation in traditional Winnebago rituals. While the Christian elements continued, as we shall see below with the extract from the autobiography of Mountain Wolf Woman, the injunction against other forms of spirituality did not.

Regardless of the tradition, the outlines of the ceremonies are actually similar. They take place over a single night and are usually held on weekends. The use of a psychoactive substance allows an intensity of experience that collapses the usual four-day rituals into a single night. Thus, this modified form of traditional religion accords with the work week of the dominant culture. Because the ritual paraphernalia—a special fan and gourd rattle, a carved staff, a whistle, and a small water drum, as described in the previous section—carried by the ritual leaders, called "roadman," are highly portable, the rituals can be put on virtually anywhere. Some forms prefer a tipi, others use a more permanent round house, but the ritual can be put on in rooms in modern buildings.

A general outline of the ritual is as follows. (For details, see La Barre in *Further Reading*.) Both men and women sit on the ground or floor in a circle, with the roadman facing east, as happens with most Native American rituals. The roadman will lay out the paraphernalia described above and prepare the drum. A large peyote button is placed on a bed of sage in the middle of the altar. This is called Grandfather or Father Peyote, and it will remain in place throughout the ritual. A person called "cedarman" will prepare the fire and throw cedar leaflets on it, thus creating purifying smoke. Tobacco and fixings for making cigarettes are passed around in a sunwise direction. The congregants will make themselves cigarettes to smoke during the opening prayer by the roadman. A bag of dried peyote buttons, usually from Texas, is incensed by cedarman and passed around the circle; alternatively, a tea made from peyote might be used. The congregants take four buttons at a time. The congregants sing songs as the drum is passed around the circle well into the night, with peyote passed around every so often. People usually take about twelve buttons in total, although some take considerably more. At midnight, water is passed around the circle, and there is a break in the ceremony, with people stepping outside. People return and prayers become more spontaneous, as the individuals are moved to speak or sing. There may be special rituals for healing at this time. At the end of the night, the roadman sings the Dawn Song, and the "water woman" comes in and passes water around. She then brings in a simple meal of traditional foods. Some last songs are sung and the ceremony comes to an end. After the ritual paraphernalia is put away, everyone leaves the ritual space and takes part in a feast.

Some groups hold monthly ceremonies; others do it more spontaneously. A Peyote ceremony can be put on for several reasons: to give thanks for a safe journey, for recovery from sickness, to celebrate a birth or to name a baby, for healing, and, for some groups, to memorialize the dead. Some traditions hold Peyote ceremonies during Christian festivals, as Christmas and Easter, or at Thanksgiving and New Year.

Peyote ritual fulfills all of the expectations and meets virtually all of the needs of traditional Native ceremonies but in a more compact mode. Given the ingestion of a psychoactive substance in a powerful ritual context, it is not unusual for the participants to have visions. It is the intense spiritual experience, the immediacy, and the reality of it, along with the enhanced sense of community, that gives the ritual its great power. The Winnebago woman, Mountain Wolf Woman, intensely remembers a ritual, the Christian version of Rave, she attended many decades before she narrated her autobiography. First she had a dark vision symbolizing the destruction of her people and culture; then within the vision, she had an epiphany:

> Then I saw Jesus standing there. I saw that He had one hand raised high. The right hand, high in the air. I saw that He was standing there. Whatever He was doing, I was to do also. I was to pray, I thought. I stood up. Though I was in the midst of all those people my thought were not on that. I stood up because I saw Jesus. I will pray to him, I thought. I stood up and raised my arm. I prayed. I asked for a good life, – thanking God who gave me life. This I did. And as the drum was beating, my body shook in time to the beat. I was unaware of it. I was just very contented. I never knew such pleasure as this. There was a sensation of great joyousness. . . .
>
> Then the drummers stopped singing. When they reached the end of the song, they stopped. Then I sat down on the ground. I knew that when I ate peyote that they were using something holy. That way is directed towards God. Nothing else on earth is holy . . . if someone sees something holy at a peyote meeting, that is really true. They are able to understand things concerning God. I understand that this religion is holy. It is directed towards God. I even saw Jesus![11]

After the Peyote Religion began to spread, it was not long before the dominant culture tried to stamp it out by making it illegal. By 1918, several states had passed laws against it and Congress was considering similar legislation. With the advice of the anthropologist James Mooney of the Smithsonian Institution, the leaders of the religion incorporated themselves in 1918 on the model of Protestant churches as the Native American Church of North America (so as to include Canada). Since that time, the various governments have tried over and over again to put an end to the religion. For a history of the religion's spread and its immense legal history, see Omer Stewart in *Further Reading*.

The most egregious recent case was the U.S. Supreme Court's decision in *Employment Division v. Smith* in 1990. Two members of the Native

American Church were fired as drug counselors because they took part in Native American Church rituals, in that they were using peyote, which the U.N. Convention lists as a drug. This was ludicrous in that the Native American Church has been notably successful in moving Native people away from alcohol and drug abuse. The majority opinion, written by Justice Scalia, held that their right to the free exercise of religion was superseded because they had violated valid laws, whether sensible or not was irrelevant. Laws, any laws, had priority over freedom of religion.

Congress was outraged and passed the Religious Freedom Restoration Act (RFRA) in 1993. The House passed the bill unanimously and the Senate passed it 97–3. Certainly Congress had made its will that Native people can now have freedom of religion abundantly clear. Yet, the Supreme Court rebuked Congress in 1997 in *City of Boerne v. Flores*. Although the case had nothing to do with Native religion, what is important is that the Supreme Court struck down the law, stating that Congress had stepped beyond their power of enforcement.

But the Supreme Court seems to have reversed itself in 2006 in *Gonzales v. O Centro Espirita Beneficente União do Vegetal*. This case concerned the use by a Brazilian religion of *hoasca* tea (ayahuasca, a very powerful psychoactive vine that is common to most Amazonian religious traditions). U.S. Customs had seized 30 gallons of the tea. The Church claimed the right to use it under RFRA. A unanimous decision written by Chief Justice Roberts found that the government was unable to detail the State's compelling interest in barring religious usage of hoasca under the strict scrutiny that the RFRA demands of such regulations. The case was sent back to the lower court. As of this writing, that trial had not yet been held. It seems that the Supreme Court now accepts the RFRA, and that may yet help Native people in the United States obtain religious freedom, especially with regard to peyote.

EPILOGUE

When I first became interested in Native religious traditions a half century ago, the common wisdom in the dominant culture was that these were traditions of the past, not the present. It was only when I began teaching related subjects over three decades ago that Native students seeking elders who were continuing the traditions in secret informed me that the traditions were not dead. With them, I came to meet elders who carried on traditional healing rituals and were teaching these traditions to youths to carry on after them. I came into contact with young Native families who were seeking to return to a traditional spiritual life, one denied them on the Christian missionary-controlled reserves. I became involved with an urban Native-way school that was bringing these values into the lives of Native children. And I met elders from different traditions as I organized an Elders Conference at my university that subsequently was taken up by an urban Native friendship center. Since that time much has changed in these regards, as outlined in Chapter 2.

There are now a number of Native-way schools and colleges. Native ceremonies are taking place openly, and secularized activities, such as powwows, are returning to their spiritual roots in a thoroughly modern form. The boarding schools have been closed; on one large reserve, the burned-out hulk of the school is left standing as a memorial to its horrid past. Spirit Lodges and other rituals are taking place on reserves where once forbidden. In urban areas, there are healing circles attached to health centers and elders working with various government services.

On many reservations and reserves, although most people are Christians, there is tolerance for those returning to the traditional religion, and some take part in both. In some areas near Native reserves, the Catholic churches have incorporated aspects of Native religion, such as the Sacred Pipe, into their own rituals. Two decades ago, I took part in a conference of Protestant church leaders and Native elders, with the church leaders, especially Native ministers, fully supporting the revitalization of Native traditions with no expectation of the incorporation of Christian elements. All took part in a Spirit Lodge.

This is not to imply that problems do not continue. On some reservations, there is deep-felt antagonism between Christians and traditionalists, which can flare into violence. In some of the revitalized modes of traditional religion, the revitalization took place one or two generations ago, and the youth feel that the tradition is overemphasizing a socioeconomic past to which return is impossible. Some long-standing traditions, the result of reforms of traditional religions a couple of centuries ago, may again need reform to be viable in the modern world.

There is also the phenomenon of casinos. In the United States, casinos have brought prosperity to many reservations; indeed, new reservations have been created for the express purpose of building a casino. The money from the casinos has led to the erection of beautiful museums of Native traditions, but the casinos have also created a cultural climate that perceives the traditions as belonging to the past and not appropriate to the present. The values of the casinos, especially those connected to organized crime, and traditional Native values are not the same, and this can lead to conflict.

In South America, the recent election of presidents with a Native or part-Native background has led to a new recognition and legitimization of Native religious traditions; this is a possibility for Mexico and Mesoamerica. Thus far, in Mexico the distant Native past is celebrated as the foundation of the country, but living Native peoples themselves live precarious lives. The insurrection in Chiapas has led to increased awareness of—but not the solution to—the problems of the Mayans there; problems that were to a degree resolved in Yucatan because of an insurrection many decades earlier.

In the United States and Canada, aspects of the governments have not given up on eradicating Native religious traditions, although the U.S. Congress has recently been supportive. In many prisons, particularly state and provincial ones, even where most prisoners are Native, there is still no fundamental right for Native people to practice their religion or for Native elders to provide succor. The courts continue to apply concepts of religion that are pertinent to Western but not Native religions and often end up denying freedom of religion to Native traditionalists. Despite regulations to the contrary, customs officials routinely confiscate sacred items from Natives as they travel to ceremonies. More recently, political correctness has been used to stop basic Native religious practices, such as smoking the Sacred Pipe during rituals, on university campuses or ritually hunting animals perceived by urbanites as cute rather than as divine.

Despite all these continuing and new difficulties, over the course of my life I have witnessed a widespread resurgence and flourishing of Native traditional religion. I see no reason to assume that this will not continue. But that is a matter for Native youth. On that topic, Jason Baird Jackson recorded part of an oration given by Newman Littlebear before the Ribbon Dance at The Duck Creek (Oklahoma) Ceremonial Ground's Green Corn Ceremony on June 28, 1996:

> How much longer can all of our ceremonials
>   continue on?
> I say to the young generation
>   it is in your hands.
> How well you respond
>   to what we still have,
>   that is the answer.
> How well you learn,
>   pay attention.
> Because some
>   of us people
>   had a little interest when we were young
>   we are still able to continue on
>   to this modern day.
> There are many things in this life
>   in this modern time that can distract you
>   gets our attention
>   and causes us
>   to forget about our ways
>   our way of life
>   that have been going on for so long.
> But nowadays we talk about it
>   we gather up
>   have meetings
>   and discuss
>   what we still have
>   and try to
>   find ways
>   that we can continue on.[1]

NOTES

CHAPTER 1

1. Lawrence C. Wroth, *The Voyages of Giovanni da Varrazzano, 1524–1528* (New Haven: Yale University Press, 1970), 141.

2. "American Indian Spiritual Traditions Exploited and Abused at New Age Workshops," *American Indian Review* Spring, no. 10 (1995), http://www.american-indian-review.co.uk

CHAPTER 2

1. Charles Hudson, *The Southeastern Indians* (Knoxville: University of Tennessee Press, 1976), 3.

2. The material on the marriage ritual was extracted from my *Through the Earth Darkly: Female Spirituality in Comparative Perspective* (New York: Continuum, 1997), chapter 9.

3. Thomas E. Mails, *Fools Crow* (New York: Doubleday, 1979), 45.

4. Peter Matthiessen, *In the Spirit of Crazy Horse* (New York: Viking Press, 1983), 37.

CHAPTER 3

1. A. Irving Hallowell, "Ojibwa Ontology, Behavior, and World View," in *Culture in History: Essays in Honor of Paul Radin*, ed. Stanley Diamond (New York: Columbia University Press, 1960), 19–52.

2. Rigoberta Menchú, *Me Llamo Rigoberta Menchú y Asi Me Nació la Conciencia* (México DF: Siglo XXI, 1985), 13; as found in translation in Ronald Wright, *Time Among the Maya: Travels in Belize, Guatemala, and Mexico* (Toronto: Penguin Books, 1989), 253.

3. *Walum Olum or Red Score: The Migration Legend of the Lenni Lenape or Delaware Indians* (Indianapolis: Indiana Historical Society, 1954).

4. Arthur Solomon, *Songs for the People: Teachings on the Natural Way* (Toronto: NC Press, 1990), 16.

5. John (Fire) Lame Deer and Richard Erdoes, *Lame Deer: Seeker of Visions* (New York: Simon & Shuster, 1972; Pocket Book 1976 edition), 4–6.

6. Ruth M. Underhill, *Papago Woman* (Prospect Heights, IL: Waveland Press, 1979), 46–47.

7. Barry Holsten Lopez, *Giving Birth to Thunder, Sleeping with His Daughter: Coyote Builds North America* (New York: Avon Books, 1977), 181.

CHAPTER 4

1. A respondent's statement in Carrie E. Garrow, "Gambling, Factions, and Sovereignty: A Pathway to Injustice" (honors thesis, Dartmouth College, 1991), 65–66.

CHAPTER 5

1. June Helm, *Prophecy and Power among the Dogrib Indians* (Lincoln: University of Nebraska Press, 1994), 83.

2. Data for the Navajo ritual, to a large part, are from the work by the ethnomusicologist, Charlotte Frisbie, *Kinaaldá: A Study of the Navajo Girl's Puberty Ceremony* (Middletown, CT: Wesleyan University, 1967). Data for the Apache ritual are synthesized from Morris Edward Opler, *An Apache Life-Way: The Economic, Social, and Religious Institutions of the Chiricahua Indians* (New York: Cooper Square, 1965 [1941]), 82–134; Keith H. Basso, "The Gift of Changing Woman," *Bulletin of the Bureau of American Ethnology* 196 (1966): 113–73 (regarding Cibecue Apache menarche ritual); Rico Leffanta, "Sunrise Ceremony," http://www.geocities.com/coqrico/apachedance.html (regarding Fort Apache Indian Reservation); and Ernestine Cody, "The Sunrise Dance: *Na'ii'ees*, The Apache Woman's Puberty Ceremony," http://www.peabody.Harvard.edu/maria/sunrisedance.html

3. Clo Mingo, "From the Research: Kinaaldá," reprint from *HSC–Women & Change*, 1, no. 2, in *Newsletter of the New Mexico Geriatric Education Center* October (1999): 3–4.

4. H. Henrietta Stockel, *Women of the Apache Nation: Voices of Truth* (Reno, NV: University of Nevada Press, 1991), 75.

5. There are two major sources for this section. For the traditional Green Corn Ceremony, it is the classic work by John R. Swanton, "Religious Beliefs and Medical Practices of the Creek Indians," in *Forty-second Annual Report of the Bureau of American Ethnology, 1924–25* (Washington, DC: Bureau of American Ethnology, 1928), 473–672. For contemporary practices, there is the excellent chapter by Ananda Sattwa, "Green Corn Ceremony," in *American Indian Religious Traditions: An Encyclopedia*, ed. Suzanne J. Crawford and Dennis F. Kelly (Santa Barbara, CA: ABC-CLIO, 2005), I, 350–5.

6. Mary Pierpoint, "Stomp Dance is Social Dance for Everyone," Indian Country Today, June 28, 2000. http://www.indiancountry.com/content.cfm?id=2528

7. *Encyclopedia of North American Indians*, s.v. "Creek (Muskogee)" (by Kenneth W. McIntosh), http://www.college.hmco.com/history/readerscomp/naind/html/na_000107_entries.htm

CHAPTER 6

1. Materials for this section, but not the interpretations, are from Gene Weltfish, *The Lost Universe: Pawnee Life and Culture* (New York: Basic Books, 1965; repr., Lincoln, NE: University of Nebraska Press, 1977) and James R. Murie, *Ceremonies of the Pawnee*, 2 vols. Ed. by Douglas R. Parks (Washington, DC: Smithsonian Institution Press, 1981). Both books need to be used with caution, given that the material was collected long after many of the rituals ceased to be practiced. But Weltfish's work has serious flaws. Although the author is female, it is highly androcentric, often discounting the religious role of women in contradiction of her own narrative. Second, the author, an anthropologist, seems to have little understanding of Native religion, assuming, for example, that "sweat lodge" is not a religious ritual. She uses Christian terminology for ritual leaders, for example, calling bundle-keepers sometimes "priests" and sometimes "ministers," while calling the ritual leaders of the hunt, "chiefs." Finally, she adds a monotheistic overlay to her presentation of Pawnee theology as well as Genesis language and concepts to the creation myths, something Parks does not do.

2. This section is a truncated version of similar material in my *Through the Earth Darkly*. For the early history of the Nitsitapi, see John C. Ewers, "The Horse in Blackfoot Indian Culture," *Bureau of American Ethnology Bulletin* 159 (1955). The following discussion is based, in order of importance, on the following publications: Beverly Hungry Wolf, *The Ways of My Grandmothers* (New York: William Morrow, 1980); Walter McClintock, *The Old North Trail: Life, Legends & Religion of the Blackfeet Indians* (London: Macmillan, 1910)—McClintock was adopted by a Blackfoot elder and initiated into rituals during the last quarter of the nineteenth century for the expressed purpose of enlightening Euro-Americans about Blackfoot religion; Ben Calf Robe, *Siksika': A Blackfoot Legacy* (Invermere, British Columbia: Good Medicine Books, 1979); George Bird Grinnell, *Blackfoot Lodge Tales: The Story of a Prairie People* (New York: C. Scribner's Sons, 1892); the monographs of Clark Wissler, based on the formal ethnology of the early twentieth century, were not relied on. Of importance are an 1897 manuscript by Robert Nathaniel Wilson, who spent most of his life on the Peigan and Blood Reserves, "Ethnographical Notes on the Blackfoot 'Sundance,'" and tapes recorded in 1969 and 1974 by George First Rider of the Blood Reserves, who was born in 1904—both sources in the archives of the Glenbow–Alberta Museum.

3. McClintock, *The Old North Trail*, 80–81.

4. In the 1970s, Siksika elders allowed a film, "Okan," to be made to record the ritual, except for the esoteric parts; this film is in the keeping of the Glenbow–Alberta Museum and not for public distribution.

5. Hungry Wolf, *Ways of My Grandmothers*, 34–39.

6. Ibid., 74–81.

CHAPTER 7

1. Gloria Cranmer Webster, "The Contemporary Potlatch," in *The Enduring Kwakiutl Potlatch*, ed. Aldona Jonaitis (Vancouver: Douglas & McIntyre, 1991), 227–48. The description of the potlatch is extracted from this article. Readers are encouraged to read the article to receive a fuller account of a typical potlatch.

2. Canada's Digital Collections, Potlatch, http://collections.ic.gc.ca/kwak wakawakw/ potlatch.htm (accessed August 4, 2006).

3. Hudson Webster, "Spirituality," http://www.nuuchahnulth.org/culture/spirituality/ culture_j_hudson_webster.html (accessed August 4, 2006).

4. "Makah Whaling Tradition," http://www.makah.com/whalingtradition.html (accessed August 4, 2006).

5. Paul Sullivan, *Globe and Mail*, May 22, 1999, D2.

6. David Hicks, "Save the Whales (for the Makah)," World Council of Whalers, http://www.worldcouncilofwhalers.com/publications/newsletters/6.htm#save (accessed August 4, 2006).

7. Canadian Press, March 10, 2006 (from its Web site).

CHAPTER 8

1. This section in large part is abstracted from my "'Sweat Lodge': A Northern Native American Ritual for Communal Shamanic Trance," *Temenos: Studies in Comparative Religion* 26 (1990): 85–94. The description is based on Edward Benton-Banai, *The Mishomis Book: The Voice of the Ojibway* (Saint Paul, MN: Indian Country Press, 1979), Chapter 12 "Sweat Lodge." The analysis is based on my own experience.

2. "Therapeutic Temazcal (Traditional Indigenous Steam Bath)," http://www. hotelhaciendaloslaureles.com/english/temascal.html (August 4, 2006).

3. From Claude E. Schaeffer, "Blackfoot Shaking Tent" (Glenbow Museum Occasional Paper 5, Calgary, Alberta, 1969), 4–5.

4. Jennifer S.H. Brown and Robert Brightman, *The Orders of the Dreamed: George Nelson on Cree and Northern Ojibwa Religion and Myth, 1823* (Winnipeg, Manitoba: University of Manitoba Press, 1988), 102–107.

5. Diamond Jenness, "The Ojibwa Indians of Parry Island, Their Social and Religious Life" (National Museum of Canada Bulletin 78, Ottawa, Ontario, 1935), 68.

6. William K. Powers, *Yuwipi* (Lincoln, NE: University of Nebraska Press, 1982).

7. This can be seen in the descriptions of late-nineteenth-century rituals. As examples, see the following works published in the *Anthropological Papers of the American Museum of Natural History*, vol. 16, part 4 (1919): Pliney Earle Goddard, "Notes on the Sun Dance of the Sarsi"; Alanson Skinner, "The Sun Dance of the Plains Cree"; Pliney Earle Goddard, "Notes on the Sun Dance of the Cree in Alberta"; W.D. Wallis, "The Sun Dance of the Canadian Dakota"; and Alanson Skinner, "Notes on the Sun Dance of the Sisseton Dakota."

8. Carl Starkloff, *The People of the Center: American Indian Religion and Christianity* (New York: Seabury Press, 1974), 133.

9. Flyingheart2, "Why We Dance," October 18, 2004, http://www.powwows.com/ gathering/articles.php?action=viewarticle&artid=1

10. Joseph D. McGuire, "Pipes and Smoking Customs of the American Aborigines, Based on Materials in the U.S. National Museum," *Annual Report of the Smithsonian Institution 1897* I (1899): 351–645/551–552.

11. Nancy Oestreich Lurie, ed. *Mountain Wolf Woman, Sister of Crashing Thunder: The Autobiography of a Winnebago Indian* (Ann Arbor, MI: University of Michigan Press, 1961), 42.

EPILOGUE

1. Jason Baird Jackson, *Yuchi Ceremonial Life: Performance, Meaning, and Tradition in a Contemporary American Indian Community* (Lincoln, NE: University of Nebraska Press, 2003), 106–7.

FURTHER READING

PROLOGUE

To keep this book to a manageable size and accepting that an introduction can but suggest the richness of a religious tradition, let alone many interconnected traditions, a number of important topics pertinent to the study of Native North American religions have not been covered. Those who have particular interests or wish to continue with a more comprehensive work may wish to consult the encyclopedias on Native American religion that have been appearing. In particular, readers are recommended to a highly readable, comprehensive compendium of articles: Suzanne J. Crawford and Dennis F. Kelley, ed. *American Indian Religious Traditions: An Encyclopedia*. 3 vols. (Santa Barbara: ABC-CLIO, 2005).

CHAPTER 1

The following books are suggested as important resources for understanding the inner fundamental aspects of Native religious traditions as discussed in the chapter:

McClintock, Walter. *The Old North Trail: Life, Legends & Religion of the Blackfeet Indians*. Lincoln, NE: University of Nebraska Press, [1910] 1968.

Horse Capture, George, ed. *The Seven Visions of Bull Lodge, As Told by His Daughter, Garter Snake*. Lincoln, NE: University of Nebraska Press, 1992. First published 1980 by Bison Books.

Radin, Paul. *The Autobiography of a Winnebago Indian*. New York: Dover Publications, [1920] 1963.

Radin, Paul. *The Road of Life and Death: A Ritual Drama of the American Indians*. Princeton, NJ: Princeton University Press, 1945.

Lurie, Nancy Oestrich, ed. *Mountain Wolf Woman, Sister of Crashing Thunder: The Autobiography of a Winnebago Indian*. Ann Arbor, MI: University of Michigan Press, 1961.

Underhill, Ruth M. *Papago Woman*. New York: Holt, Rinehart and Winston, 1979.

Simmons, Leo W., ed. *Sun Chief: The Autobiography of a Hopi Indian*. New Haven, CT: Yale University Press, 1942.

CHAPTER 2

An excellent introduction to the Native traditions of North America is Alice B. Kehoe's *North American Indians: A Comprehensive Account* (Englewood Cliffs, NJ: Prentice Hall, 1981). Also very useful, if read with care as some of the anthropological theories are dated, is Carl Waldman, *Atlas of the North American Indian* (New York: Facts on File Publications, 1985). A brief compendium of essays on the history of Native religious traditions will be found in Joel W. Martin, *The Land Looks After Us: A History of Native American Religion* (New York: Oxford University Press, 2001).

For northern Athapaskan-speaking traditions, see June Helm, *Prophecy and Power among the Dogrib Indians* (Lincoln, NE: University of Nebraska Press, 1994). A northeast tradition is covered in the following work, although the reader should take into account the dated nature of the study, as is evident in the belittling wording of the subtitle: Frank G. Speck, *Naskapi: The Savage Hunters of the Labrador Peninsula* (Norman, OK: University of Oklahoma Press, 1935). For the western Great Lakes, see Paul Radin, *The Winnebago Tribe* (37th Annual Report of the Bureau of Ethnology, Smithsonian Institution, Washington, DC, 1923; reprinted by the University of Nebraska Press, 1970). A comprehensive introduction to the area focusing on the early contact period is W. Vernon Kinietz, *The Indians of the Western Great Lakes, 1615–1760* (Ann Arbor, MI: University of Michigan Press, 1940). Finally, the following work is not limited to the precontact period, but it does provide a variety of interesting aspects that will flesh out the brief presentations: Elizabeth Tooker, ed. *Native North American Spirituality of the Eastern Woodlands: Sacred Myths, Dreams, Visions, Speeches, Healing Formulas, Rituals and Ceremonials* (New York: Paulist Press, 1979).

Because of the extensive, albeit skewed, writings from the Jesuit mission to the Huron, which both established contact and led to their demise from the smallpox that the missionaries brought with them, there have been major studies on Huron culture, including religion. A compendium of digested Jesuit writings will be found in Elizabeth Tooker, *An Ethnography of the Huron Indians, 1615–49* (Bureau of American Ethnology, Bulletin 190, Smithsonian Institution, Washington, DC, 1964). A *tour de force* on the subject is Bruce G. Trigger, *The Children of Aataentsic: A History of the Huron People to 1660* (Montreal, Quebec: McGill-Queen's University Press, 1976).

The best and most comprehensive study of the Southeastern cultures remains Charles Hudson, *The Southeastern Indians* (Knoxville, TN: University of Tennessee Press, 1976). For the Mississippian cultures, particularly illustrations of religious artifacts, see David S. Brose, James A. Brown, and David W. Penney, *Ancient Art of the American Woodland Indians* (New York: Harry N. Abrams, 1985). For Cahokia, see Timothy R. Pauketat and Thomas E. Emerson, *Cahokia: Domination and Ideology in the Mississippian World* (Lincoln, NE: University of Nebraska Press, 2000).

Because the adoption of the horse had a major impact on Plains traditions, studies of the religion in precontact times for that area are not feasible. Two general works, however, do capture essential aspects of these traditions that are far older than the shift to horse nomadism: Howard L. Harrod, *Renewing the World: Plains Indian Religion and Morality* (Tucson, AZ: University of Arizona Press, 1987); and Lee Irwin, *The Dream Seekers: Native American Visionary Traditions of the Great Plains* (Norman, OK: University of Oklahoma Press, 1994).

There are a number of books on Northwest Coast cultures, particularly renditions of myths. Two early works by ethnographers on specific traditions, including discussions of religion, are Aurel Krause, *The Tlingit Indians*, trans. Erna Gunther (Seattle, WA: University of Washington Press, 1956; original title, *Die Tlingit-Indianer*, 1885) and Franz Boas, *Kwakiutl Ethnography*, ed. and abr. Helen Codere (Chicago: University of Chicago Press, 1966; from manuscripts based on fieldwork carried out in the 1880s).

For the Pueblo traditions of the Southwest, the studies that best reflect the continuation of precontact religion are those of the Zuni and the Hopi. For the former, see Ruth L. Bunzel, *Zuni Ceremonialism* (Albuquerque, NM: University of New Mexico Press, 1992; reprint of 1932 edition) as well as a superb rendition of contemporary Zuni understanding in Barbara Tedlock, *The Beautiful and the Dangerous: Dialogues with Zuni Indians* (New York: Penguin Books, 1992). The best book on Hopi religion, despite its seeming limited scope from the title, remains Armin W. Geertz and Michael Lomatuway'ma, *Children of Cottonwood: Piety and Ceremonialism in Hopi Indian Puppetry* (Lincoln, NE: University of Nebraska Press, 1987). See also Armin W. Geertz, *Hopi Indian Altar Iconography* (Leiden: E. J. Brill, 1986) and Mischa Titiev, *Old Oraibi: A Study of the Hopi Indians of Third Mesa* (Albuquerque, NM: University of New Mexico Press, 1992; reprint of the 1944 edition) as well as Simmons, *Sun Chief*, discussed above with regard to Chapter 1. The many cultures of California are outlined in A. L. Kroeber, *Handbook of the Indians of California* (Bureau of American Ethnology, Bulletin 78, Smithsonian Institution, Washington, DC, 1925; reprinted by Dover, 1976).

There is a vast literature on the religions of Mesoamerica; many, particularly with regard to the Maya, are out of date, as discussed in the text. A brief but excellent introduction will be found in David Carrasco, *Religions of Mesoamerica: Cosmovision and Ceremonial Centers* (San Francisco: HarperSanFrancisco, 1990). Specific to the Huichol mentioned in the chapter is Kathleen Berrin, ed. *The Art of the Huichol Indians* (New York: Harry N. Abrams, 1978); this book has excellent articles on the religion of the Huichol and is a superb compendium of art arising from the ritual use of peyote. For the culture and religion of precontact Puerto Rico, see Jesse Walter Fewkes, *The Aborigines of Porto Rico and Neighboring Islands* (New York: Johnson Reprint, 1970; originally part of the 25th Annual Report of the U.S. Bureau of Ethnology, 1903–04).

Concerning the effects on religion following contact, the great debate at the Spanish court is analyzed in Lewis Hanke, *Aristotle and the American Indians: A Study of Race Prejudice in the Modern World* (Bloomington, IN: Indiana University Press, 1959). The early interaction in the French-controlled area is well discussed in Alfred Goldsworthy Bailey, *The Conflict of European and Eastern Algonkian Cultures 1504–1700*, 2nd ed. (Toronto: University of Toronto Press, 1969). The story of the Shawnee Prophet is told in R. David Edmund, *The Shawnee Prophet* (Lincoln, NE: University of Nebraska Press, 1983).

An excellent book on the Prophet Dances of the Plateau is Robert H. Ruby and John A. Brown, *Dreamer-Prophets of the Columbia Plateau: Smohalla and Skolaskin* (Norman, OK: University of Oklahoma Press, 1989). James Mooney studied the Ghost Dance while it was still quite active and interviewed many of the participants; his book on the subject remains a classic: *The Ghost-Dance Religion and the Sioux Outbreak of 1890* (Chicago: University of Chicago Press, 1965; reprint of Fourteenth Annual Report of the Bureau of Ethnology, 1892–93). Black Elk's Catholicism has been the subject of several articles by Clyde Holler and his book, *Black Elk's Religion: The Sun Dance and Lakota Catholicism* (Syracuse, NY: Syracuse University Press, 1995).

The best book on American Indian Movement (AIM) remains Peter Matthiessen, *In the Spirit of Crazy Horse* (New York: Viking Press, 1983). Other suggested readings relevant to the revitalization will be mentioned with regard to specific traditions or rituals for subsequent chapters. A good study of the theft and confiscation of Northwest Coast ritual items will be found in Douglas Cole, *Captured Heritage: The Scramble for Northwest Coast Artifacts* (Vancouver: UBC Press, 1985).

CHAPTER 3

Many of the topics covered in this chapter will be found more fully developed as well as in a comparative setting in my *The Deities are Many: A Polytheistic Theology* (Albany, NY: State University of New York Press, 2005).

A highly readable version of the Nanabozho myth-cycle, one generalized from several versions and written for children, can be found in Dorothy M. Reid, *Tales of Nanabozho* (Toronto: Oxford University Press, 1963). An analysis of the underwater spirit will be found in Theresa S. Smith, *The Island of the Anishnaabeg: Thunderers and Water Monsters in the Traditional Ojibwe Life-World* (Moscow, ID: University of Idaho Press, 1995). The Navajo myth summarized will be found in detail in Paul G. Zolbrod, *Diné Bahanè: The Navajo Creation Story* (Albuquerque, NM: University of New Mexico Press, 1984).

The development of Lakota theological thought can be traced through the conversations recorded by James R. Walker between 1896 and 1914 in his *Lakota Belief and Ritual*, ed. Raymond J. De Mallie and Elaine A. Jahner (Lincoln, NE: University of Nebraska Press, 1980). It is suggested that readers note the age of the various speakers to perceive the generational differences. The most accurate and readable translation of the *Popol Vuh* to date is the one by Dennis Tedlock (New York: Simon & Schuster, 1996).

A thorough discussion of the animal spirits of a single tradition will be found in Joseph Epes Brown, *Animals of the Soul: Sacred Animals of the Oglala Sioux* (Rockport, MA: Element, 1992). A work that successfully introduces the living Zuni understanding of the sacred, including the dead, is Barbara Tedlock, *The Beautiful and the Dangerous: Dialogues with the Zuni Indians* (New York: Penguin Books, 1992).

Perhaps the best rendition of Native myths of the culture hero/trickster is Barry Holston Lopez, *Giving Birth to Thunder, Sleeping with His Daughter: Coyote Builds North America* (New York: Avon Books, 1977). This book is not a translation of stories, nor full myths; rather it is a sympathetic retelling by a master English-language storyteller. The stories are from many traditions, but all the mythic figures–Coyote,

Crow, Spider, and Hare–are transformed into Coyote, which is quite appropriate given that they are all shape-shifters. The Anishnabe Nanabozho myths can be found in *Tales of Nanabozho* mentioned above. Many versions of Raven myths have been published; one of the most digestible will be found in Ralph Maud, ed. *The Porcupine Hunter and Other Stories: The Original Tsimshian Texts of Henry Tate* (Vancouver: Talon Books, 1993).

CHAPTER 4

The most important book on the modern Midewiwin is Edward Benton-Banai, *The Mishomis Book: The Voice of the Ojibway* (Saint Paul, MN: Indian Country Press, 1979). Written by the present-day ritual leader of the Midewiwin, the book is intended to be used in native-way schools, and the general science to be found within it would date to the author's own junior high-school education. Selwyn Dewdney, *The Sacred Scrolls of the Southern Ojibway* (Toronto: University of Toronto Press, 1975) is a useful compendium on the sacred scrolls and mythic aspects of the Midewiwin. Michael Angel, *Preserving the Sacred: Historical Perspectives on the Ojibwa Midewiwin* (Winnipeg: University of Manitoba Press, 2002) analyzes the works written on the Midewiwin but is seemingly oblivious of the Midewiwin being a living tradition rather than an historical one.

The classic text on the Longhouse Religion as an example of revitalization is Anthony F. C. Wallace, *The Death and Rebirth of the Seneca* (New York: Alfred A. Knopf, 1970). Arthur C. Parker, *The Code of Handsome Lake, the Seneca Prophet*, first published in 1913, has been republished along with *The Constitution of the Five Nations* and other writings in William N. Fenton, ed. *Parker on the Iroquois* (Syracuse, NY: Syracuse University Press, 1968). Twentieth-century Longhouse ceremonies are described in Elisabeth Tooker, *The Iroquois Ceremonial of Midwinter* (Syracuse, NY: Syracuse University Press, 1970). William N. Fenton, *The False Faces of the Iroquois* (Norman, OK: University of Oklahoma Press, 1987) is the definitive work on the subject.

CHAPTER 5

Further information on Diné menarche rituals will be found in Chapter 10, if my *Through the Earth Darkly: Female Spirituality in Comparative Perspective* (New York: Continuum, 1997). In this work, there are other chapters concerning female spirituality with regard to the Anishnabe, the Hopi, and the Pikuni. There is also a relatively recent hour-long film (2000) by Lena Carr: *Kinaalda*.

The special herbal preparation for the Green Corn Dance and other medicines will be found in David Lewis, Jr., and Ann T. Jordan, *Creek Indian Medicine Ways: The Enduring Power of Mvskoke Religion* (Albuquerque, NM: University of New Mexico Press, 2002). Late-twentieth-century oratory and myths now being told during and around the Green Corn Dance and other related rituals will be found in Jason Baird Jackson, *Yuchi Ceremonial Life: Performance, Meaning, and Tradition in a Contemporary American Indian Community* (Lincoln, NE: University of Nebraska Press, 2003). The Cherokee version of the Green Corn Dance will be found in Frank G. Speck and Leonard Broom, *Cherokee Dance and Drama*, in collaboration with Will West Long (Norman, OK: University of Oklahoma Press, [1951] 1983). For the history of the stick-ball game, see Thomas Vennum, Jr. *American Indian Lacrosse: Little Brother of War* (Washington, DC: Smithsonian Institution Press, 1994).

CHAPTER 6

Full descriptions of the ceremonies discussed in the Pawnee section, along with many photographs of the relevant ritual items and bundles, will be found in James R. Murie, *Ceremonies of the Pawnee*, ed. Douglas R. Parks. 2 vols. (Washington, DC: Smithsonian Institution Press, 1981). The manuscript Parks wrote, whose mother was Pawnee, was completed in 1921, but sat unpublished for many decades.

Sources utilized in writing the section on the Nitsitapi included the following recommended works: Beverly Hungry Wolf, *The Ways of My Grandmothers* (New York: William Morrow, 1980); Walter McClintock, *The Old North Trail: Life, Legends & Religion of the Blackfeet Indians* (London: Macmillan, 1910)–McClintock was adopted by a Blackfoot elder and initiated into rituals during the last quarter of the nineteenth century for the expressed purpose of enlightening Euro-Americans about Blackfoot religion; and Ben Calf Robe, *Siksika': A Blackfoot Legacy* (Invermere, British Columbia: Good Medicine Books, 1979).

For the Cheyenne Sun Dance, see Peter J. Powell, *Sweet Medicine: The Continuing Role of the Sacred Arrows, the Sun Dance, and the Sacred Buffalo Hat in Northern Cheyenne History* (Norman, OK: University of Oklahoma Press, 1969). Powell provides a detailed account (245 pages, including photographs) of the Oxheheom; but as Powell, in his own words, is an Anglo-Catholic priest, he plays down the role of the Sacred Woman. For contrary views, see Karl H. Schlesier, *The Wolves of Heaven: Cheyenne Shamanism, Ceremonies, and Prehistoric Origins* (Norman, OK: University of Oklahoma Press, 1987).

CHAPTER 7

For a thorough analysis of one Northwest Coast Potlatch tradition of the past that can be recommended, see Sergei Kan, *Symbolic Immortality: The Tlingit Potlatch of the Nineteenth Century* (Washington, DC: Smithsonian Institution Press, 1989). Although prepared as an exhibition catalogue, Aldona Jonaitis, ed. *Chiefly Feasts: The Enduring Kwakiutl Potlatch* (Vancouver: Douglas & McIntyre, 1991) remains an excellent resource on the Potlatch, both past and present. It has superb articles, a large number of photographs of Potlatches, and, of course, illustrations of the best examples of Potlatch ritual paraphernalia to be found anywhere.

CHAPTER 8

For a brief but thorough introduction to the "Sweat Lodge," see Joseph Bruchac, *The Native American Sweat Lodge: History and Legends* (Freedom, CA: Crossing Press, 1993). The Lakota Yuwipi (binding) ritual is detailed in a readily digestible form, along with briefer but detailed descriptions of sweat lodge and fasting by William K. Powers, *Yuwipi: Vision & Experience in Oglala Ritual* (Lincoln, NE: University of Nebraska Press, 1982). A sympathetic account of the nineteenth-century northern Cree version of the Shaking Tent by a Euro-American trader living in Cree territory can be found in Jennifer S. H. Brown and Robert Brightman, *The Orders of the*

Dreamed: George Nelson on Cree and Northern Ojibwa Religion and Myth, 1823 (Winnipeg: University of Manitoba Press, 1988).

Two works on the Thirst Dance mentioned in the text are George Catlin, *O-kee-pa*, ed. John C. Ewers (New Haven, CT: Yale University Press, 1967) and Joseph G. Jorgensen, *The Sun Dance Religion: Power for the Powerless* (Chicago: University of Chicago Press, 1972). Detailed descriptions of ceremonies will be found in Fred W. Voget, *The Shoshoni-Crow Sun Dance* (Norman, OK: University of Oklahoma Press, 1984). The books by Ben Calf Robe and Peter Powell mentioned with regard to Chapter 6 provide descriptions of the Siksika Okan and the Cheyenne Thirst Dance, respectively.

For the dream dance drum, see Thomas Vennum, Jr. *The Ojibwa Dance Drum: Its History and Construction* (Washington, DC: Smithsonian Institution Press–Smithsonian Folklife Studies 2, 1982). For drums in general and other instruments, see Beverly Diamond, M. Sam Cronk, and Franziska von Rosen, *Visions of Sound: Musical Instruments of First Nation Communities in Northeastern America* (Waterloo, Ontario: Wilfrid Laurier Press, 1994). Several essays on a variety of topics concerning the powwow can be found in Clyde Ellis, Luke Eric Lassiter, and Gary W. Dunham, *Powwow* (Lincoln, NE: University of Nebraska Press, 2005).

Parts of the section on the Sacred Pipe are taken from my *Offering Smoke: The Sacred Pipe and Native American Religion* (Moscow, ID: University of Idaho Press, 1988) which has detailed material and analyses of many aspects of the Pipe.

Two books on the Huichol use of peyote are outstanding. Kathleen Berrin, ed. *The Art of the Huichol Indians* (New York: Harry N. Abrams, 1978) is a catalogue of an outstanding exhibition of art that is inspired by peyote ingestion and used in peyote rituals with many excellent articles, particularly one by Peter Furst. Barbara G. Myerhoff, *Peyote Hunt: The Sacred Journey of the Huichol Indians* (Ithaca, NY: Cornell University Press, 1974) provides an analysis of peyote in Huichol religion. Of the many books on the Native American Church, three books are particularly recommended. The definitive study originally published in 1938 and expanded over five editions is Weston La Barre, *The Peyote Cult*, 5th ed. (Norman, OK: University of Oklahoma Press, 1989). The best history is the thorough Omer C. Stewart, *Peyote Religion: A History* (Norman, OK: University of Oklahoma Press, 1987). The best analysis from the perspective of religious studies is the more recent Åke Hultkrantz, *The Attraction of Peyote: An Inquiry into the Basic Conditions for the Diffusion of the Peyote Religion in North America* (Stockholm: Almqvist & Wiksell International, 1997).

REFERENCES

Basso, Keith H. "The Gift of Changing Woman," *Bulletin of the Bureau of American Ethnology* 196 (1966): 113–73.

Benton-Banai, Edward. *The Mishomis Book: The Voice of the Ojibway*. Saint Paul, MN: Indian Country Press, 1979.

Brown, Jennifer S. H., and Robert Brightman. *The Orders of the Dreamed: George Nelson on Cree and Northern Ojibwa Religion and Myth, 1823*. Winnipeg: University of Manitoba Press, 1988.

Calf Robe, Ben. *Siksika': A Blackfoot Legacy*. Invermere, British Columbia: Good Medicine Books, 1979.

Ewers, John C. "The Horse in Blackfoot Indian Culture," *Bureau of American Ethnology Bulletin* 159 (1955).

Frisbie, Charlotte. *Kinaaldá: A Study of the Navaho Girl's Puberty Ceremony*. Middletown, CT: Wesleyan University, 1967.

Grinnell, George Bird. *Blackfoot Lodge Tales: The Story of a Prairie People*. New York: C. Scribner's Sons, 1892.

Hallowell, A. Irving. "Ojibwa Ontology, Behavior, and World View." In *Culture in History: Essays in Honor of Paul Radin*, edited by Stanley Diamond, 19–52. New York: Columbia University Press, 1960.

Helm, June. *Prophecy and Power among the Dogrib Indians*. Lincoln, NE: University of Nebraska Press, 1994.

Hudson, Charles. *The Southeastern Indians*. Knoxville, TN: University of Tennessee Press, 1976.

Hungry Wolf, Beverly. *The Ways of My Grandmothers*. New York: William Morrow, 1980.

Jackson, Jason Baird. *Yuchi Ceremonial Life: Performance, Meaning, and Tradition in a Contemporary American Indian Community*. Lincoln, NE: University of Nebraska Press, 2003.

Jenness, Diamond. *The Ojibwa Indians of Parry Island: Their Social and Religious Life*. Ottawa: National Museums of Canada Bulletins, No. 78, 1935.

Lame Deer, John (Fire), and Richard Erdoes. *Lame Deer, Seeker of Visions*. New York: Simon & Shuster, 1972.

Lopez, Barry Holston. *Giving Birth to Thunder, Sleeping with His Daughter: Coyote Builds North America*. New York: Avon Books, 1977.

Lurie, Nancy Oestreich, ed. *Mountain Wolf Woman, Sister of Crashing Thunder: The Autobiography of a Winnebago Indian*. Ann Arbor, MI: University of Michigan Press, 1961.

Mails, Thomas E. *Fools Crow*. New York, Doubleday, 1979.

Matthiessen, Peter. *In the Spirit of Crazy Horse*. New York: Viking Press, 1983.

McClintock, Walter. *The Old North Trail: Life, Legends & Religion of the Blackfeet Indians*. London: Macmillan, 1910.

McGuire, Joseph D. "Pipes and Smoking Customs of the American Aborigines, Based on Materials in the U.S. National Museum," *Annual Report of the Smithsonian Institution 1897* I (1899).

Mingo, Clo. "From the Research: Kinaaldá," *Newsletter of the New Mexico Geriatric Education Center*, October (1999): 3–4.

Murie, James R. *Ceremonies of the Pawnee*. Edited by Douglas R. Parks. 2 vols. Washington, DC: Smithsonian Institution Press, 1981.

Opler, Morris Edward. *An Apache Life-Way: The Economic, Social, and Religious Institutions of the Chiricahua Indians*. New York: Cooper Square, [1941] 1965.

Paper, Jordan. *Offering Smoke: The Sacred Pipe and Native American Religion*. Moscow, ID: University of Idaho Press, 1988.

———. " 'Sweat Lodge': A Northern Native American Ritual for Communal Shamanic Trance," *Temenos: Studies in Comparative Religion* 26 (1990): 85–94.

———. *Through the Earth Darkly: Female Spirituality in Comparative Perspective*. New York: Continuum, 1997.

———. *The Deities are Many: A Polytheistic Theology*. Albany, NY: State University of New York Press, 2005.

Sattwa, Ananda. "Green Corn Ceremony." In *American Indian Religious Traditions: An Encyclopedia*, edited by Suzanne J. Crawford and Dennis F. Kelley, I, 350–55. Santa Barbara: ABC-CLIO, 2005.

Schaeffer, Claude E. *Blackfoot Shaking Tent*. Calgary: Glenbow-Alberta Institute, 1969.

Solomon, Arthur. *Songs for the People: Teachings on the Natural Way*. Toronto: NC Press, 1990.

Starkloff, Carl. *The People of the Center: American Indian Religion and Christianity*. New York: Seabury Press, 1974.

Stockel, H. Henrietta. *Women of the Apache Nation: Voices of Truth*. Reno, NV: University of Nevada Press, 1991.

Swanton, John R. "Religious Beliefs and Medical Practices of the Creek Indians," *Forty-second Annual Report of the Bureau of American Ethnology, 1924–25* (1928): 473–672.

Underhill, Ruth M. *Papago Woman*. Prospect Heights, IL: Waveland Press, 1979.

Voegelin, Carl F. *Walum Olum or Red Score: The Migration Legend of the Lenni Lenape or Delaware Indians*. Indianapolis, IN: Indiana Historical Society, 1954.

Webster, Gloria Cranmer. "The Contemporary Potlatch." In *Chiefly Feasts: The Enduring Kwakiutl Potlatch*, edited by Aldona Jonaitis, 227–48. Vancouver: Douglas & McIntyre, 1991.

Weltfish, Gene. *The Lost Universe: Pawnee Life and Culture*. New York: Basic Books, 1965.

Wright, Ronald. *Time among the Maya: Travels in Belize, Guatemala, and Mexico*. Toronto: Penguin Books, 1989.

Wroth, Lawrence C. *The Voyages of Giovanni Da Verazzano, 1524–1528*. New Haven: Yale University Press, 1970.

INDEX

ABOUT THE AUTHOR

JORDAN PAPER is Professor Emeritus at York University. He is the author of *Offering Smoke: The Sacred Pipe and Native American Religion*, *The Spirits are Drunk: Comparative Approaches to Chinese Religion*, *Through the Earth Darkly: Female Spirituality in Comparative Perspective*, *The Deities Are Many: A Polytheistic Theology*, and other titles, articles and presentations.